NUMBER 208

THE ENGLISH EXPERIENCE

ITS RECORD IN EARLY PRINTED BOOKS
PUBLISHED IN FACSIMILE

JEAN FRANÇOIS LE PETIT

THE LOW COUNTRY COMMONWEALTH

1609

DA CAPO PRESS
THEATRVM ORBIS TERRARVM LTD.
AMSTERDAM 1969 NEW YORK

The publishers acknowledge their gratitude
to the Governors of the John Rylands Library
Manchester, M3 3EH
for their permission to reproduce
the Library's copy.
(Shelfmark: 6970(2))

S.T.C. No. 15485
Collation: A^4, $B-V^8$

Published in 1969 by
Theatrum Orbis Terrarum Ltd.,
O.Z. Voorburgwal 85, Amsterdam
&
Da Capo Press
- a division of Plenum Publishing Corporation -
227 West 17th Street, New York, 10011
Printed in the Netherlands
ISBN 90 221 0208 4

THE
LOW-COVNTry
COMMON WEALth
Contayninge
An exact discription
of the Eight vnited
Prouinces. Now Made fire
Translated out of french
by
ED GRIMESTON a h

Printed by G Eld. 1609

TO THE WORTHIE
Knight Sir *Peter* *Manwood.*

Sir.

Fter the Edition of the Ne-
therland *Historie*, I was in-
treated to peruse and translate
this discourse, being a description of the vnited Prouinces,
written by Iohn Francis Petit, one of the cheefe Authors
of that *Historie* ; who (as he
himselfe doth auerre) hath
made a particular suruay of all the Prouinces, townes
and forts, which are now vnder the gouernment of the
Confederate Estates. And finding it likely to giue
some contentment to the Reader, and necessarie, as
well for his better vnderstanding of the Historie, as
for his knowledge of the strength and state of those
Prouinces, which haue maintained so long and difficult
a warre, against so potent a Monarke : I haue spent

A2   such

such houres as I could well spare, from my more necessarie imployments (since my comming into France) in
the traduction thereof, that it might bee printed as
an Appendix to the History. The which I cannot re
commend to any Gentleman better deseruing of mee
then your selfe, vnto whom I am much bound for many
kind fauors and respects. Accept it good Sir, though
not worthy of your view, ye as a testymonie of his
loue and thankesfullnesse, who will
alwaies remaine

Orleans Aprill 10.
stilo nouo. 1609.

Yours, deuoted to doe
you seruice.

Edward Grimeston.

A table contayning all the names

of Citties, Townes, Castles, Burgs and Villages in these
eight vnited Prouinces, with the Townes and
Forts out of the said Prouinces and yet
included in their vnion: and first
of Geldres.

A 3

FINIS.

The Belgick Common-weale,

Or

A particular defcription of the eight vnited Prouinces of the Netherlands

The Duchie of Gelders.

 Here is great contradicti-on of opinions betwixt b th ancient and moderne writers touching the firft beginning of the *Geldrois*, the which they can hardly reconcile , neither will I vnder-take the charge. *Marlian* faith, that in *Iulius Cæfars* time, the con-trie which is now called *Gelders*,was inhabited by the *Menapiens* Others hold that it was the aboad of the *Sicambrians*, where-vnto I will yeeld, and that vnder that name the *Cleuois* were compre-hended : through whofe country , as well as through *Gelders* the riuer of *Rhine* doth runne : the which doth caft one of his branches betwixt the Duchies of *Gelders* and *Cleues* , being called *Wahal*, at the diuifion of the I'and of *Sgrauen-weerdt*,where that mighty fort was firft built by Collonell *Martin Schenck,*and at this day in great efteeme.For which Iland there hath bin long de-bate betwixt the Dukes of *Gelders* and *Cleues*. the

B   which

which is not yet decided, & was begun betwixt
the Emperor *Charles* the fift, and *William* duke of
Cleues, father to this laft Duke. The *Battauians* or
Hollanders did alfo hold a part of that which is
now called *Gelders*. There is no doubt, but in *Cæfars* time, the *Sicambrians* did inhabit on either-
fide of the *Rhine*, in the countries of *Cleues* and
Geldres : as *Wezel* on the one fide, with *Burich*,
Cleef and others of the other fide are of the Duchy of *Cleues*: And of *Geldres*, *Nymegen* lies of the
one fide and *Arnham* on the other, fo as we may
rightly fay that the riuers of *Rhine* and *Wahal* do
run through thefe two Prouinces: for the *Sicambrians* hauing often bin defeated by the *Romains*,
Auguftus (who fucceeded *Cæfar* as *Strabo*, *Sueto-
nius* & others do write) to be the better affured
of them, and to keepe them in awe, tranfported a
good number of them with other people on this
fide the *Rhine*, and there planted them. I will not
deny that the *Menapians* did not firft inhabit all
that country which lies along the riuer of *Rhine*,
to whom the *Sicambrians* did afterwards fuc-
ceed, who enioyed a great continent of ground,
on the one fide as far as the *Vbiens*, and on the o-
ther vnto the ocean fea. The which *Marlian* con-
firmes by thefe words. The *Sicambrians* planted
wheras the two great riuers of *Rhine* and *Meufe*
do meet and ioyne, extend themfelues vnto the
ocean fea: And in another place he faith. The *Sicambrians* are people wholy *Germains*, inhabiting
beyond

beyond the riuer of *Rhine* nere vnto the *Vbiens* and *Eburones*, which are the people of *Cologne* & *Liege*. So as wee cannot fay that thofe which at this day are called *Geldrois* had the name of *Sicambrians* onely, but that vnder that name were alfo comprehended, they of *Cleues*, *Monts*, *Marck* & *Iulliers*, all neighbors to the *Rhine*, and on the other fide a part of the riuer of *Meufe* which paffing by the country of the *Eburones* and the moderne *Geldrois*, comes & ioynes with the riuer of *Wahal* (which is a branche of the *Rhine*) nere vnto *Loueftein*, and then retayning the fole name of *Meufe*, wafhing the townes of *Dordrecht*, *Rotterdam*, *Schiedam*, *Vlaerdingen* and the *Brill*, it falls into the *Britifh* fea, and fo into the great Ocean. The which *Sydonius Appolinaris*, an excelent Poet in his time doth witneffe by thefe verfes.

Sic Ripa duplicis tumore fracta,
Detonfus Vahalim bibat Sycamber.
So when the double fwelling breakes the brinke
Wahal fhalbe the thorne *Sicambrians* drinke.

But no man can directly fay when or how thefe *Menapians* & *Sicambrians* were diuided in thefe Prouinces thus diftinguifhed, by which diftinction they haue loft their ancient name. This Prouince is at this day called *Geldres*, and the others *Cleues*, *Iulliers*, *Monts*, *Marck*, *Lieg*, yea & *Weftphalia*: the *Etimology* of which name of *Geldres* feems

ridi-

ridiculous vnto me, as it is fet downe in the chronicle of *Holland*: I would rather hold with them
which maintaine that the whole countrie hath
taken his name of *Gelduba*, a towne in old time
feated vpon the *Rhine*, wherof *Tacitus* makes honorable mention, but at this day there remaines
no memory thereof: *Munfter* holds it for moft
certaine, that the firft Lords of this country
(who long after carried no higher title then of
Aduocates, then of Earles, and in the end of
Dukes)were two brethre, iffued from the French
Wvncard and *Lvold du Pont*, who built a Caftell
called *Pont Gelder*, which caftle hath long retained that name of Pont, and is now ioyned to the
towne of *Geldre*, which hath giuen the name to
the whole Prouince, hauing at this day towards
the North the countrie of *Frifland*, to the Norweft the *Zuyderzee:* vpon the South the riuer of
Meufe ioynes vpon it, and diuides it from the
Duchie of *Brabant*: to the South eaft is the Duchie of *Iuilllers*. Towards the Eaft is a part of the
riuer of *Rhine*, and the duchie of *Cleues*, the which
diuides it into two very vnequall parts : & to the
Weft is *Holland* and the fiegneurie of *Vtrecht*.

This Prouince is plaine and of a goodly fcitu-
ation, hauing few mountaines, but maine heaths,
& great ftore of woods, which are both pleafant
and profitable : among the which is that of *Ech-
terwald*. All their foile or ground for tillage is very fertile in corne : and the pafture fat for cattle,
                                                                especially

eſpecially that which lies vpon the bankes of the
riuer of *Rhine*, *Wahal*, *Iſſel* and *Meuſe*. *Lewis Gui-
chardin* and other writers of our time, confound
the Earldome of *Zutphen* with the Duchie of
Geldres, as we will ſhew in the particular deſcription, and not confound it with that of *Gelders*.

The Duchie of *Gelders* and the Countie of *Zutphen*, containe the townes of *Arnhem*, *Zutphen*,
Nymegen, and *Ruremond*, which are the foure
chiefe of the whole country, making the foure
quarters of theſe two Prouinces, & are ſcituated
(as we will ſhew) vpon foure diuerſe riuers, and
are ſubiect to foure ſeuerall Biſhops. Then are
the townes of *Venlo* vpon the *Meuſe*: *Geldres*: *Stralen*: *Wachkendonck* and *Erkelens* in the champiar
country. Then there is *Hatten* vpon the *Iſſell*,
Elbruch, and *Harderwyck* vpon the *Zuyderzee*, *Wageningen* vpon the *Rhine*, *Tyel* and *Bomel* vpon
the *Wahal*. There are many townes which in ancient time were walled in, but through diuerſe accidents and diſaſters they are now wholy or in
part ſpoiled, & in theſe laſt warres ſome haue bin
vtterly ruined : yet as touching that little which
remaines they doe ſtill enioy their ancient priuiledges of townes, as *Keppel*, *Burch*, *Ghendt*, *Baten-
burch*, *Montfort* & *Eche* with others, whereof we
will make mention comming to their quarter,
with the which there are aboue three hundred
villages, hauing ſteeples & the rights of pariſhes.
The Eſtates of this Duchie conſiſts vpon three

chiefe

chiefe members of the Barons, whom they call
Vvv Heren; of the Nobles whom they call *Red-
derfchap*, and of the foure forefaid chiefe townes,
which Eftates fo farre as they are fallen from the
Princes of *Auftria*, hold their Colledge in the
towne of *Arnham*, whereas in like manner the
Chancerie and the Chamber of accoumpts remaines, as well for the Duchie as the county of
Zutphen. Wherefore although it may difpleafe
Nymegen, as the laft member added to the Duchy
of *Gelders*, wee will begin with *Arnham* as the
chiefe towne, and defcribe all the other townes
in particular, according to their dignities.

Arnham.

THis towne was in old time called *Arnacum*, it
is a good towne and fomewhat fpacious, feated vpon the right banke of the riuer of *Rhine* :
halfe a league from the which is *Foffa Drufiana*,
which is now called *Iffel Dort* : whereas *Drufus*
(to keepe his foldiers from idleneffe)caufed them
to begin to dig a channell, which drawing the water out of the *Rhine*, it fell into a little riuer called
Iffell neere vnto *Dousbourg* in the countie of *Zutphen*, the which hee did build, and called it by his
owne name, that he might haue a fhorter paffage
by water to go and make warre againft the *Frifons*: which channell, or little riuer did fo increafe
in a fhort time, as at this day it is growne very
great, & is called *Iffel*, paffing before the townes
of

of *Dousbourg*, *Bronchorst*, *Zutphen*, *Deuenter* and
Campen, where it falls into the *Zuyder* sea. This
towne of *Arnham* is the chiefe of the Estate and
siegneury of the *Veluwe*, which is one of the foure
quarters of the Duchie of *Gelders*: vnder which
towne are the townes of *Hattem*, *Harderwyck*, *Elbruch* & *Wageningen*, all walled; with many villages, burrowes and castels, with their iurisdictions
and particular officers, subiect to the iustice of the
Drossart or Lieutenant generall of that quarter,
compassed in by the *Zuyderzee*, the *Rhine*, and the
riuer of *Issel*, for which cause fish abounds there,
and is very good cheape: besides there is great
store of woods, vnder-woods and bushes, full of
game for the pleasure of hunting. Neere vnto the
said towne of *Arnham*, is an other member of the
duchy, called *Velwe Zoom*, the which extends neer
vnto *Zutphin* on the one side, and on the other it
reacheth neere to *Wageningen*: in all which soile
there are nothing but meades, and very pleasant
and fertile pastures: which quarter hath a particular officer, which is the Iudge of *Arnham*, with
foure assistants: and as for the *Veluwe* the *Drossart*
hath ten assistants or councellors whereas hee
keepe his courts of pleas. But touching the spiri-
tualtie, the towne of *Arnham* with the whole iurisdiction, before the troubles was subiect to the
Bishoprick of *Vtrecht*. In this towne the Dukes
of Geldres did in former times make their resi-
dence, and there they were intombed in the
great Church before the market place, from

B 4   whence

whence they go vnto the Port which leads vnto
the riuer of *Rhine* . The Chancery & the councel
of *Gelders* were eſtabliſhed there by the Emperor
Charles the fiſt in the yeare 1543. when as hee
conquered it from *william* Duke of *Cleues*, who
maintained himſelf to be true and lawfull heire
to *Charles* of *Egmont* laſt Duke of *Gelders*, which
councell did ſerue as well for the Duchy of *Gelders* as the County of *Zutphen*, ioyntly conſiſting of a Chancellor and ten councellors, that is,
foure of the Nobility of the foure quarters a-
boue mentioned, and ſixe Lawiers or others, the
which adminiſter Iuſtice with great authority,
hauing an Attorney generall, a Regiſter and o-
ther Officers, from whoſe ſentence there is no
appeale. In which towne the Chamber of accounts was alſo placed by *Philip* the ſecond King
of *Spaine* and Duke of *Geldres*, ſucceeding the
Emperor *Charles* his Father in the yeare 1559.
whereas all the Officers of *Geldres* and *Zutphen*,
as well of Iuſtice, as of the treaſure, muſt yeeld
an account of their charges and offices. This
towne within theſe thirty yeares is wonderfully
changed, as well in fortifications and Boul-
warks, as otherwiſe: it hath beene often threat-
ned and attempted to be ſurprized by the *Spaniſh*
faction, but it was fruit-leſſe; the which might
ſeeme ſtrange, conſidering the eaſie acceſſe they
had. when as they held the townes of *Deuenter*
and *Zutphen*.

                                                  Nymc-

Nymegen.

IT is a free towne and a fee of the Empire, of ancient foundation: Of the which we read that *Magus* King of *Gaule*, the Sonne of *Dis*, had beene the firſt founder, who called it *Maga*, by his owne name : And that afterwards *Batto* King of the *Catthes* (as we will ſhew more amply in the deſcription of *Holland*) comming into that quarter, pleaſing himſelfe in the ſcituation, and in the remarkable antiquity, cauſed it to be repaired, and did both ampleſie and fortefie it with new walls, wherevpon it was called *Nouiomagum* the which in the country ſpeech, anſweres to *Nyenmegen*, vnleſſe that in fauoring the little town of *Megen* ſeated vpon the riuer of *Meuſe*, prefering it in antiquity, we will maintaine that *Nymegen* hath beene built ſince vpon the riuer of *Wahal*, by the ſame *Magus*, or his ſucceſſor the which I leaue doubtfull. *Heſſel* Sonne to *Batto* fauored this towne of *Nymeghen*, for that he was borne there, and did ſo inlarge it, as the lower part of the towne is called *Heſſel-marckt* vnto this day . Among all the ſingularities and antiquities of this towne the caſtle is yet ſtanding, vpon the toppe of a little hill, and ouer lookes the towne, the which ſome affirme was built and re-edefied by *Iulius Ceſar*, to diſcouer the Country there-aboutes, and to commaund it;
Neither

Neither is there any place in all that quarter to be found, which yeelds so goodly a prospect of the country, riuers, townes and villages, as this Fort doth, the which vnto this day they call *Des Wallicks Hoff*, which is as much to say, as *the Gaules Court*, the which is a probable argument, that *Magus* or some other of the *Gaules* haue built it. They haue found in this towne & about it within few yeares, memories of the *Romans* antiquity, as medals and goodly stones of sumptuous buildings and sepulchers, with inscriptions and Epitaphes of some Captaines *&* famous men. There are also many ruines of the *Romaines* time along the riuer of *Wahal*, where as some thinke they planted their campe, and placed their garrisons: so as the passage which is neere vnto the towne, is at this day called in the country language *Roomsche Vort*, which signifieth a *Romaine Fort*. So as they haue found great stones in the wall of the chiefe Port, which they call *Hessell-Port*, whereas these words are grauen; *Hic pes Romani Imperii* : Here is the foote of the *Romaine* Empire. And on the other side; *Hic finis regni Stauria*, Here is the end of the command of *Staurius*, whereof we will speake here-after in the description of *Frisland*. There was also found in S^t. *Stephens* church-yard a great stone, on the which these verses were grauen.

Anno milleno postquam salus est data seclo,
Centeno iuncto quinquageno, quoque quinto,

Cæsai

Cæſar *in orbe ſitus,* Fredericus *pacis amicus*
Lapſum, confractum, vetus, in nihil ante redactum
Arte, nitore pari reparauit opus Neomagi,
Iulius *in primo tamen extitit eius origo*
Impar pacifico reparateri Frederico.
Twelue hundred years (wanting but forty fiue)
After Saluation did appeare to men,
Frederick (then peacefull Emperor) did reuiue
The Priſtine fame of ruin'd *Nymegen,*
Iulius did build it long before; as then,
His firſt foundations ſtood; but farre vnlike
To the repaires of peacefull *Frederick.*

This was when as the Emperor *Frederick* cauſed
the old ruines to be repaired. Vnder this towne
are comprehended (as making one quarter of the
Dutchie of *Gelders)* the townes of *Bomel* and *Tyel*
which are walled in, and *Ghendt* which lyes open,
but yet it enioyes the priuiledges of a towne. The
iuriſdictions are firſt that of the *Bourgraue,* that is
to ſay, the Vicont of *Nymegen,* & of the officers of
the ſaid two townes, and of *Bomelweerd:* then that
of the higher and lower *Betuwe,* and afterwards
they that lye betwixt the riuers of *Wahal* and
Meuſe. In the yeare 1248. this towne came vnder
the ſubiection of the Princes of *Gelders* by the
meanes which follow. *Otto* Earle of *Gelders* did
lend vnto *William* King of the *Romanes,* Earle of
Holland, Zeeland, &c. the ſumme of 21000.
markes of pure ſiluer, vpon condition, that if
within a certaine time limited, hee did not pay
the

the fayd fumme , hee fhould inioy the fayd
Towne with the iurifdiction as his owne proper inheritance. The which the Emperor *Rodolphus* did continue fince , & did augment the conditions for the Earles aduantage. And withall the
faid money was not fatisfied : whether it were
through the negligence of the Princes of the
Empire , or that they had not meanes to pay
it;wherby the Vicontie and Seigneury of Nymeghen hath remained incorporated vpon certain
conditions to the Duchy of Gelders, retaining
the iurifdiction , foueraignty and prerogatiue
to coyne money, as an Imperiall Towne. In the
yeare 1 5 8 9. Collonell *Martin Schencke* of *Ny-
deck* , made an vnfortunate enterprize vppon the
towne, who retyring vnto his boate beeing ouer-
laden, it funke and he was drownd : Since the vnited Eftates hauing built a mighty fort called
Knotfenbourg on the other banke of the Riuer of
Wahal, oppofite vnto the Towne , the which did
hinder their nauigation and much anoy them
with their Canon , the townfe-men did preffe
the Duke of *Parma* to free them from this Fort,
and to befeege it : But Prince *Maurice* comming
thether out of *Friefeland* , and hauing defeated
fome of the Dukes men, hee was forced to raize
his feege , and to retyre with his Army into Brabant,he him felfe going to the *Spaw* : The Prince
feeing him retyred , made hafte to befeege the
fayd towne , which he foone forced to yeeld vn-
                                                    to

to the vnited Eftates. In the yeare 1 5 9 2. vnder
whofe obedience it hath euer fince continued.

Ruermond.

IT is a reafonable good towne, feated vpon the
Riuer of *Meuze*, ioyning to the mouth of that
of *Ruoer*, For *Mondt* in the duch tongue fignifies
mouth or entrance, and fo of that word and of *Ru-
er* the name of this towne is compounded, as many others are found in the Netherlands of the
like definitions, as *Dendermond* in *Flanders*, *Iffel-
mond* in *Holland* and others: in Latin it is called
Ruremunda, fiue leagues from *Maiftricht*, & three
from *Venloo*: A towne well peopled, rich & well
built, ftrong both by nature and by art of fortifications of rampars and bulwarkes. It is one of
the foure chiefe Townes of *Gelders*, chiefe of one
of the quarters, vnder whofe Iurifdictiõ are comprehended the Townes of *Venlo*, *Gelder*, *Stralen*
Wachtendonck and *Erckelans*, al walled and ftrong,
with three fmall Bouroughes, *Montfort*, *Vucht*
and *Nyeuftadt*, one a league diftant from another,
which are vnder the Iudges and Officers of the
faid townes, as alfo they of *Keffel*, *Middeler* and
Creykenbeeck. Within fixty yeares this town was
appointed to be the Bifhops Sea for the whole
Duchy of *Gelders*: And there are at this day more
Prieftes and Monkes in i then in any other
Towne in the Country They haue had their
                                    fhare

share of troubles in these last wa⸗res , but not in so great a measure as many others.

A good league from *Ruremond* is the goodly Village of *Keſſell*, with a strong Castle built vpon a Mountaine, belonging to a priuate Lord, from which Village there is a little Angle of the Country, called *Landt-van-Keſſell*, which is of the demaines of the Duchie. This place of *Keſſell* was sometimes a towne of great importance, the which *Ptolomey* calleth *Caſtelleum*, & makes it the Metropolitaine of the *Menapians*. This towne of *Ruremond* with the whole Iuriſdiction , is at this day subiect to the Princes of *Auſtria*.

Venloo.

IT is vppon the right banke of the riuer of *Meuſe* , three leagues from *Ruremond* and halfe a league from *Stralen* , it is a good and a strong Towne, the people are martiall and giuen to Armes , and hath in former times reſiſted an Imperiall Armie. And although it hath often had garriſons of *VVallons*, *Germaines*, *Spaniards* and *Italiens* , yet they haue alwaies found meanes to free them-ſelues by ſome deuice , and to ſette the garriſon at diuiſion one againſt an other, the Citizens fortefying one of the parties , and chaſing away the other ; then finding them ſtrong ynough for that which remained and which had fauoured them, they expelled them alſo; as it hap

ne

ned in the yeare 1578. to the Seignior of *Es-stournelles*, and in the yeare, 1591. to *Otto Bentinck* their Gouernor : remaning notwithstanding alwaies faithfull to the Princes of *Austria*, to whom they knew wel how to excuse them selues. In the yeare 1601. Prince *Maurice* made a gallant enterprize vpon the said Towne ; but beeing ill seconded, the Burgers hauing taken armes and recouered their Ports , it succeeded not ; so as he was forced to retyre, with the losse of two of his Captaines. In this Towne *VVilliam* Duke of *Cleues*, hauing lost all his Duchy and a good part of *Iuilliers* and *Cleues*, came in the yeare 1543. and submitted him-selfe to the mercy of the Emperor *Charles* the fift , where he was receiued into grace , renouncing the league which hee had with the *French* , and marrying the daughter of *Ferdinand* King of the *Romaines* the Emperors brother , & absolutely renounced al his interest to the Duchy of *Gelders*, as we haue shewed more amply in another place.

Guelder.

THe Towne of *Gelder* is (as we haue said) that which hath giuen the name to the whole Ducthy, being within two smal leagues of *Stralen*, it hath a Castle which was wont to be without the towne , but now it is comprehended within the fortification. This was wont to be the

Court of the Lords of *Pont*, Aduocats, and afterwards Earles of *Gelders* : it is deuided into two
habitations, seperated by a water, vppon the
which there is a bridge, which giues accesse from
one to the other, seated in a country some-what
Moorish, and not very accessible to plant the Canon. This towne in the beginning of the last
troubles, was vnder the obedience of the vnited
estates. But the Earle of *Lecester* Lieutenant to
the Queen of *England*, Protectresse of the vnion,
hauing placed Collonel *patton* a *Scottishman* for
Gouernor there, hee sold it for thirtie thousand
crownes in ready money to the duke of *Parma*,
in the King of *Spaines* name, retaining to him-self
the horses and moueables of Collonel *Schenck*,
and the ransomes of some of the ritchest and best
Cittizens. And so this towne returned vnder the
power of the Princes of *Austria*, as it is yet at this
day.

Stralen.

THis towne is but a league and a halfe from
Wachtendonck, a small towne, but sufficiently fortified for the importance thereof, beeing
too neere to *Venlo*, in the which the Princes of
Austria intertaine an ordinary garrison vnder
some Gouernor or Captaine whome they place
there.

VVachtendonck

Wachtendonch.

IS alfo a fmall Towne with a Caftle belonging to a priuate Lord: the which in the yeare 1588. holding the party of the vnited Eftates, the duke of *Parma* after that hee had fayled at the feege of *Berghen vp Zoom*, fent Cont *Charles* of *Manffeldt* to befeege it, where in the end hee forced them to yeeld. In the yeare 1600. Cont *Lodowike* of *Naffau* furprized it for the vnited Eftates. After which the garrifon of *Gelders*, *Stralen* and others thereabouts furprized it againe, but not able to take the Caftle, they were forced to abandon it: So as in the yeare 1605. the Marquis *Spinola* went and befeeged it, who receiuedit by compofition for the Arch-Dukes of *Auftria*.

Erchelens.

SOme will fay that this towne hath taken his name of *Hercules Allemanicus* : It is fituated vpon the fronters of the Duchy of *Iuilliers* foure leagues from *Ruremend*, it is a reafonable good towne. obedient with the like garrifon vnto the Princes of *Auftria*. But lette vs now come vnto the townes which are feated as wel vpon *Zuyder-zee*, as vpon the riuers of *Rhyne*, *Wahal*, *Meuze* and *Iffell*. Firft,

Echt

IT is a league from the *Meuze*, and as far from *Montfort*, on the side of that goodly Wood which they call *Echterwout.*

Montfort.

IT is a Castle of importance, the which was in ancient time a smal towne: it lies a league from R*uermond.*

Harderwick.

IT is a an indifferent good towne lying vppon the *Zuyderzee* : yet the hauen is bad, so as the shippes are forced to lye in the Road : Notwithstanding *Charles* Duke of *Geldrs* , sending fiue shippes well manned with soldiers out of that towne, thought to surprize the Towne of *Horne* in *West-Freezeland* , whereof he sayled. In the yeare 1503. this towne was by chance sette on fire , the which was so violent , as in lesse then three houres it was all consumed to ashes, except fiue or sixe houses , with the losse of all their goods , and the death of many persons which were surprized by the fire, or smothered vnder the ruynes of the houses and walles the which was a fearefull and pittyfull sight.

Since

Since it hath beene in a short time new built, and made more beautifull and stronger then before. There are some rich and ciuil people in it: The Magistrate intertaines a good Schoole there : It hath not much tasted of the miseries of these last warres : sometime it hath maintained a small garrison of horse and foote, without any great charge vnto them.

Elburgh.

IT lyes vppon the *Zuyderzee* like vnto *Harderwick*, from the which it is distant two good leagues, and as much from the Towne of *Campen* in *Oueryssell* It is a little town of smal trafficke, but yet good cheap to liue in, and hath during these warres followed the same party that *Harderwick*. did

Hattem.

WAs in ancient time a good towne, though none of the greatest, seated vppon the left banke of the riuer of *Yssell*. There is a goodly strong Castle, which hath tasted of the miseries of these last warres, for the Drossart or Lieutenant of the Country thinking to deliuer it into the *Spaniards* handes, being discouered, they thought to make it good in this Castle,

whereas

wheras the Estates befeeged them, and the Castle was fo battered and torne with the canon (wherof the marks are yet to bee feene) as they were forced and carryed prifoners to *Arnham* whereas they loft their heads.

Wagheninghen.

IS a fmall ancient ftrong towne, and is the very fame which *Cornelius Tacitus* called *Vada* , as to fpeake the truth it may properly be fo called, being in a manner compaffed in of all fides with moores and bogs, which makes it in-acceffible on thofe parts , it lies not far from the riuer of *Rhyne* , beeing of an equall diftance from the townes of *Arnham* and *Nymeghen* , and foure leagues from *Culenbourg.*

Tyel.

THis Towne is the chiefe place of the Iurifdiction or *Bayiwick* which they call *Tyeler-weerd*, the which was wont to be *a Peninfula*: But fince thefe laft warres *Derick-vick* Seignior of *Soulen* Bailiffe of the town and iurifdiction, hath caufed a chanell to be cutte through the Commune to fayle from the riuer of *Meuze* into the *Wahal* vppon the right banke wherof the faid towne is built : by which meanes the faid *Tyel-weerd* is now made an Iland , for that there is no

entrance

entrance into it but by water, or through the towne: It is ſtrong by nature and by art, through the dilligence of the ſaid *Amptman or* Bailyffe, who ſince the laſt troubles hath made ſharp wars againſt the *Spaniards,* by the meanes of that garriſon: In the yeare 1528. holding the party of *Charles* Duke of Gelders their Prince, the *Burguignons* beſeeged it in the Emperors name, but it was ſo well defended, as they were forced to raiſe their ſeege, to the great honour of the Inhabitants, and the few ſoldiers that were within it.

Bommel.

IT is a faire ſtrong place, the cheefe towne of all the Territory of *Bommell-weerd*, which the *Rhyne* and *Meuze* doe compaſſe in, making it an Iland, the which they ſay was called by *Cæſar, Inſula Batauorum* (if it extend no farther) the which wee may ſay is now the higher and lower *Betuwe*, on the other banke of the riuer of *Ryne*, as farre as *Tyel*, and beyond to *Haerwerden*, where at this preſent is the mighty fort of Saint *Andrew* (whereof wee will preſently make mention) whereas the *Wahal* and the *Meuze* kiſſing as the paſſe, ioyne together at *Loueſtein* at the end of the ſaid *Bomelſ-weerd* in one body, the which ſoone after from *Gorrichom* takes the name of *Meruue*, vntill that

C 3   hauing

hauing paſt *Dordrecht*, it reſumes his name of *Meuze*, and beneath *Bryell* runnes into the *Brittiſh* Seas.

In this Iland there are many fayre Villages and Caſtles, among others *Roſſem*, whereas *Martin van Roſſem* Seignior of *Puydroyen* was borne; a famous Captaine in his time, hauing beene Marſhall of the field to the Duke *Charles* of *Gelders* and *William* of *Cleues*, who in the yeare of our Lord, 1534. did terrifie the Towne of *Antwerp*, and thinking to doe the like to them of *Lovuain* was forced to retyre

In the yeare of our Lord 1598. Arch-Duke *Albert* of *Auſtria* beeing gone into *Spaine* to fetch his ſpouſe, the *Infanta Iſabella*, daughter to King *Philip* the ſecond, and ſiſter to King *Philip* the third now raigning; left (during his abſence) Cardinal *Andrew* of *Auſtria* to gouerne the *Netherlands*, which were giuen in marriage to the ſayd *Iſabella*, and *Don Franciſco de Mendoza* Admirall of *Arragon*, for generall of his armie: the which hee ſent vnto the frontiers of *Germanie* to make warre againſt the vnited Eſtates that way, where hauing done what hee liſted, and taken from the Eſtates by ſeege the townes of *Rhynberch* and *Deutecom*, and then the Fort of *Creuccœur*, hee paſt to the ſaid Iland of *Bommell*, with an intent to beſeege the towne, the which by reaſon of their workes at the fortification

fortification lay halfe open. The which Prince *Maurice* vnderstanding, he posted thether with all speed , and assured it with his presence and forces, causing a trench to bee cast without the towne , from one side of the riuer vnto the other, whereas hee lodged the greatest part of his Army , where-vppon the Admirall seeing there was no way to force them, hee retired farther into the Iland busiyng him-selfe about the building of Saint *Andrewes* Fort, so as the towne of *Bommel* was freed.

In this towne was borne that learned man *Elbert Leoninus*, Doctor of the Lawes, who dyed in the yeare 1601. being Chancellor of *Gelders* and deputy for the general Estates of the vnited Prouinces, being aboue 80. years old: he was sotimes Tutor to the Prince of *Orange* which now liueth.

S. *Andrew.*

THis Fort was so named by *Andrew* of *Austria* Cardinal of *Constance*, being Gouernor of the *Netherlands* (as wee haue said) in the absence of the Arch-duke *Albert.* It is the mightiest fort that hath bin made in al the *Netherlands* , for the building whereof the Admirall of *Arragon* disfurnished the whole Iland of trees: It is comprehended in fiue Bulwarks , after the forme of the Cittadel of *Antwerp,* wherof three are vppon the bankes of *Mewze* and *Wahal* , and the two others

C 4 towards

towards *Haerwerden*, either of them hauing a ca-
ualier or plat-forme to defend it, with broad and
deepe ditches, without the which is a counter-
fcarpe, the which hath alfo a ditch round about
it, and fmall forts to warrant it, efpecially wheras thefe two riuers imbrace one an other, towards *Tyler-weerd*, whereas the Fort of *Naffau*
is fet oppofite to that of Saint *Andrew*, in a corner, which is alfo made an Ifland by art, beeing
called *Voorne*, and is herd by the Eftates: which
two Forts did daily falute one an other with
their Ordinance. Tne Admiroll hauing fynifhed
this Fort, thinking thereby to keepe the riuers
of *Wahal* and *Meufe*. and the whole Ifland in fubiection, left a garrifon of 1500. men in it,
with ftore of artillerie and munition, and then
retired with his army to refrefh it in *Brabant*.
But Prince *Maurice* did not diffolue his armie,
but kept it togither all the winter, as well in the
towne of *Bommel*, as in the trenches and fhips
which he had lying by: The fpring time beeing
come, hauing recouered the Fort of *Creuecæur*,
he went to befeege that of Saint *Andrew*, the
which through want of victualls, was yeelded
vnto him, with all the artillery and munition,
the fouldiers being about 1100. and fome 400.
out of *Creuecæur* remained in the Princes feruice, who afterwards at the battaile of *Nieuport*
fhewed themfelues both valiant and faithfull.
And fo this Fort of Saint *Andrew* hath vnto
this

this day remained vnder the obedience of the v-
nited Eſtates

Culembourg.

ALthough this towne be a fee of *Gueldres*, yet
there is a queſtion made whether it bee of
that territory . It is ſcituaed vpon the left banke
of the riuer of *Lecke*, a league from *Buren*, & two
leagues from *Vianen*, on the ſame ſide of the riuer . It hath a goodly caſtle, whereas the Lord
doth ordinarily reſide, and a large iuriſdiction,
wherevpon King *Philippe* the ſecond erected it
to an Earldome, whereof *Florent* of *Palant* was
the firſt Earle, beſides many other great poſſeſſions which hee enioyed, whereof his ſonne is
now Lord and Earle.

Battenbourg.

ALthough this towne (at this preſent ruined)
and the caſtle, bee within the limmits of the
Duchy of *Geldres*, ſeated vpon the banke of the
riuer of *Meuſe*, whereby the Barron of that place
makes a great reuenew of the toule and cuſtome
which is paied by all the ſhips that paſſe that
way : yet the ſaid ſigneury is merely held of the
Empire, as *William* of *Bronthurſt* did take it vppe
of *Maximillian* the Emperour : His Sonne
ſucceeded him, and dying without heires,

Maxi-

Maximillian of *Bronckhurst* his coufin Germaine did inherit , and is now Lord of it. This place is of very great antiquity. The Chronicles of *Holland* affirme , that it was the firft Caftle which Prince *Battus* (of whome *Batauia* or *Holland* tooke his name) did build vppon the *Meuze* in the Countie of *Sicambrians* , which now is *Gelders.*

Buren.

THis Towne is neither a fee, nor of the territory of *Gelders,*but a little country of it felfe, which holdes of the Empire , carrying the title of an Earle with great Iurifdiction , a large territory and many Villages , and yet fhut vp in the lymits of the Duchy of *Gelders.*

This place is feated neere vnto the riuer of *Lingen* , vppon a little Brooke which in old time was called the ditch for mufcles , a league from *Tyl,*it is not very bigge , but hath a very ftrong Caftle ioyning vnto it, where there is an ordinary garrifon for the vnited Eftates. That valiant and famous Prince *Maximilian* of *Egmont* was Earle of this place , who for his great feruices done vnto the Emperor *Charles* the fift, (whereof diuers hiftories make mention) left his memory immortall to pofterity : Dying at *Bruffels* in the yeare one thoufand four hundred & nine,to whom fucceeded his only daughter

ter the fole heire by her mother of the houfe
of *Lannoy* : Who was the firft wife of *William* of
Naffau Prince of *Orange*, by whom fhe left a fon
and a daughter, that is *Philip William* of *Naffau*
now Prince of *Orange*, Earle of *Buren* , Seignior
of *Lannoy* &c. And the Lady *Mary* of *Naffau*
widdow to Cont *Philip* of *Hohenlo*.

This may fuffice for the defcription of the
Townes and cheefe Forts comprehended in
the Eftate of the Dutchy of *Gelders*.

The people of this Prouince are valiant and
warlike, from whence they were wont to draw
a good part of them at Armes and Archers
of the bandes of Ordinance of the *Low-countries.*

Thefe were the laft among the *Belgick Gaules*
that fubmitted them-felues to the yoake of the
Romane Empire, & the firft when this Monarchy
began to decline , that freed them-felues from
their fubiection. Afterwards they were made
fubiect to the *French* : yet imbracing the occafion when it it was offered , they did fhake of this
yoak, and began to be gouerned by priuat Lords
of the country it felfe : the which hapned in
the time of the Emperour *Chalres* the bald
King of *France* : Which Lords were fimply
called Tutors or Aduocats of the country:
The which according o their vertues and merits
were chofen & created by the people , the firft of
which was *Wrinchard* (as we haue fhewed before)

to

to whome fucceeded his fonne *Gerlach* in the
yeare 9 1 0. fo as there were feauen Lords or
Feofes fucceffiuely iffued from this familie,
the laft whereof was alfo called *winchard* , who
left but one daughter called *Aleyd* or *Alix* , mar-
yed to *Otto* Earle of *Naffau* : who was the firft
which carryed the title of the Earle of *Gelders*
giuen him by the Emperor *Henry* the third, in
the yeare 1 0 7 9.

But the fayd *Aleyd* beeing dead hee marryed
with the daughter of *Gerlach* Earle of *Zutphen*,
who was flaine in a battaile giuen betwixt *Con-*
rard Bifhop of *Vtrecht* and *Thiery* the fixt Earle
of *Holland*. Where-vppon (as wee haue fayd)
the Earldome of *Zutphen* was alfo vnited vnto
the Duchy of *Gelders*. *Otto* eft thefe Earles after
him, *Gerrard* , *Henry* , *Gerrard* & *Otto* the fecond,
furnamed the ftump-foot. It was he which did
purchafe the Seigneury of *Nymeghen* , as wee
haue fayd before, which hee did wall in with diuers others, which were but Burroughs, as *Rure-*
mond, *Arnhem* , *Harderwicke* , *Bommel* and *Wage-*
ninghen all in the Prouince of *Gelders* , and aboue
it *Goch* in the country of *Cleues* : to the which he
gaue goodly priuiledges, as to great Citties.

To this *Otto* fuceeded his fonne *Renald*, and to
him a fonne of his owne name , who obtained in
the yeare 1 3 2 9. the dignity and title of Duke
of the Emperour *Lewis* of *Bauaria* in an imperiall Dyet held at *Francfort* : As in like manner the
County

Countie of *Iuilliers* was by him erected into a Dutchy. Af er this *Reginold* the second, *Geldres* was gouerned by *Arnold* & *Edward* his two sons, but not without great contentions. Both of them dying, *Arnold* left two daughters of diuers beddes, *Ioane* and *Isabell*, who continued the diuision which had beene betwixt their Father and Vncle: but *Isabell* dying without children, *Ioane* remained sole and peaceable Dutchesse, to whom succeeded *William* her sonne, who was the fourth duke of *Geldres*, but dying without heires, *Reynold* his brother the fourth Duke of *Iuilliers* succeeded him, and was the fift Duke of *Geldres*, who dying without issue male, the succession went to his only daughter, married to *Arnold* of *Egmond*, issued from a daughter of the first Duke of *Geldres*, by which meanes the sayd *Arnold* came vnto the principality, whose Sonne called *Adolphe*, (who is numbred for the seauenth Duke) repyning that his Father liued so long, by the perswasion of his own Mother, caused him to bee seazed on in a night, and to bee put in prison in the castle of *Buren*, where hee detained him many yeares. Pope *Paul* the second and the Emperour *Frederick* the third, not able to suffer so great an impiety, gaue authority to *Charles* the *Warlicke*, Duke of *Bourgongne* to free this miserable Father by force of armes out of the hands and tyranie of his sonne: The which *Adolph* vnderstanding, and

and feeing that the Pope and Emperor did imbrace the caufe, and that he was not able to refift Duke *Charles* his forces, he drew his father out of prifon, and hauing obtayned a pafport from the Duke, he came vnto him with his father to *Dourlans* in *Picardy* : before whome the father cafting his gloue, defied the fonne: But the Duke who loued this *Adolph*, labored to perfwade the father to refigne the Duchy vnto his Sonne, and that being now very old, he fhould retire to *Graue*, and content him-felfe with that peece and three thoufand florins rent, wherevpon *Adolph* like an vnnaturall and barbarous fonne hearing this propofition made by Duke *Charles* of *Bourgongne*, anfwered, that he had rather caft his father head-long into a wel, and him felfe after, then accept of that compofition.

That it was reafon, feeing his father had gouerned, forty foure yeares, that he fhould alfo come in his rancke to the Principality, and enioy it as his father had don. Adding that he was well content his father fhould haue 3000 florins yerely for his entertainment, but he muft depart out of the country and fiegneury of *Gelders*, and neuer enter more into it : Duke *Charles* hearing thefe fpeeches and noting the cruelty of a fonne towards his father, feemed fo much incenfed thereat, as *Adolph* fearing his fury, fled in a difguifed habit, thinking to faue him-felfe in *Gelders* ; but beeing knowne, neere vnto *Namur* hee was taken and put in prifon

at

at *Villevord*, & from thence carried to *Courtray*, where hee remayned till after the death of Duke Charles. In the mean time the father to be reuē-ged of his son, sought to dif-inherit him ; resig-ning his Duthcy of *Gelders* & County of *Zutphē* vnto Duke *Charles* vppon certaine conditions. By which resignation the Princes of the house of *Austria* haue so much pretended vnto the sayd Dutchy, as in the end after the death of the laſt Duke *Charles* of *Egmont*, they haue inioyed it, al-though by right it ſhould deſcend to *VVilliam* Duke of *Cleues*, whome the Emperor forced to yeeld it vnto him. And to return to *Adolph* he was freed from his priſon at *Courtray* by the *Ganthois*, who made him their Generall againſt the *Frēch* king *Lewis* the 11. where this vngrate-ful ſon was ſlaine before *Tournay*, receiuing the fruits of his deſert, hauing bin ſo cruel, to his fa-ther. Duke *Arnould* dying afterwards at *Graue*, he inſtituted (vpō caution) the ſaid duke of *Bour-gongne* to be his heyre, diſ-inheriting his ſon *A-dolph* of the ſucceſſion, as *contumax*, ingrat & re-bellious: But the *Geldrois* refuſing to accept of Duke *Arnolds* diſpoſition & teſtament, the duke of *Bourgongne* went with a mighty army and by force took poſſeſſion of the country, receiuing their othes of fealty & homage, whervnto he for-ced the townes & the Nobility of *Gelders*: And the better to aſſure this new Eſtate he purchaſed from *Gerard* Duke of *Iuilliers* and his children,

II

all the intereſt they had or might hereafter pretend vnto the Duchie of *Gelders*. This done hee
ſent *Charles* and *Philip* the ſons of *Adolph* whome
he had by a Princeſſe of the houſe of *Bourbon*, to
be bred vp in *Flarders* ; and by that meanes the
Duke of *Bourgongne* remained in quiet poſſeſſion
of the Eſtate of *Gelders*, and dying left the ſucceſſion to his onely daughter and heyre, who was
married to the Emperor *Maximillian*, but the
Geldrois refuſing to obey him, he raiſed a mighty
Army, and came to *Boiſleduc*, where-with the Eſtates of *Gelders* being terrified, they acknowledged him for their Prince in the right of his wife,
and did ſweare obedience vnto him. And ſo
Maximillian gotte the quiet poſſeſſion without
any effuſion of blood, the which he inioyed vntil
that *Charles* the ſonne of *Adolph* (who had bene
taken priſoner with the Earle of *Naſſau* in an incounter neere vnto *Bethune* by the *French*, and
afterwards by reaſon of his Allyance by the
mothers ſide, ſet at liberty) with the helpe of the
French King and his Kinſmen and friendes, returned into *Gelders* with a ſmall Army, where without any reſiſtance or difficulty, hee was receiued
by the people, as their lawful Prince, and numbred for the eight Duke of *Gelders*.

This Duke *Charles* of *Egmont* was in his time
a valiant and warlike Prince: making war againſt
all his neighbors, eſpecially againſt *Albert* duke
of *Saxony* feudatary of *Freezland* & of *Groning*:

Gouernor

Gouernor of a part of the *Netherlands* for the Emperour *Maximillian*, and the Arch-Duke *Philip* his fonne, who marryed the Lady *Ioane* of *Caftile*, and was afterwards Queen of *Spaine*, after the death of the King *Don Ferdinand* of *Arragon* and of Queene *Iffabelle* of *Caftile*, her father and mother : whereby the Realmes of *Spaine* came vnto the houfe of *Auftria*, and haue continued vnto this day.

The faid Duke had alfo great warre againft the Lieutenant of the Emperor *Charles* the fift, fonne and fucceffor to the faid Arch-Duke *Philip*: fo as in the end there was a peace made betwixt them at *Gorcum* in the yeare 1528. and afterwards in the yeare 1536. there was an other generall peace made in the Towne of *Graue* : The conditions whereof were in fub-ftance that Duke *Charles* of *Egmont* fhould hold the Dutchy of *Gelders* and the County of *Zutphen* in fee of the Emperor or Duke of *Brabant*, and Earle of *Holland*, for him and his lawful heirs: But if hee dyed without iffue, his Eftates and Seigneuries fhould accrue vnto the Emperor and his heirs. This duke died without children in the yeare 1538. And fo according to the faid Accord and tranfaction, and the rights which his great grandfather the Duke of *Burgongne* had gotten, thefe countries fhould defcend vnto the faid Emperor : But *Iohn* Duke of *Iuilliers* pretending an intereft by reafon of their ancient rights,

D   (renounced

(renounced and fold as we haue fayd by his Anceftors) was not receiued by the *Eſtates* , ſo that after the death of Duke *Charles* of *Egmont* the *Cleuois* had laboured to draw ſome by loue and others by force vnder the ſubiection of the King, and to make them his vaſſals , where-vppon they tooke armes againſt him. And worſhipping the ſunne riſing more then the ſunne ſeting , neglecting the old Duke , they did choſe and receiue his ſonne *William* , who was made ſure to the daughter of the Duke of *Alòret* and heire to the Crowne of *Nauarre* : which election was confirmed and better eſtabliſhed in the yeare of our Lord 1 5 3 9. by the death of the ſaid Duke *Iohn* : at which time neither the Emperors title nor authority could preuaile any thing to make him to be acknowledged Lord of this Prouince. But this was not all , for the Emperor being in *Spaine* , his countries were ſodainly inuaded by the *French* King and this Duke *William* : Where-vppon the Emperour beeing returned from his laſt vnfortunate voyage of *Affricke* , hee went into the *Netherlands* with a mighty army , and ſodainly ſubdued in a a manner all the townes of the Dutchy of *Cleues* and *Iuilliers*, and among others thoſe of *Duren* & *Sittant*. Where-with Duke *William* being amazed , and fearing this mighty enemy , by the perſwaſion of the Princes of *Germany*, his Allies, he went and humbled him-ſelfe vnto the Empe-

ror

ror in the towne of *Venlo*, to whom he was reconciled, yeelding abfolutely vnto him the faid Dutchy of *Gelders* and Earldome of *Zutphen*, renouncing alfo the league which hee had with the
French King, and his pretended marriage with
Ioane of *Albret* Princeffe of *Nauarre*, and marrying with the daughter of *Ferdinand* King of *Romanes*, the Emperors Brother. In confideration
wherof all his other Countries which the Emperors men had taken from him were reftored
againe. To which Accord the Eftates of *Gelders*
did willingly confent, vpon certaine conditions
conteyned in their pattent. And fo *Gelders* and
Zutphen returned againe to the houfe of *Auftria*
vnder the Emperor *Charles* the fift in the yeare
1543. and in the yeare 1549. there was receiued
for Prince and homage done vnto *Philip* of *Auftria* Prince of *Spaine*, the only fon vnto the Emperour, as future and lawfull Lord of the faid
Duchy & Earldome: who gaue the gouernmēt
thereof vnto *Charles* of *Brunen* Earle of *Meghen*.
Vntill that in thefe laft wars the faid Prouinces
hauing entred into the general vnion of the *Ne-
therlinds*, by the pacification of *Gandt*, they haue
(notwithftanding the dif-vnion of them of *Arthois*, *Henault* and others) continued alwaies con-
ftant in the faid vnion, and fo remaine at this prefent, hauing tafted the bitter fruites of the faid
wars, as the hiftorie of the *Netherlands* makes
mention.

D 2   The

The Earldome *of* Holland *and of* VVeft-Friefland.

BEfore I vndertake to defcribe *Batauia* (which is now called *Holland*) in old time the mother of good horfemen , and the miftreffe of martiall difcipline , not tributary , but companions and allyes to the people of *Rome,* I thinke it fit in the relating the originall of the nation to make a repetition of that which hath bin collected of their antiquity by anciết records,& redeeming them from forgettfulneffe to reftore them to their ancient glory and honour. To which effect as I hold it very abfurd to abufe the reader with fables and lyes , fo will I not altogether reiect that which hath beene deliuered by our Anceftors. I know that the curious reader affects new things more then ancient , the memory wherof is almoft extinct : but I will intreat them to giue mee leaue to remember the honour which the *Batauians* haue purchafed by armes, regiftred by al ancient writers , whereof we wil prefently make mention.

Firft of all it is well knowne that the *Batauians* are originally defcended from the *Cattes* a people of *Germany* , whoe driuen from their natiue foyle by inteftine diffentions , hauing paft the *Rhyne* fought a new habitation , and ceazing vppon the borders of *Belgia* which were

inhabited

inhabited, they planted them-selues in the Iland which the *Rhyne* doth enuirō. The which *Tacitus* a Knight and a faithfull *Romaine* writer doth witnesse in his booke which hee hath written of the manners of the *Germains. Omnium* (saith hee) *harum gentium virtute precipui* Bataui , *non multum ex ripa , sed insulam Rheni amnis incolunt,* Catorum *quondam populus,et seditione domestica in eas sedes transgressus , in quibus pars Romani Imperii fuerūt: manet honos & antiquæ societatis insigne &c.* That is to say: of al the natiōs (meaning the *Germaines*) the *Batauian* are the most valiant not farre from the bankes , but inhabiting of the Iland of the riuer of *Rhyne.*

In ancient time a people of the *Cattes,* and by their ciuill dissentions transported into these parts to make a portion of the *Romaine* Empire, they yet inioy the honour thereof. Bataui *donec trans Rhenum agebant pars* Cattorum*, seditione domestica pulsi extrema Gallicæ oræ vacua cultoribus simulá, insulam inter vada sitam occupauere : quam mare Oceanum a fronte , Rhenus amnis tergum ac latera circumluit.*

The *Batauians* whilst they remained beyond the *Rhyne* were a part of the *Cattes* , chased away by Ciuill dissentions , planted them-selues vppon the extremities of the *Gaulish* fronters In an Iland lying among the marishes hauing the Ocean Sea in Front , and the Riuer of *Rhyne* behinde and on either side. By these
wordes

words wee are taught that the *Battauians*
muft fetch their firft beginning from the *Catthes*;
but it is queftionable in what part of *Germany*
the *Catthes* did dwell; for *Iohn Stella* who hath
written the *Philippi* peregrination, fayth, that
they did refide at *Heidelberg*, *Heilbrunen* and the
Othonian forest. *Schonerus* the *Mathematician*
makes them *Saxons* : *Marlianus* fends them
to the foreft of *Hongary*, *Irenicus* will haue
then *Turingians*, all which opinions are full
of obfcure errors. But *Stella* flying a heigher
pitch like vnto *Icarus*, one error drawing on
an other, makes the *Vifipiens* to be neighbors
vnto the *Catthes*, affigning thofe of *Fancford*
and *Conflens*, euen vnto the riuer of *Mofelle*
whereas it falls into the *Rhine*. Hee affirmes
more-ouer that the *Teucteres* neighbors to
the *Catthes* now called a part of *Heſſen*, remayning along the riuers of *Lane* and *Lippe*. For
my part I hold them to be of *Heſſe*, with the
which many learned writers doe concurre, for
Tacitus doth make them to bee neighbors to
the *Cherufques* (which are the people of *Luxe-
bourg*) and to the *Hermodures*, which were
they of *Mifnia*, beginning their iurifdictions
from the forreft *Hircinia* : whereof the riuer
Sala is a good witneſſe for the enioying whereof the *Catthes* were in continuall quarrell a-
gainft the *Hermodures*, which diuiding the
Bifhop-

Bifhopricke of *Naumburg* and *Merfpurg* falls into
the riuer of *Elbe* limiting in old time the *Signieu-
ry* of the *Cattes.*The riuer of *Eder* is alfo a witneffe
running through the country of the *Cattes*, which
(as the fame author doth report)the yong men of
the *Cattes* did fwim through when as *Cæfar Germanicus* did charge them fodenly. This riuer falls
into that of *Fulda*, vpon whofe banke *Battenburg* is
feated, from whence we may coniecture that our
Batto, or at the leaft they of the houfe of *Battenburg* are iffued. The which alfo they of *Catfenelle-
bogen* doe teftefie, hauing a *Caftle* vpon the banks
of the riuer of *Rhine* of that name, fhewing the antiquitie of the name of the *Cattes Meliboces*:
In the countrie of *Heffen*, wee haue alfo for reliks of this nation two villages of the *Cattes*,
the one vpon the fea, called *Catwyck vp Zee*,
and the other neere vnto the village of *Rinf-
burg* called *Catwycke* vppon the *Rhine*, both of
them of the iurifdiction of *Holland* ; and *Cattes* a towne of Zeeland, which fome feuenty
yeares paft was drowned, And fince, with *Cort-
geen* and the ile of *Northbeueland* (an *Ifland* of
Zeeland)within this ten yeares recouered from
the fea. There are fome that affirme that the
caufe why the *Cattes* remooued from the place
of their birth was, for that they loft a battayle a-
gainft the *Hermodures*, being in continuall quarrell for their falt, which (as we haue faid before)
was made of the water of the riuer of *Sala*,

whereby

whereby the *Hermodures* became more puiffant; but I hold it a detraction from the *Batauian* honour for that they by the affiftance of the *Romans* hauing obtained a great victory , conftrained the *Cattes* to change their place, and to come to inhabit this Iland of the *Rhyne*. For which caufe the *Cattes* may with great reafon bee faid to bee the beginning andfirft Fathers of the *Batauians*, or *Hollanders*. A people renowned for their fkill in warre , *Cornelius Tacitus* attributing much to their induftry and dexterity in the difpofing of an armie , and alfo in obeying their Commaunders , to take or put of the combat as it fhould be thought fit ; of great courage , firme and hard bodies, wel lymmed, of a fierce and menacing afpect , fearefull for the horrible length of their beardes and hayre , which fafhion and countenance hee faith was not lawfull for them to leaue off, or change although they had brought victory from their enemies.

Some fay that *Batto* iffued from the royall bloud of the *Cattes* , was moued to change his naturall abode to a new one , not for the defire hee had to finde a better or more fertile country , or in regard of too great a multitude of people (which are the two maine occafions that nations remoue their ancient habitations) but that his ftep-mother laid diuers ambufhes for him , and fearing to bee poyfoned (beeing at oddes with her) his father confenting thereto,

or

or at leaft not oppofing it: By reafon whereof, what with the fplendor of his heroicall vertues, his gratious and amiable carryage, and his condition truly royall , hee drew vnto him a good part of the Nobility , and a great number of the people , who beeing out of hope of better times followed him willingly ; and by the councell of the King of *Tongres* (his good father) hee addreft him-felfe to the confines of *Belgia* there to inhabit: and hauing paft the *Rhyne*, not farre from the riuers of *VVahal* and of *Meuze*, hee happily built the Caftle of *Battengbourgh* vppon the riuer of *Meuze* , which hauing paft at the parting of the *Rhyne*, where the *VVahal* retyres and takes his courfe apart, hee inioyed all the whole circuit, euen to the *Ocean* Sea , parting the land amongft the Nobles and common people fo that of his name it was called *Battauia*, which fignifies nothing elfe but the heritage of *Batto*, as if one fhould fay *Batous Haue* , for *Haue* in the old Dutch, and yet at this prefent fignifies heritage: So that then this Prouince hath taken his name and that lawfully, from a Prince , the fon of a King: al which is witneffed by diuers authors, amongft whom the moft worthy of beleefe is *Cornelius Tacitus*, a *Romaine* Knight , a rare writer of the Story of *Auguftus*, and Commiffary for *Gaule Belgique*, who makes mention of *Claudius Ciuilis* defcended from *Batto*, iffued from a royal branch of the *Batauians* or *Hollanders*.

Here

Here you may fee that *Plyny*, not without great reafon, called this Ifle the moft noble Ifle of *Batto*: The which name of *Batto* hath heretofore fpread it felfe very far amongft the *Allemans* and *Dalmatians*, and *Dion* a *Romaine* Hiftoriographer makes mention of two *Battoes*; the firft *Batto* duke of *Bruces* (which is a part of *Pannonia*, which I now hold to be the country of *Pruffia* confining *Poland* & *Hungary*:) the other *Batto Defidiate*, who ftirred vp the *Dalmatians* (beeing too much exacted vpon by impofitions) to take armes againft the *Romanes*, to whom hee gaue many affronts. The fame *Dion* reports in his 55. & 56. booke a memorable anfwere that the faid *Battus* gaue *Tyberius Cæfar*, who demaunding of him why he had ftirred vp the people to fo long and bloody a war? Anfwered that the *Romães* thē-felues were caufe, in that they had fent them wolues for their gardiens, not dogs & fheapheards. But as it commonly happens amongft thefe barbarous natiõs, through the weaknes or ignorãce of the men of thofe times, wee haue nothing left vs whereby wee may know who were the kinfmen or fucceffors to this *Batto* of *Holland*; fo that we know not any thing for certaine of their cuftomes or manner of liuing, but that *Tafitus* hath toucht at thē, as if it were in paffing by, and that breefly. Some fay that this *Batto* re-edefied the Caftle of *Nymeghen*, and compaft the town with wals, & that he being dead his fon *Hefus* augmented it by adding therto that quarter which is called *Hefelbergh*, or
                                                         the

the hil of *Hesus.* The which town the Kings that
succeeded after him caused to be the metropolitaine of *Batauia* or *Holland,* and their seege royal.
Al which *Gerard* of *Nymeghen* recites, affirming
that he had drawn them from the commentaries
of Princes. *Strabo* the Geographer makes mention of one *Peremire* king of the *Batauians*, who
had a daughter called *Rhamis,* married to the son
of *Siquter* Duke of the *Cherusques,* who afterwards was led in triumph to *Rome* by *Germanicus
Cæsar.* I haue not known any man that hath writ
how great the limits were, or how far the inheritance of *Batto* extended; some haue made it too
little, in taking away a gr at part from it; wherefore I wil assigne him his confines to a haire (as
it were) to remaine firme and stable for euer.

Batauia then which I cal the antient, took heretofore his beginning from the separation of the
Rhyne at the castle of *Lober,* & was inclos'd on one
side with that which we properly call the *Rhyne,*
(which had wont to sal neer unto *Catwick* into the
Brittish Ocean, which gulph is now choakt vp,
as wee will shew hereafter) and the *Wahal,* from
whence falling again into the *Merwe*, and from
thence into that which we cal the *Meuze,* passing
by *Bryel* renders him self into the same Sea: In
which cōpasse and circuit of the *Rhyne* ther are a
great number of Townes, and to beginne aboue,
first, *Huessen*, *Tyell*, *Buiren*, *Wicktarduirsted,*
Vtrecht, *Viane*, *Culembourg*, *Aspeney*, *Henclom,* *Leerdan*, *Iselsteyne*, *Montfort*, *VVoerden*
Ondewater

Oudewater, *Gorcum* , *Wandrichom* , *Schoonhouen*, *Dordrecht*, *Goud*, *Leyden* , *Delft* , *Rotterdam*, *Schie-dā* and the *Bryell*. I wil not meddle with *Nieuport* right ouer againſt *Schoonhouen* and *Haesrecht*; for that by their ruines other townes haue beene augmented. If any oppoſe to the deſignements of the limits , ſaying that the *Betuwe* (which is a part of the Dutchy of *Gelderland*) is that which properly ought to bee called *Batauia* : I will ſend him to the iudge and principall defender of the cauſe, *Ptolomeus* of *Alexandria* , who puts *Lugodunum* (which is *Leyden*) amongſt the *Batauians*, where hee ſayes expreſly λιγοδεινον βαταβῶν *Lugodunum Battauorum* , which is a Towne diſtant foure thouſand paces from thence. What will this controuler ſay of *Cæfars* meaſuring of it , who reckons it to bee fourſcore thouſand paces after it parts from the *Rhyne* before it enters into the Sea ; between which two riuers hee cannot deny but that the *Batauian* Iſle is incloſed : *Tacitus* him-ſelfe ends it at the *Meuze* , from whence it deſcends to the Sea. This inheritance of *Battus* which I willingly cal the old *Batauia*, for that certaine hundreths of years after his death *Drufus*, of two branches or gulphs made three , the 3. falling into the middle ſea cōmonly called *Zuyderzee* firſt paſſing by *Campen* in the country of *Oueryſſell*, amplifying therby the territory of *Batauia* : the which he did to excerciſe his army to preuent idleneſſe in
them

them;beginning at *Iseloort*, which bräch is called the riuer of *Isell*, it seemes also that he gaue them an other *Isle* of the *Rhyne* more large and spatious which we may cal a new *Batauia*. To expres this name, al that is comprized between the gulphes of the *Flye*, the old *Rheyne* and the *Meuze*, render them-selues into the *Brittish* sea, the firmnesse of this middle gulph of the *Rheyne* being the cause that al this land holds together. The which (by reason of the continual ditches or downes made to resist the rage of the Sea) seperates *Batauia* from *Freezland*. *Pomponius Mela* the *Geographer* calls it a great Lake , which is not so vntil the flowing of the Ocean come into the *Zuyderzee*, and so to *Amsterdam* and *Sparendam* , and from thence by *Scluses* to *Harlem*: Al which agrees very well with *Tacitus* , who saies it is but a short passage from one side to the other , & yet it is so large from *Encuysen* to *Harlinghen*, that with a faire season and a good wind it will aske some foure houres passage.

To conclude who wil know the manners, fashion of liuing and military vertue of the ancient *Batauians* or *Hollanders* , let him read for the ancient, perticularly *Cornelius Tacitus*, and for the moderne *Hadrianus Iunius* a Phisition of the towne of *Horne*, in his *Batauia* : wherein I doubt not but he shall find much to content him.

Concerning their vertue and military discipline, I dare affirme that the *Hollander* at this

day

day, doe not only equall their predeceſſors but farre exceed them (both by Land, and Sea, wherein their Aunceſtors had no experience) as it hath well appeared for theſe forty yeares a-gainſt all the attempts of that puiſſant Monarch of *Spayne*.

Dordrecht.

THis towne is the firſt in order of 28. in the County of *Holland*, & hath the firſt voyce in the aſſembly of the Eſtates for that County. It is ſeated vpon the *Merwe*, but ſo as this riuer is cõ-poſed of the *Rhyne*, the *Wahall*, the *Meuze* and *Ling*, which all being ioined in one, paſſe before the town, ſo as we may ſay it is ſeated vpon 4. ri-uers, the *Merwe*, *Wahal*, *Meuz* & *Ling*. And ſo they repreſ̃ed the portrait of it by theſe two lattin verſes at the happy entrance of king *Philip* the 2. into their town in the yeare of our Lord 1549.

Me Moſa, et Wahalis, *cum Linga*, Meruaꝗ, cingũt *Æternam* Batauæ *virginis ecce fidem.*

Guirt with the *Meuſe, Wahal*, the *Merwe* & *Ling* See *Hollands* virgin faith vn-altering.

THere are great diuerſities of opinions about the etimologie of the name of it, ſome there are that would haue it called *Durdrecht* and not **Dordrecht**, ſaying that this word *Drecht* was
heretofore

heretofore as much as to say a *Fayre* or a free
market, called in lattin *Forum* : Of the which
name there are diuers townes after the names of
great perfonages , as *Forum Varronis* not farre
from *Milan*; *Forum Cornelii* in *Emilia*, which is
now called *Imola*. *Forum Claudii* now called *Ta-
rentaife*, *Forum Iulii*,*Forum Liuii* and others, and
fo by that reafon *Durdrecht* fhould haue its
name from fome certaine man called *Duret* ; yet
the *Annals* of *Holland* make but fmall mention
of any fuch. The fame may bee fayd of *Haes-
strecht* three thoufand paces from *Tergoude*,
heretofore a towne that had three Caftles, and
two Monafteries , now a Village in the middeft
of the Earldome of *Blois* , between the townes of
Schoonhouen and *Goude*,which three townes were
the proprietary inheritance of the Earles of
Blois,as you may more amply read in the general
hiftory of the *Netherlands*.

The fame may likewife be faid of *Moore-drecht*,
Papendrecht,*Suyndrecht*,*Barendrecht*,and *Slydrecht*
all Villages of *Holland* not farre from *Dordrecht*,
which is alfo witneffed by the old feale of the
faid towne ; the circumfcription is *Sigillum
oppidanorum* in *Durdrecht*:The feale of the townf-
men of *Durdrecht*.

It is alfo found in records, & amongft others in
the Bull of the Emperor *Henry* the fourth,*Thure-
Drecht*. Be as it may be in regard of the ancient-
neffe of the vfe and that it lafts to this day,

we

we wil giue it no other name but *Dordrecht.*

This Towne is long in forme of a compaſſe rich and well peopled, and indeed a very ſtore-houſe of all things neceſſary for mans life : being ſince the yeare of our Lord, 1 4 2 1. become an Iland : the *Wahal* the *Meuze*, and the *Sea*, by the breach of a ditch filleth all the gulph (which be-fore was firme land and ioyning to the Dutchy of *Brabant*) and drowned 72. Villages, where there periſhed aboue an hundreth thouſand ſoules, with al their ſubſtance. The time of this deluge is expreſſed by theſe two lattin verſes.

DurDreChto InCVBVIt VIs atroX InCIta VentIs
Vrbſ quâ dIſsILVIt protInVs haVſta MarI.

In one thouſand four hundred twenty and one *DORT* felt that feareful diſſolution.

THis deluge hapned by the wickedneſſe of a country-man that enuying the proſperity of his neighbour, aſſayed to drowne his land that lay neere the Sea, or at leaſt to ſpoyle it, not thin-king what would follow : and to accompliſh this his curſed reſolution, he wrought a hole through the earth and made a gutter, that the water of tho Sea might drowne his neighbours land; but the vehemency of it was ſo great, that of a little ſtreame, the Sea gayning more, it made ſuch a gap, that it was vnpoſſible to be ſtopt, and

ſo

fo all the country about *Dordrecht*, as it is yet to bee feene was loft. Notwithftanding fince by little and little *Adrian Cornellis vander Mylen* a Bourguemaiftet of the faid town and his children haue recouered, and yet dayly doe recouer a good part of it, by vertue of a grant giuen by *Charles* the fifth Emperour to the faid Bourguemaifter, fo that at this day there are fayre feeldes, in firme land, adioyning to the fayd Towne, with the little Caftell of *Craefteyne*, belonging to the faid *Vander Mylen*.

This Towne efpecially the ftreete called *Den Langen-dike* hath the moft fayre and lofty buildings that are to bee found in all *Holland*, with their ftore-houfes and caues for Wines all vaulted, fo that they neuer fee neither Sunne or Moone. There is a fayre great Church where there had wont to bee a Colledge of *Chanons*. The hiftory of *Holland* fets downe certaine foolifh fables of the foundation of this Church, which I forbeare to repeat for that they are too ridiculous.

A Faucon fhotte from that part of the towne towards *Papendrecht*; there are high and eminent reliques of the Caftle of *Merwe* neere to the ditch where before the Inundation was, as alfo of the Village and Barony of *Merwe*, from whence the Lords of *Afperen* and *Langueraeck* haue their Barony, inioying yet
E   both

both profits and preheminences in the towne of
Dordrecht.

Holding vppon certaine dayes in the yeare,
either in his owne perfon or by his Bailyffe
or sheriff, as large power in iudging caufes
as the Bourguemaifter and Councell of the town
whofe authority in cafe of iustice at this day
ceafes.

In this drown'd land and in the *Merwe*
there are great store of *Salmons* and *Sturgeons* taken, befides it abounds in fundry other
fort of fifhes, the water beeing for foure or fiue
leagues fweete.

The priuiledge and right of the staple
for all forts of Marchandife, as Wine, Corne,
Wood and other commodities that paffe by
them comming out of *Germanie*, *Gelderland*,
Cleues and *Iuilliers* belonging to this towne of
Dordrecht.

VVell feeing wee haue made mention of
this word *Staple*, it followes neceffarily for the
true vnderftanding of it, that we fay fomething
both for the name and vfe of it.

The word *Eftaple* is a *French* word, deriued
from the lattin word *Stabulum*, fo that the word
Staple is a market or publicke place in a towne
ordained for the beftowing of VVine, Corne,
VVood and other Marchandife that comes fró
other countries; euery Towne hauing their feuerall priuiledges, according to the graunt of the

Prince

Prince. Not without great greefe and vexation
to others both Marchants and Marryners that
bring them thether. As for example, The towne
of *Arras* is the *Staple* for *Arthois*, and *Valenciennes*
for *Henault*, for Wines that are brought out of
France by land into the *Low-Countries* : So that
the Marchants or Carryers are conltrained
to bring them thether before any other place,
and there to bee ftayde a certayne time
in the *Staple* to fee who will buy in the
Market , the which beeing done they
may carrie them away whether they thinke
beft.

The towne of *Middlebourgh* in *Zealand* is
the *Staple* for Wines that come from *France*,
Spayne, *Portugal* and other Countryes brought
thether by Sea. But the priuiledges of the town
of *Dordrecht* are more ftrickt and compelling;for
they are of fuch force and vertue, that what-fouer
is brought either by the *Rhyne*, or *Meuze*, be it
corne, wine, pitch, cole or any other Marchandife
paffing by them , they are compelled (vppon
paine of forfeyture of all , if they bee taken,
not hauing payed their duty) to difcharge their
boates or barkes in their Hauen , and to paie
all rights , cuftomes , impoftes and other
duties what-foeuer , and alfo to difcharge
their Marchandzfe in Shippes of the towne
or of the Cittizens and free Marryners: or
elfe to make fome agreement with them and fo
E 2　　　they

they may paſſe them in thoſe that belong to the
cuſtome or impoſt. And notwithſtanding that
the priuiledges are at this preſent diuers , and
vary one from another , according to the nature
of the marchandiſe and condition of the townes
to whome ſuch priuileges are graunted, yet they
haue euer from the firſt beginning beene called
by the name of *Eſtaple.* The which(being ſometimes in one towne,ſometimes in another,either
for the ſcituation or ſome other occation)cauſe
a great commodity and benifit to the country
both in generall and particuler , and a faire reuenew and large profit to the Prince of the ſame.

This towne as the firſt in rancke hath power
to coyne both ſiluer and gold,a priueledge deni-
ed to any other towne of Holland what-ſo-euer.
In this towne the Prince or Earle of Holland is
put in poſſeſſion of this county , taking his oth to
the ſtates of the country , and receiuing their homage and feallty.

Harlem.

THe ſecond towne of Holland in rancke and
prerogatiue is the towne of *Harlem* , which
within this thirty yeares , before *Amſterdam* was
made greater, was the greateſt and faireſt of all
Holland, as well in faire buildings,as ſweete and
good temperature of ayre, hauing neither the
Sea nor Mariſhes or Fens to annoy it; ſeated in
the

the middeſt of a good land fit both for tillage and for paſture, enuironed with faire country houſes, Farmes, little woods and many caſtles and villages, and to conclude ſeated reaſonable high, and very pleaſant. It hath one very great Church with a high ſteeple ſupported with great columnes or pillars, and much longer then any other in the Low-countries. There paſſeth now through it a riuer called Sparre, which falls out of a lake of freſh water into the chanell that runnes towards the townes of *Amſterdam* and *Leyden*, which is called the ſea of *Harlem*; which riuer hath bene drawne with great labour and charge from that of *Tye* by the ſluces of *Sparendam*, about halfe a league from thence: before the towne on that ſide towards *Leyden* there was heretofore a very pleaſant wood which during the ſeege of the *Spaniards* was cut downe by the *Allamaines* that were quartred on that ſide in the village of *Hemſted*; But within a few yeares after the Magiſtrate of the towne cauſed it to be replanted, ſo as in a ſhort time it became as pleaſant as it was before, ſeruing the inhabitants of the towne for delightfull walkes for the excerſiſe of their ſpirits, and keeping many people of the towne from the Tauernes and ſuch other places, in paſſing their time there. There is there likewiſe made very great ſtore of fine white linnen cloth, much deſired and ſought for from *Spaine*, *Italy*, and other countries, and alſo good wollen

E 3   cloth,

cloth, which for the dye equalls any other country, and is like-wise transported into forraine
regions.

Touching the *Etymology* or deriuation of the
name, I may not rely vpon *Lewis Guichardine*,
who hath followed the old Dutch chronicle of
Holland, but rather follow that learned Phisition
and Histoand Historiographer of *Horne*, Doctor *Adrianus
Iunius*, who affirmes that the *Harlemois* are if-
sued from the bloud of the Kings of Freezland,
who first built both the their towne and castle in
the yeare of the natiuity of our Sauiour Iesus
Christ fiue hundred and sixe. The castle was
seated vpon the chanell that runnes towards
Egmont, not farre from *Heimskirk*, all built of
great and large bricke, as yet at this day is to be
seene by the ruines and ground worke of the
walls. The demolishment whereof some attribute to the tyrany of the Lord of the place, o-
thers to the fury of the people, who sought to
extirpe and roote out the Nobility. This castle
alone at this time was not demolished, but like
a violent thunder they threw downe all to the
ground. Seeing wee are speaking of this
castle, I thinke it not amisse (although it be set
downe in the history of the Netherlands) to relate a memorable accident that then hapned, as
a strange note of true coniugall loue. And thus
it was.

The

The Lord of the place hauing by his exaction and cruelty made him-selfe odious to all his people, and he and his wife being beseeged, and so prest for want of victualls, that he was compelled (hauing no other meanes to escape) to enter into treaty for the rendering of the towne. His wife(a true mirror of piety and loue towards her husband) among other articles for the rendring of the towne, capitulated that shee might haue as much of her most pretious mooueables as she could carry out at one time, the which being graunted, shee (with the helpe of her chamber-maide) carried her husband lockt in a chest out of the castle, leauing all her rings and iewells behind her : In imitation of the wife of *Guelphe* Duke of *Bauaria*, who in the like necessity prayed the Emperor *Conrad*, that she and her Ladies might carry out that which they held most deare and pretious : the Emperor imagining it was nothing but their rings and iewels, shee(and all the Ladies after her example) tooke her husband on her shoulders and her little childe in her armes and so issued forth . But let vs returne to *Harlem* ; to the which (and that iustly) wee may attribute the noble inuention of the Art of printing, although some (to selfe-willed) maintaine that it came from *Mogunce* or *Mentz*, an imperiall and electorall towne of *Germany*; but it is for certaine confirmed by many notable and auncient personages

E 4 of

of the said towne of *Harlem* that from father to sonne they haue held, and yet to this day doe hold it, that about a hundreth and seauenty years agoe there dwelt in the sayd Towne in a very fayre house, which is yet to bee seene standing right againft the royall Pallace, one *Laurence Ians* surnamed *Sachriftain* (which was a good and honourable hereditary office in his family) to whome this place of honour (which some other heretofore haue robd them off) belongs. This man walking forth for his recreation into the Wood of *Harlem* (as it was the custome of the beft *Burgers* after dinner & supper) began to cutte in little peeces of wood the letters of his name, printing them on the backe of his hand, which pleasing him hee cutte three or four lines, which he beat with Inke and printed them vpon paper, wherewith beeing much ioyd (as it is said the worekman delights in his worke) he determined to find out an other kind of inke more fasting and holding, and so with his kinsman *Thomas Peterse* (who left foure sonnes; that came to the place of *Burguemaifters* which I speak to that end that I would haue no man thinke that so noble an inuention could haue beginning from low-spirited and mechanical men)found out an other way to print whole sheetes, but of one side only, which are yet to be seene in the said towne, and besides a booke in *Flemifh* called the Mirrour of health; which hee did in the instancy of this art,

(no

no inuention being brought to perfection at the firft affay) and affaying to print the fheet on the other fide, the right fide tooke not, and fo hee fpoyled the impreffion. Afterwards he changed his letters of wood into lead, and after that into tinne to make them more firme, leffe plyant and more durable, the remainder of which Caracters are yet to be feene in the houfe of the faid *Laurence*, fince poffeft and dwelt in by *Gerard Thomas* an honourable old Cittizen, who died within this fifty yeares. This new Art neuer feen before made euery one fo inamoured of it; that it yeelded him much profit, and his bufineffe fo increafed that he was conftrayned to take feruants to help him, but in the choyce of them he was fo curious, that hee intertained not any, but hee took an oth of the not to difcouer the art to any body, beeing very defirous to keepe the principall fecret to him-felfe; yet notwithftanding al his care, one of his feruants called *Iohn* of his owne furname, who hauing learnt to compofe, caft the letters, and other things belonging to this Art, fpyed his time and oportunity to runne away, the which he did vppon Chriftmas day at night when euery body was at Euen fong, and his maifter abfent, taking away the Caracters & other thinges belonging to this Art, running away like a Domeftique theefe with the goods and honour of his maifter to *Amfterdam*; from thence to *Cologne*, and afterwards to *Mogunce* or

Mentz

Mentz where he might liue more safe and keepe open shop of his theft. *Laurens Ianse* printed the Doctrinall of *Alexander*, a grammar then much in vse, and the treatises of *Peeter* of *Spaine*. Behold then what hath beene affirmed from time to time by many ancient and honorable personages of the first inuention of it, besides the good and sufficient proofes that they of *Harlem* haue; wherefore it were a great wrong to robbe them of the honor of this inuention, as that theese did his Maifter, to make his name famous in the towne of *Mentz*.

Polidore Virgili in his treatise of the inuention of things, attributes it to one *Iohn Gutttenbergh* a gentleman of *Germany*. I must needs grant that the art by succeffion of time was brought to a greater perfection then in *Holland*, but they like infants suckt their milke from *Laurence Ianse* of *Harlem* the first inuentor. Well wee see that it was sufficiently diuulged, for in the yeare one thousand fiue hundred, fourty eight, one *Conrade* (a *German* also) carried this art into *Italy* and so to *Rome*. After him *Nicholas Iohnson* a *French* man inricht it merueloufly; but aboue all *Aldus Manutius a Roman*, a man well read and very learned in the *Greeke* and latin tounges, brought this art to perfection, by his extreame dilligence & great trauail, neuer shrinking at any charge or trouble but only respecting his honor & the publique good, so that euery man desired his bookes

of

of *Aldus* edition, they were so neate and exactly printed, hee beeing the first that euer sette vp a printing presse for the *Greeke* tongue.

The people of this towne of *Harlem* had the honour of the taking of *Pelusium* (now called *Damiette* a famous towne in *Ægipt*) which the Christian princes had long time beseeged, among whome was *William* Earle of *Holland*: While the Princes were consulting how they might first get the hauen of the town, wnich was shut vp with 2. great chaines of yron, fastned to two strong Towers from one side to the other, they of *Harlem* caused a hulke or two bee armed from the toppe to the bottome with sawes made of yron a purpose to cut the chaynes, and with a good gale of wind at the returne of the Sea, ranne with full sayles spread against the chaines, which they broke : and notwithstanding all the arrowes and other shotte made at them from the two Towers, past on and got the hauen, making passage for the rest of the Christian ships and so the towne was wonne The honour whereof was giuen to them of *Harlem*, and in memory of their valour their armes (which before was a dry *Tree*) were by the Emperour changed to a *Swoord* compassed with sixe stars, to the which the Patriarke of *Ierusalem* added vpon the point a crosse *Patteé*, which are at this day the Armes of the towne of *Harlem*.

This town was greatly afflicted and distressed

in

in the yeare 1 5 7 2. the *Spaniards* lying before it eight moneths to their great losse, yet in the end by reason of famine it was constrained to yeeld to the mercy of the Duke of *Alua*, the violent fury of whose soldiars brought it well neere to ruine. During this seege there was obserued in the *Bourgers* and inhabitants a meruailous resolution to defend, and constancy to maintaine them-selues; the garrison soldiers & they neuer dif-agreeing, which gaue example to the other townes of *Holland* to arme them-selues against the *Spanish* fury, as we will shew hereafter in the description of the towne of *Alcmar*.

Delf.

THe Towne of *Delf* (heretofore renowned) (but now much more) for brewing good beere which they transporte through all *Holland*, *Zeeland* and other neighbour countries, not much inferior to that of England) holdes the third ranck and suffrage in the session of the Estates for the County of *Holland*. This Towne hath his name from his situation, being seated vpon a chanell that comes from the *Hage*, and falls into the Riuer of *Meuze* at *Delfs-Hauen*, which chanel cut in a right line cost a great deal of labour and charge before it was made.

This town was first founded by *Godfrey* called the crooke-backe Duke of *Lorraine*, who beeing
called

called in and affifted by the Bifhoppe of *Vtrecht*,chafed out of *Holland* Earle *Robert* the *Frifon*,the Lady *Gheertruyd* his wife and hir little fon that fhe had in her firft marriage by *Florent* the firft of that name and fixth Earle of *Holland*.

This Duke of *Lorraine* inioyed the faid Earldome aboue foure yeares, during which time he built the towne of *Delf*.

But the little fonne of *Geertruyd* being growne fomewhat bigger with the helpe of neighbour Princes, both *Germaines* (in regard of his mother)and others , re-entred with a goodly army into *Holland* to giue him battaile,where he ouerthrew him,and hauing chafed him out recouered al his coútry:But fhortly after one of his feruants as hee was at the priuy run him into the fundament with a Iauelin , of which hee died in the towne of *Maeftricht*.

This towne of *Delf* was ftraightly befeeged by Count *Albert* of *Bauaria* (as you may read more amply in the hiftory of the *Netherlands*) fo as being conftrained to yeeld,the Earle caufed a great part of the wall to bee throwne down. Yet notwithftanding fhortly after they did him great feruice in the warre hee had with the *Frifons* (the other Townes refufing to ayd him) and couragioufly releafed certain *Englifh* foldiers engaged in a Fort befeeged by the *Frifons* , for which duty and valour of theirs , the Earle confented to the re-building

of

of their walles. There befell a pittifull accident to this towne in the month of *Maie* 1536. being set on fire by cafual:y & the fire fo difperft that it was almoft burned before there could bee any helpe, yet they wanted not water, for it hath two chanels that paffe through the towne.

But the wind being very vehement, fo difperft the fire, that there fcarce could any thing be faued; yet like the *Phænix* renuing out of her afhes, this Towne was built againe more fayre and magnificent then euer before, remedying their error in the firft building (which was the cheefe caufe of their ruine) by not fuffering one houfe to bee thatcht with ftraw; but high and ftately buildings without, with their inward ornaments and furnitures fo neat and fitting that in the whole *Netherlands* it is not to be parraleld; the ftreets likewife fo cleane and well kept, that notwithftanding the greateft rayne there is no durt to touch the fhoo, fo as indeed they feem to be alwaies wafht.

In this fire there hapned fo memorable an accident, that (happily) the like hath not beene recorded in antient or moderne ftories: It is moft true that *Pliny* and other authors fet downe (as a matter of notable and great confideration) that the young *Storkes* when the old ones are growne in yeares and paft helping of themfelues fupply that want by feeding them, and when their winges fayle in paffing the Sea,

the

the young ones take them on their backes: But that which hapned of the fame birds in the towne of *Delph* is of greater confequence and more remarkeable.

This towne is fo feated for the feeding and bringing vp of thefe birdes that it is hard to fee any houfe vppon the which they are not nefted to breed in: This fire hapned vppon the third of *Maie* in the yeare aforefaid 1 5 3 6. at which time the young *Storkes* are growne pretty and big, the old ones perceiuing the fire to approch their nefts, attempted to carry them away but could not they were fo waighty, which they perceiuing neuer ceafed with their winges fpread couering them, till they all perifhed in the flames. *Gafpar Veldius* (an author of reuerent efteeme) in his booke of *Storkes* recountes the fame, and alfo *D. Adrianus Iunius* in his hiftory of *Holland*, from whom I haue drawn thefe lattin verfes following.

Candida et obftreperis inuifa Ciconia *ramis.*
Pignora ab ardenti viderat igne premi.
Æripatne fuos, et aperta pericula tentet?
Hinc fuadet Pietas, vitæ amor inde vetat,
Hanc luctam pietas generofa diremit, et vrna
Effe cadem, et fobolis vult libitena fuæ.
Iam minor Affyrium Phænicem *fama loquatur*
Viuere quæ bufto quærit, at ifta mori.

The

The white hu'd *Storke* that neuer fits on bowe
Seeing her young in flames; ah how it paines her!
Shall fhe for them aduenture life to loofe?
Piety bids her trye, but feare reftraines her:
Yet piety her feare foone ouerthrowes,
And fo one tomb with her poore yong containes her,
Giue place thou *Phænix* then: thou feeks new breath
By being Burnt: but fhe fought onely death.

AT *Delf* there are excellent clothes made
both great and fmall that are much defired
in other countries, commonly called in their language *Delfs puyck.*

In this towne was borne that abhominable
Monfter for herefie and impofture called *Dauid
George*, but his right name was *Hans van Burcht* a
painter of glaffes and the fonne of a painter, one
that infeded with the poyfon of his herefie the
towne of *Munfter* in *Weftphalia*; A man altogether
vnlearned, yet of fo fubtile a memory and vnderftanding and withall fo eloquent, accompanied
with a kind of grauity, that hee could perfwade his
followers to what hee thought good, whereby
he not onely made him-felfe chiefe head of a new
fed, but caufed him-felfe by his defciples and
followers to bee adored as GOD him-felfe,
perfwading them that hee was the true *Mef-
fias.*

This Gallant (or rather Diuell) was married and
had children, gouerning his familie in outward
fhew indifferent honeftly, but in effed had neither

her religion, vertue or any goodneſſe whatſoe-
uer : notwithſtanding(the people being for the
moſt part light and inconſtant, louers of no-
uelties, wicked and contentious, feeding their
ambition by the firſt occaſion offered)hee ſowed
and diſperſed his hereſie vnder colour of diuers
extrauagant lawes throughout the lower *Germany*,being already ſo far aduanced in this buſineſſe
that diuers that followed him as his deſciples
bound them-ſelues to the will of this damnable
Arch-hereticke : But this impiety beginning to
bee diſcouered and the Magiſtrate making dilli-
gent purſuit and ſeuere inquiſition after it,as the
caſe required, this monſter fled to *Baſil* in *Suit-
zerland* with his wife,children, houſhold and all
other his baggage, where being ariued hee was
taken to be a rich Marchant of the *Netherlands*
fledde thether for his religion, and to auoyd the
fury of the Imperial P*lacarts*,where by his friends
and confederates hee was welcomed and much
made off. When hee went to Church with his
wife and children hee was accompanied (like a
great Lord) with a troope of followers and
ſeruants, ſhewing at his firſt comming great
liberallity to the poore, which made him to bee
much admyred. Being well prouided of money
he bought a fayre houſe in the towne, and a Caſtle called *Benningen* halfe a league out of the
towne,dwelling ſometimes in the one and ſome-
time in the other : To augment his loue and

reputation with the Cittizens hee matcht fome
of his children with the principall of the towne
endowing them very ritchly, ftill aduancing
and teaching in priuate his moft damnable herefie, confirming thofe that were abfent by letters
and bookes which hee caufed to bee printed in
his Caftle of *Beningen* : Hee dyed in the fayd
towne of *Bafil* in the yeare of our Lord 1 5 5 6.
for meere greefe that one of his followers was
reuolted, fearing that by his meanes hee might
be difcouered and fo punifhed. Before his death
his difciples that thought him to bee God feeing
him draw towards death, hee refolutely fayd vnto them, bee not amazed, I goe to beginne to
fhew my power. Chrift my predeceffor (to fhew
his power)rofe again the third day, and I to fhew
my greater glory will rife againe at three yeares.
O horrible blafphemy ! The Magiftrate beeing
throughly informed of his life and doctrine caufed his proceffe to be drawn after his death, & by
a fentence his body was taken out of the ground,
and iuftice done as if he had bin aliue; his goods
being confifcated,& his books burnt : fome of his
followers acknowledged & abiured their errors,
and imbracing again the reformed religion were
with al courtefie and gentleneffe pardoned, and
the whole hiftory of it fet forth in print, both in
lattin and dutch to the view of the world. In oppofition to this wicked monfter the town of *Delf*
hath brought forth many excellent perfonages &
among

among the reſt *Ioos Salſbout* an excellent Poet and
Chancellor of *Gelderlãd*; *Arnoult* his ſon who ſucceeded his father in the ſame office of Chancellor, and ſince Preſident of the priuy Counſell at
Bruſſels, and from that to be Preſident for the affaires of the *Netherlands* in *Spaine*: *Cornelius Muſa*
Prouoſt of S. *Agatha*, a man of rare vertue and
knowledge, a great Diuine & an excellent Poet.
who was vniuſtly put to death by the Earle of
March about thirty-fiue yeares ſince.

Leyden.

THere hath bin much diſpute and great diuerſity of opinions about the deriuation of this
name of *Leyden*, but I will content my ſelfe that
Ptolemy called it *Lugdunum Battauorum*, & *Antoni-*
nus in his Itinerary or guide for waies to *Rome*,
cals it *Lugdunum Caput Germanorum*, the head citty of the *Germaines*, or the firſt Citty of the *Ro-*
maine Empire, from it beginning his Iourney to
Rome; concerning the lattin and dutch woord
of *Leyden* I will content my ſelfe with the antient vſe, for that many learned lattin Authors
haue alſo called it *Leyda*; bee it as it may, yet
this is moſt certayne that it hath beene here-tofore a towne of great importance, for the *Ro-*
main Prætor that gouerned that quarter kept alwaies his reſidence and garriſon in that towne;
and the hiſtoryes of *Holland* recount that from

the

the firſt Earles and long after it was called the chamber of *Holland.*

It is ſeated in a low and euen coumtry, full of ditches and chanels, beutified with farmes, gardens and other delights round about. It incloſes in it ſelfe thirty one Iſles, paſſing from the one to the other in boates, beſides nineteene more that haue bridges to paſſe ouer.

To conclude there are in this towne 145 bridges, an hundreth and foure built of free ſtone, and the reſt of wood : It is one of the ſix chiefe townes of *Holland*, and the fourth in preheminence and ſuffrage: It is the cheefe for that quarter of *Rind-Land*, hauing vnder it 49. townes and villages, the moſt part of which bring their commodities thether (as butter, milke, cheefe, lard , foule , fruites and other neceſſaryes) to bee ſold in the Market, abounding in all thinges elſe that the earth may bring forth, and ſufficiently ſtored with fiſh, the Sea being not aboue a league from it and compaſſed with many freſh waters. It is likewiſe ſo ſtored with ſundry kinds of fowle , that it is incredible but to them that know it.

This town is fairly ſeated in a delicate proſpectiue, euen in the heart of *Holland*, neatly built and fit for the muſes to dwel in; for which cauſe the Sates of *Holland* in the yeare of our Lord 1575 after they were releaſed of their long and dangerous ſiege erected an vniuerſity there, furniſhing

it

it with profeſſions in all languages, giuing them
good and ſufficient ſtipends, drawing to them
the ſufficients men in all profeſſions that can be
found in Chriſtendome, as at this day the Seignior of *L'eſcale*, *Cluſius*, *Baudius*, and others profeſ-
ſing Phyloſophy, Phyſicke and the lawes : They
want not alſo moſt excellent and learned Di-
uines, hauing within this tenne yeares loſt
three as rare ones as any were in Chriſtendome, to wit the Lord of Saint *Aldegond*, D.
Francis Iunius and *Trelcatius*, profeſſors in
the greeke and lattin tongues, and in Di-uinity.

In the middeſt of this towne there is an old
Caſtle ſeated vppon a higher mote, in the
which there is a great large and deepe Well all
of ſtone, but now dry, there is not a houſe in
this Caſtle to dwell in, but compaſſed about
the mote and aboue with ſome trees, and although it bee of no vſe, yet it is reſerued for
the antiquity of it. *Ianus Douza* a learned Gentleman and Poet of *Leyden*, hath written of it in
theſe verſes.

> *Putatur Engiſtus*, Brittanno *or be*
> *Redux, poſuiſſe victor.*

> Tis held, victorious *Hengiſt* builded me
> At his returne from conquered *Britanie*.

SInce called *Bourg* of which came the name of
Burgraue (which is as much as to ſay an Earle

of a Towne , which wee call Vifcounts) the
title remained long in the Noble family of the
Lordes of *Waffenare* , who held the Viconty
of *Leyden* and the Iurifdiction of *Rhyn-landt,*
with the Dependances both of it and *Ter-goud,*
vntill the yeare of our LORD 1 2 5 1. after the
death of Vicont *Iames* , his daughter *Chriftien-
ne* beeing vnder the protection of the Earle of
Holland who vtterly fpoyled it , yet the poffeffion thereof was deliuered againe by the
Counteffe *Iaqueline* , vnto the fayd family of
the *Waffenares* , but *Philip* Duke of *Burgondy* fuc-
ceeding in the faid County tooke it away againe;
where-vppon Vifcount *Iames,* the fonne of *Henry* in a full affembly of the Eftates contefted
againft the Duke, demaunding againe his antient patrimony , but his meanes beeing too
weake againft fo puiffant a Prince , hee was conftrayned to ceafe his title , and to content
him-felfe with what it pleafed the Duke to
giue him , which was but the bare title of Vifcount.

There are in this Towne three parifh Churches, in Saint *Pancratius* there is a company
of Chanoins , and in Saint *Peeters* there is a lofe
of bread turned to a ftone, fafely kept in a place
yrond about for a perpetuall remembrance of
the ftrangeneffe of the accident , and this it was:
In the yeare of our Lord 1 3 1 6. a great famine
happening in the towne, a poore woman went
to

to her owne fifter that was very rich to borrow a loafe of bread, to faue her and her children from ftaruing, her fifter denyed that fhee had any in the houfe, fhee infifted that fhee had, where-vppon her ritch fifter fell a fwearing and curfing, praying God that if fhe had any it might bee turned into a ftone, which God miraculoufly fuffered to bee done, to the confufion of this pittileffe and periured woman, it is not long fince there were two loaues, but now there is but one.

Two little leagues from *Leyden* is *Waffenare* a fayre and beautifull Village, with the two *Catwicks*, *Voorburch* and *Voorfcoten*, belonging now to the Counts of *Ligne*, the mafculine lyne of the Vicounts of *Leyden* and Lords of *Waffenare* being vtterly extinct. In this towne *Hans van Leyden* a knife-maker by his trade was born a moft difloyal Anabaptift, and one that by ftrange and extraordinary meanes fo befotted the people that hee made him felfe King of *Munfter* in *Weftphalia* to the great and pittifull ruine of it. In the end he was befeeged by the Bifhoppe (affifted by the Princes of *Germany*) and after almoft a yeares fiege this King of perdition and his complices were taken and punifhed according to their merites. This Kinge and one of his cheefe Councellors (called *Knipperdolinge*) were putte into two Cages of yron and hung out of a high Tower, where they

F 4   ended

ended their cruell and moſt miſerable liues and reigne.

This town in oppoſition to this il hath brought forth many vertuous and learned men , as *Iohn Gherbrand* an excellent hiſtorian : *Engle-bert* of *Leyden* a rare Poet and Gramarian; *Nicholas Leonce* a good Retorician , and aboue all *Ianus Douza* Lord of *Noortwick* a moſt know-ing man in the tongues and a moſt famous Poet, as his printed workes teſtifie.

In the yeare of our Lord 1574. this towne was ſtraightly beſieged by the *Spaniards* and blockt vp with ſome thirty-ſixe fortes to fa-miſh them , wherein there dyed aboue ſeauen-thouſand men of famine and the peſtilence: the raizing of this ſeege and deliuerance of this towne can bee attributed to none but to GOD , although the Prince of *Orange* and the States of *Holland* did what they could as well by breaking of ditches and drawing vp Scluſes as otherwiſe, drowning all the countrie almoſt to the towne , but not ſo deepe that it would carry boates , vntill GOD ſent a ſtrong South-weſt-winde which draue the Sea into the riuers and land that great boates paſt a floate and victualled the towne : Which the *Spaniards* perceiuing they quitte all their Fortes and fledde for feare of beeing in-trapped.

But behold the wonderfull and re-markeable worke

worke of GOD who two daies after the Towne
was victualled sent as strong a North-west-wind
that beat backe the Sea againe from whence it
came, as you may read more at large in the history of the *Netherlands.*

Amsterdam

LEt vs now come to the towne of *Amsterdam*,
which within these hundreth yeares is become so rich and opulent that the very name of
it is famous throughout the whole world. It
takes name from the Riuer of *Amstell* that runnes
cleane through the towne, and fals into the *Zuyderzee,* from whence they sayle into all Seas, yea
the most remote and farre off of the whole
world.

They of the family of *Amstell* heertofore most
rich and opulent (now vtterly extinct) were the
first that compassed it with pallisadoes and held
the proprietary Lordship of it.

This towne since the decay of *Antwerpe* is become the most renowned of all the *Netherlands;*
ritch in people and of all sorts of Marchandises,
situate in the middest of *Holland* in a marish
country : It is strong by reason of the situation,
but stronger by art , the foundations of their
houses being made of piles of wood armed with
yron and other necessaries for that purpose, so
that the charge of building of most houses is
more

more chargeable vnder ground then aboue. The ordinary courfe of their Nauigation is to all other parts of the *Netherlands*, as *France*, *England*, *Spayne*, *Portugall*, *Germany*, *Poland*, *Denmarke*, *Lif-landt*, *Sueden*, *Norway*, *Oftlandt* and other feptentrional parts, where one may fee twice a yeare, foure or fiue hundred great fhippes arriue from *Dantzick*, *Rye*, *Reuell* and *Varna* with diuers and innumerable quantity of Marchandifes; fo as this Towne is become a wonderfull port or Staple, to the amazement of the beholders to fee fo many great hulkes belonging to the Cittizens and Inhabitants of the towne arriue there , and within fiue or fixe dayes to be all vnladen and ready for a new voyage.

There is yearely builc there a great number of tall & warlike fhips as wel for trade in Marchandife as for the war: Within this 2 5. or 30. yeares the town hath bin made greater (as wel in the circuit of the walls as in beautifull and faire building) by the halfe with a new church built where Saint *Anthonies* gate heretofore ftood: It is flanked about with great bulwarks , that anfwering one na other makes it inpregnable: what with the waters about it and the induftry of man it is warranted towards the Sea with a long double pallifadoe from the Eaft to the Weft, in which aboue a thoufand great fhips and innumerable of leffer **forts may fafely lye out of daunger.** There hath
beene

bene of long tyme two churches, the one called Saint *Nicholas* the old, the other our *Lady* the new.

To conclude this towne is a moſt ritch Store-houſe, not onely for the Low-Countries, but in a maner for all Chriſtendome, where al thinges neceſſary for the vſe of man are as ſoon to be foũd as in al the world beſids. *D. Adrianus Iunius* in his hiſtory òf *Holland* hath writ certaine accroſtique verſes in praiſe of it, which I thinke not vnfit to bee here inſerted both in lattin and Engliſh.

A ureus, vt perhibent, quondam ab Ioue perpluit imbar
M agnificis. turgentem opibus Rhodon: horrea Romæ
S icaniam eſſe Ceres, victuro munere ceſſit.
T orſit et huc occulos facilis Deus ipſe benignos,
E t me mactam opibus iuſſit, florereq, rebus
L ætis: at circundor aquis, pigraq, palude
O bſita: roboreoq, ſolo ſtant culmina nixa
D epactis alté trabibus, ſurgentia cælo.
A lternanſq, ſtatis vicibus, maris eſtus aperti
M ænia ſubcingit, qua parte exotica puppes
V ellifera inuectant onera, exportantq, frequenti
M ercatu, Heſperias *qua ſe dimittit in vndas*

B arbaraq, Eous *pandit quà littora Titan.*
E xpedio, quos noſtra tamen non area verrit,
L egifere cumulos Ceraris, *genitalia dona,*
G argara prouentu tanto non farris abundant.
I nferior fuerit, vel Momo *iudice, mecum,*
C ontendit locuplete penu ſi Trinacris *ora,*
Æqualeiſque ferax non Affrica *ſtipat aceruos,*

                                              Horreum

H orreum et agnoscit me non male Belgica *fælix,*
O mnigenas,vt opes sic vitæ alimenta ministro.
R ecte vt quis faturæ similem me dixerit aluo
R obore defectos succum quæ didit in artus.
E ximia hinc adeo Cæsar *me ferre coronam*
V ertutis decus,ac munus spectabile Iussit.
M ateriem at linquo scribendi vatibus amplam.

A fhowre of gold fell once from *Ioue*,men fay:
M any commend *Rhodes* wealth. *Sicilia*
S ay diuers) was the Store-houfe vnto *Rome?*
T rue,once;but *Ceres* now is hether come;
E uen fhe,and all the Deities haue laid
R itches on me. Be euer ritch they faid:
D rown'd is my feate thereof in fenny ftrand
A nd on wood-piles doe all my buildings ftand:
M y walls are wafht with waues that ebbe and flow

B ut from thofe waues doth mine aduancement grow.
E ach quarter of the world fends fhips to me
L aden with wares of worth,for vfe,for eye.
G reat is my gaine by trades,but greater yet
I s that which by my vent of Corne I gette.
A ffrica,*Sicilia* and the *Idæan* field
S et paralels with me for that muft yeeld:

S uch is my ftate,recorded by fames hand,
T o be the Store-houfe of all *Netherland.*
O f all things man doth need (nay rather more)
R itch,needy,here may all haue choyce and ftore.
E uen as the ftomachs fole digeftion,
H elps Mans whole forme with growth of flefh & bone.
O ur worth thus tryde,made *Cafar* fet a Crowne
V pon our fheeld,as badge of due renowne.
S tay , now no more;but leaue againft our will
E ternall matter for a purer quill.

                r   **They**

They of *Amſterdam* made a great preſent of money to the Emperor *Maximillian* the firſt of that name, for the which hee graunted them eaue to beare an Imperiall Crowne vppon the Armes of their Citty, a dignity neuer granted to any Towne before. There is yet to bee ſeene in a glaſſe window of the old Church certaine purſes painted with their mouths downeward, ſcattering gold and ſiluer, ſignifying this liberallity of the *Amſterdammers*.

All ſorts of people of moſt nations haue recourſe and free leaue to dwell in this towne: as *French, Germã, Italian, Spaniard, Portugeſſe, Engliſh, Scottiſh, Cymbrian, Sarmatian, Sueden, Dane, Norweghian, Liflander*, and other of the Septentroniall parts.

At the ſame time or ſhortly after that the Anabaptiſts domineerd in *Munſter*, there was a commotion of the ſame kinde of people in this towne, who one night after they had beene at their priuate aſſembly, tooke armes and poſſeſt them ſelues of the Market place and the Magiſtrates houſe, killing ſome Burgeſſes, and among the reſt one Burguemaiſter, but they were repulſt and cauſed to flye ſome here and ſome there, by Boates into *Freezeland* and other places: Some of them both men and women as they ranne vppe and down the ſtreetes all naked were taken and executed after diuers and ſundry faſhions. An antient Cittizen of this
towne

towne hath alſo made theſe verſes follow'ing in honour of his country.

Hæc illa eſt Battauæ non vltima gloria gentis
Amnis cui nomen, cui cataracta dedit,
Dicta prius Dammum, ràris habitata colonis
Cum contenta caſis, ruſtica vita fuit.
Hinc Amſterdamum, iam facta celebrior, atq̃
Fortunæ creuit tempore nomen item:
Vrbs bene nota prope, atq̃ procul dictantibus oris
Dotibus innumeris ſuſpicienda bonis.
Diues agri, diues precioſe veſtis et auri,
Vt pleno cornu copia larga beet.
Quod Tagus atq̃ Hermus vehit, et Pactolus in vnum
Verê huc congeſtum dixeris eſſe locum.

Belgiaes bright glory we this towne may call
Which had the laſt name from the riuers fall
VVhiIom the name was *Dam*, the people ſuch
As had they meat & clothes, thought they had much.
Hence hight it *Amſterdam*, and with the name
The Fortune hath increaſed and the fame
T'is known vnto far Coaſtes and Continents
And may be well ſo, for the good it vents.
Tis ritch in Corne, in Coyne, in Fleſh, in Fiſh
And all aboundance that the world can wiſh.
Breefely it is ſo ritch, it ſeemes to hold
All *Tagus*, *Hermus* and *Pactolus* gold.

Goude.

ALthough the Hiſtoriographers do diſpute much about the name of this town, ſome ſaying that it came frõ a Lady ſo called, heretofore inheritrix of it, others from the golden leaues where-with the Steeple of their church was couered

uered to shew their ritches and magnificence: for
Goude in the dutch tongue signifies gold, yet it
seemes to me most probable, that it is deriued frō
a certain water called *Goude*, beginning from the
sluce of *Goude* neere vnto *Alphen*, where heretofore the *Romains* had their abode, calling it *Castra
Albiniana*, running euen to the riuers of *Yssule*,
vppon the which at the entry of that water is the
said town built, It is a strong town, populous and
pleasant, enuironed with goodly feelds & farmes,
strong wals and deep ditches, and within beauti-
fully furnished with faire houses, but especially
vppon both sides of the hauen and the Market
place: Abounding in all sorts of victuals by reasō
of their commodious situation, and the continual
passing of such infinite number of shippes whereby they haue this aduantage, by reason of their riuers and chanels, that they may victual thē-selues
and serue the Prouinces of *Holland, Zealand, Brabant* & others, the greatest part of their wealth
cōming in by that meanes. The aire by reason it
is far from the Sea is more healthsome then any o-
ther part of the Prouince; there runs a chanell of
fresh-water through euery streete of the towne,
by reason whereof (here-tofore) there hath
beene in this towne 3 0 5. Brewers, who serued
all the rest of the Prouinces, their beere being called for the goodnesse of it the reuenew of *Goude*; but the neighbour townes (notwithstanding the goodnesse of it) haue taken that
                                                    commodity

commodity from them. It hath a faire and
fpatious Market place in an Ouall forme, and in
the middeft thereof a great and magnificent
State-houfe, which the Lady *Iaquelin* Counteffe
of *Holland* caufed to be built, when at the purfuit
of *Phillip* Duke of *Burgondy* (being abandoned by
almoft all the townes of *Holland*) fhee was forced
to retyre to the Caftle of this towne; yet notwithftanding it feemes this State houfe was fini-
fhed after her death, in the yeare of our Lord
1440. I haue feene at the *Hage* a chaire of wood,
vpon the backe whereof their were two *A. A.* in
gold, and thefe words **Trou aen din.** Thefe two
A. A fignifie *Gouda*, which is in Dutch *A.* of gold
& **Trou aen din.** faithful to thee, which was the
deuife of the faid Counteffe, confeffing that they
of *Gouda* had beene alwayes faithfull and true vnto her : vnder the State-houfe is the Shambles of
the towne, curioufly feated vppon pillars not
wrought by the hands of a fimple Architect; and
on the backe part is a high place built vppon the
like pillars which is the place of execution, be it
either beheading by the fword or otherwife. The
parifh-Church of this towne is very magnificent
& efteemed to be greater then any one in the *Netherlands*, exceeding both in length and greatnes
the Archiepifcopal Church of *Cologne*, paffing al
beleefe in the beauty of glaffe windoes, made by
two brothers borne in this towne, whofe equals
in this art of painting haue not to this houre bin
found

found: The 12.of Ianuary 1552. the fteeple of this Church was burnt by thunder and lightning, of the date whereof *D. Adrians Iuuius* in his *Batauia* hath made this diftique.

LVX bIſſena fVIt IanI hora veſpere nona,
CVM ſacra IohannIS VVLCano CorpVIT ædes.

The tWeLfth of IanVarIe SaInt Iohns SpIre,
At nIne a cLoCk was MVCH Impaird with fire.

The which mifchieuous fire burnt nothing but the faid fteeple, and a part of the church, notwithftanding that it was enuiron'd with houfes. But about an hundreth yeares before in the *l* yeare of our Lord 1438. the 18. of Auguft vpon Saint *Lewis* his day, the towne was wholy burnt, except three houfes vpon the Hauen, the old ruines of them being yet to bee feene. At this time the old charters and priuiledges of this towne were burnt, wherevpon this diftique was made.

FLetIbVs Id dIdICI qVIa GoVda CreMat
LVdoWICI.

Sorrow allowde with fighes proclaimes,
That *Lodowicks Goude* is all on flames.

It is not long fince, that about halfe a league from the faid towne were found diuers peeces of filuer with this circumfcription on the one fide, HLVDOVICVS IMP. and on the other

G   CXRIS-

CXRISTIANA RELIGIO, which feeme
to haue beene coyned in the time of the Emperor
Lewis the Debonaire , the fonne of the Emperor
Charlemaine , and the Father of the Emperour
Charles the bauld, who after he had fetled Chriſti-
an religion in thoſe parts, gaue the Earldome of
Holland to *Thierry* of *Aquitaine*, the firſt of that
name.

There is mention made in the ancient charters and priuiledges of this towne, how *Florentius*
the fift of that name Earle of *Holland* told a Knight
called *Nicholas van Cats*, that this towne had beginning in the yeare 1272. Others, and among
the reſt Doctor *Adrianus Iunius* 1262. notwithſtanding that the said towne hath beene knowne
to haue beene long time before, whereof many
Gentlemen haue taken their names, and chiefly
among the reſt *Thiery Vander Goude*, one of the
priuie councell to Earle *William* King of the *Ro-*
maines, and the priuiledges granted to them of
Vtrecht in the yeare 1252. fhew the like. A quarter of a league out of the towne is yet to be feene
the place where the Church ſtood, and is commonly called the old Church-yard, where during
the *Romiſh* fuperſtition, they vſed to goe on pro-
ceffion in Rogation weeke ; and likewiſe a way
called the old *Goude*. But for that this place was
too farre from the riuer of *Iſſell*, the Inhabitants
for their more commodity remooued from their
former dwellings to the place where the Towne
now

now ftands.

The freedome and iurifdiction of this Towne at the beginning was no more then the compaffe of it within the portes and walls, with very little land without, but was afterward in the yeare of our Lord 1484. much amplified by the Emperour *Maximillian* the firft, and the Arch-duke *Philip* his fonne, with at leaft a league of land in compaffe on both fides the riuer of *Iffell.*

The gouernment of this towne appertained heretofore to the Earles of *Blois*, Lords of the fame, and was feated in the center or middeft of the fayd Countie : *Iohn* of *Beaumont* Earle of *Blois* by his wife, was made Lord of it and *Schoonhoven* with their dependances, by his brother *william the Good* Earle of *Holland*, to augment his reuenews, in the yeare 1306. who by the confent of his brother, inftituted the firft payments and rights of cuftomes, with the houfes and fluces where hee receiued his right : hee inlarged and much beautified the Caftle of the fayd towne, the which long time after was chofen by the Eftates of *Holland* (as a place very ftrong) for the keeping of the charters, priuiledges and lawes of their Countie ; which Caftle (except the Tower where their charters were kept) was in the yeare 1577. demolifhed, at which time there were many others throwne downe in the Low-eountries.

G 2 *Iohn*

Iohn of _Beaumont_ Lord of _Blois_, died in the yeare
1456. leauing one onely fonne likewife named
Iohn, who being a Knight of the _Teutonique_ or
Dutch order,went into _Pruſſia_ againſt the Inſidels,
and there died,ˡeauing two fonnes, _Iohn_ and _Guy_,
Earles of _Bloys_ and of _Soyſon._

   Iohn of _Chaſtillon_ Lord of _Goude_ , riche and
ſtrong , iſſued by his father from the Earles of
Holland, and by his mother from the Kings of
France, matried Madam _Mathilda_ Dutcheſſe of
Gelders and Counteſſe of _Zutphen_, at that time
when the houfes of _Bronchorſt_ and _Heeckers_ aſſai-
ed to ſhutte out the fayd Lady from her patri-
moniall inheritance. To remedie the which the
Earle of _Blois_ came into _Geldres_, accompanied by
many Lords and Knights , and a good troope of
ſouldiers befieging _Wagheningen_ and _Groenſ-
voerdt_,which he tooke,and afterwards in the right
of the Lady his wife , was receiued into _Arn-
hem_ and acknowledged for Lord and Prince.
This Lord and Lady as Dukes of _Gelders_, gaue
priuiledge to the Citizens of _Goude_ , to faile with
their Marchandize through-out the Dutchie of
Geldres and Earledome of _Zutphen_ freely , without eyther taxe or toll. This priuiledge was giuen in the towne of _Arnham_,in the yeare of our
Lord 1372

   Iohn of _Chaſtillion_ dyed in the yeare 1381.
without children,leauing all his goods to his brother _Guy_ of _Blois_, who married _Mary_ the daughter
                                                    of

of the Earle of *Namur* (by whom hee had one
fonne called *Lewis* Earle of *Dunois* , who dyed
young at *Beaumont*) the two and twenty of De-
cember 1397. After whofe death the right line
of *Iohn* of *Blois* was extinct; fo that the Signeuries
of *Goude* and *Schoonhouen*, with their dependances
(which were called the *Baliage* of the countie of
Blois) returned to the countyı of *Holland* , in the
time of *Albert* of *Bauaria*: notwithftanding *Guy*
of *Blois* left a baftard called *Iohn* of *Blois* Lord of
Treflon and *Henault*, who(as the hiftory of the Netherlands makes mention)had by his wife ſix fons.

It is apparent that the townes of *Goude*, *Dordrecht*
Harlem, *Delft*, and *Leyden* , with the Knights and
nobles of the country, reprefented the Eftates of
Holland and *Weftfreezeland* long before the towne
of *Amfterdam* was receiued for a member , as it
appeareth by diuers records and letters of ftate,
paft vnder the feales of the faid fiue townes, together with the iniuries that they of *Amfterdam* haue
done to them of *Goude* vpon the fame . The faid
towne of *Goude* for the good order which they
haue alwaies held in difcipline and Scholafticall
inftruction hath brought forth many great & learned perfonages , to their eternall fame: as *Henry*
and *Iohn* of *Goude* , whom *Trithemius* Abbot of
Spanheim puts in ranke of the rareft writers. *Willi-*
am Herman of *Goude*,whom *Erafmus Roterodamus* in
his Epiftles calls *his delight*, a moft excellent Poet
and Hiftoriographer. *Hermanus Goudanus* a great

G 3   diuine

Diuine. *Iacobus Goudanus* a famous Poet : *Theodo-
rus Gerardi*, *Reincrius Suoy* a Phifiuion and hiftoriographer, who haue all written learned workes
worthy to be confecrated to pofterity. But *Cornelius Aurelius* likewife borne in this towne furpaft
them all in excellent Poefie, as appeareth by the
Lawrel crowne that the Emperor *Maximillian* the
firft fent him by his orator *Stephanus* of *Crecouia*. It
was he that firft controlled *Gerard* of *Nymegen* in
his booke that he writt of the true fituation of *Batauia* or *Holland*, betweene the *Hornes* of the *Rhine*,
which the faid *Gerard* of *Nymegen* would haue attributed to the *Betuwe*, a part of *Gelderlana*; wherein the faid *Aurelius* liuely expreffes the honor of
the *Hollanders*, who in his youth was brought vp by
that fo much renowned *Erafmus* of *Rotterdam*, being begotten at *Goude*, but by remooue of dwelling
borne and brought vp at *Rotterdam*.

There are many other learned & famous perfons
fprung from this towne, too long here to rehearfe,
of whom *Iuftus Lypfius*, *Ianus Gruterus*, and *Domini-
cus Baudius* of *Lille* in *Flanders*, haue amply written
in their workes. Notwithftanding that throughout
all the townes of the Netherlands many bloody
decrees haue beene executed for religion on both
parts, yet they of this towne haue bin fo moderate
euen to great Papifts their neighbors and in their
power, that in a hundreth years & more there haue
bin but three executed vpon thofe placarts or decrees, whereof one was an Anabaptift, who being
                                                        fecretly

secretly aduertifed by the Magiftrat that he fhould retire himfelfe,yet hee came and rendred himfelfe into the hands of the officer : whereby it may appeare that they of *Goude* haue euer detefted tyrannie and perfecution,beleeuing that it belongs onely to God to command the confcience.

ENCHVYSEN.

THis towne of *Enchuyfen* hath taken name from the fewneffe of houfes it had at the firft, being by little and little become a great towne, as is to be feene at this day : this word *Enckle huyfen* fignifying little or fimple houfes. It is a faire towne and by the naturall fituation very ftrong, oppofed to the rigor of the fea, ftanding vpon a corner of the land, their traffique by fea makes them riche and opulent,it is for the moft part built of faire mafonrie,hauing very few houfes of wood , for feare of fire, which they haue once or twice before had experience of ; for you may read in the Annales of *Holland*, that in the yeare of our Lord 1297. the Lords of *Arkell* & *Putten* burnt it all, and yet within twenty yeares after it was made greater by the halfe, for all the falt pitts that were along the fea banke and the marifhes behind,are now within the walls,with many faire gardens & fifh-ponds.There are two paffages out to fea , and three hauens, at one of the which entrances there is a great tower, wherevpon is engrauen a Lattin diftique made by *D' Adrianus Iunius*,vpo the attempt ŷ *Charles* the laft

G 4   **Duke**

Duke of *Gelders* made for the surprize of it that he
might get an entrance into *Holland* , it expresses
the time of the attempt, and is this.

EnChVſaM InſtdIIs taCitIs ſVb noCte ſILentI.
Obı Vere adnI Xa eſt Ge Lr ICa perfıdIa.

The trecheroVs GeLDroIs ſoVght by Violent Might
T' haVe tane EnchVIſen, through the Vayle of nIght.

This town is rich in ſalt pits, the Inhabitāts fetch-
ing groſſe ſalt from *Brouage* by *Rochel*, or in *Spaine*,
and ſome-times from the ſalt Ilands where they
haue it for nothing, and after boile it again, and re-
fine it, multiplying it with ſea-water brought them
in boates, taking the heate away & making it white
fit for the table, their are as ſufficient ſtore of ſluces in this town and about it for the paſſage of ſea-
water as in *France* or *Spaine* but the ſharpneſſe of
the ſunne is not of that force to congeale and har-
den it as in other places; heretofore they made
great aboundance of ſalt of the aſhes of turues &
ſea-water, after ÿ manner of making of ſalt-peeter
at this day, which they call *Silt-ſout*, whereof they
make a great traffick: but ſince that they haue traded to *Spaine* and *France* , & from thence brought
in their great ſhippes what quantity the will, this
maner of making it is come to nothing, it beeing
vnpoſſible ÿ that which they made in diuerſe places ſhould be ſo good as that which is made of the
pure ſea-water. This towne may very fitly be called *Neptunes* ſeate, for that their ſhips paſſe all the
ſeas

seas of the world, and haue had the honor to carry and bring backe the Emperor in diuerse of his
expeditions, and likewise sundry times King *Philip*
his sonne, and since *Anne* of *Austria* his wife the
daughter of the Emperor *Maximillian* the second.
They carry in their armes three herrings argent
and two stars or, in a field *Azure*, as a fatall and
certaine Augure presaging that after the manner
of herrings they should cut through all seas, and
trade to the one and other pole, which at this time
they doe: In this towne dwelt Doctor *Paludanus*
an exquisite Phisition and great gatherer together
of strange and rare antiquities, to such an Infinite
number that they could hardly bee seene peece by
peece in three daies, the maruelous workes of nature as well proceeding from the land as the sea,
and the secret workes of God being therein to bee
contemplated & admired, but I vnderstand since,
a great part of them haue bin sould to the Lant-
graue of *Hessen*.

HORNE.

ABout the yeare 1316. in the time of Count
william the third of that name called the
good Earle of *Holland*, *Zeeland*, *Henault* and *west-
freezeland* this towne tooke his little beginning in
this manner: When the towne of *Veronne* neere
Alckmar was destroyed by the *Frisons*, there
was a great sluce in the ditch where at this day
                                                the

the market place of the fayd towne ſtands which
was called *Roeſtein* by the which the country people entred into the ſea with their barkes.It happened that three brothers cittizens of *Hambourgh*
came and went thither with ſhippes laden with
beere,who cauſed three high houſes of ſtone to be
built there for the *Friſons*,for the *Danes* came thither ordinarily with oxen,kine, horſes and other
marchandiſe,paſſing the ſea with their little ſhips,
from the *Cimbrique Cherſoneſus*, or the coun·ry of
Holſtein, ſo that from time to time by little and
little it began to augment in buildings , & firſt became a village , afterwardes a towne , and at laſt a
good city : one of theſe three houſes remained en-
tire 220. years after,vntill the yeare 1430.The o-
ther two beeing ruined were built againe but not
with ſo great ſtones as this third.

There is ſome diuerſity of opinion about the e-
tymology of the name of *Horne*,which ſignifies as
well a hunters horne as otherwiſe , ſome ſay it is
of the hauen of the towne that turnes in forme of
a little horne ; others ſay that this ſame place was
full of bogges , where now the ditches and walls
of the towne are , and that there grew there certaine plants in great quantity in forme of a horne,
the which beeing cut either aboue or below one
might winde as of a cornet.

The ſtreete of the ſaid towne that is called the
New Dam, where the woodmongers and ſhooma-
kers dwell , and where the turue boats arriue was
made

made in the time of the Count *William* when there
was not water inough without the Sluce of *Horne*,
but that the great fhippes of *Denmarke* and *Ham-
bourge* were forced to ftay at the fea ditch , and
therefore they caufed a little long ditch to bee
made which they called the *New Dam*, beginning
at the great ditch a good diftance from the mouth
of the fea, from whence they brought their horfes and oxen to the towne. All this is now within the towne ; fairely built , and called the *New
Damme*.

In the yeare of our Lord 1350. Duke *William* of
Bauaria the fonne of the Emperour *Lodowick* and
Marguerite Counteffe of *Holland* gaue to the
Burgefes of *Horne* as large and ample priuiledges as they had giuen to them of *Medenblick*
which to this day they enioy . There is a ftreete
in the faid towne called *Heer Gerits Landt* fo called of *Gerard* of *Hemskerke* who caufed a faire
houfe to bee built in a large garden now full of
houfes, the which *Gerard* died in the fayd towne
in the yeare of our Lord 1398. after hee had ferued Duke *Albert* in his wars againft the *Frifons*.

In the time of the Lady *Iaqueline* Counteffe of
Holland &c certaine townes of *Weft-Freefland* re-
belled againft her , and called in *Philippe* Duke
of *Burgundie* the Sonne of her Aunt , vnwilling
to bee gouerned any longer by a woman , wherevpon grew great warres , the *Kennemers* taking
part with their Princeffe and making warres
againft

againſt the *Waterlanders*, and *Eaſt Friſons*, the *Hornois* by reaſon of their ritches and great traffick that they had from North to South, being growne proud.

It happened at this time that a young man of the ſaid towne, the ſonne of one of the cheefeſt marchants called *Ian Lambrechts Cruyf*, being in the towne of *Goude*, where the Counteſſe *Iaqueline* kept her reſidence, ſeeing the ſaid Counteſſe paſſe by, ſaid, without thinking any hurt : *It is great pitty and ſhame to vſe ſo noble a Dame in this ſort, as if ſhe were a common woman.*

Theſe words were worſe taken then they were meant. Where-vpon hee was committed to priſon. *Lambert Cruyff* hearing of his ſonnes reſtraint, poſted thether with a good ſumme of money to redeeme him. Hauing treated with the Iudges, and preſented this money, they gaue him good words, telling him that his ſonne ſhould not dye, but ſhould be onely lead to the place of execution : Whereas the executioner drawing out his ſword, the Counteſſe ſhould crye out, which ſhould cauſe the headſ-man to ſtaye, and ſo his ſonne ſhould bee freed.

The father was ſomewhat comforted with this anſwer, and ſeeing there was no other meanes, hee recommended the cauſe vnto God. The ſonne being vpon the Scaffold, and the executioner hauing drawne his ſword, the Counteſſe made no ſhew of crying out, ſo as this poore young

man

man was vniuftly executed., wherewith the father being much moued, he fayed vnto himfelfe, being vnderftood by fome other . *Thou fhalt not remaine Conteffe of Holland neither fhalt thou hereafter enioye that Country in peace.* And therevpon he returned with his money to his owne houfe . Beeing come, to *Horne* hee acquainted the Magiftrates and the Bourgers with the wrong which the Conteffe had done vnto his fonne , in the towne of *Goude*, wherevpon a councell was held of all the chiefe of the towne, who concluded ioyntly neuer more to acknowledge her for their Princeffe, and to fortefie themfelues againft her . The father of this young man that was executed, full of difcontent and defire of reuenge, did giue or lend a great fome of money, to beginne the fortification of the towne.

And this beeing in the yeare 1427. they began to compaffe in this towne with goodly walls and deepe and large ditches . Doctor *Adrianus Iunius* (a curious fercher out of Antiquities, as appeeres by his hiftory of *Battauia*) was borne in that town, fonne to *Peter de Iouge* a Bourguemafter . This towne abounds with all forts of victualls, halfe of it all along the fea , is defended with good paliffadoes, and banks, made of a fmall graffe which they call *Vlyer*, in Latin *Alga*, wherewith moft of the bankes in that quarter of *Weftfrifland* are armed, for that it fettles clofe together, and doth not rot in a long time , and being rotten it becomes firme

earth

earth. They gather fhippes ladings of this graffe in a certaine feafon of the yeare, in the fea about the Ifland of *Wyeringhe*, from the which it is named, and they keepe great heaps thereof in ftore, to repaire their bankes at neede when as they are any way decaied. It is ftrange that is reported of this herbe, that wild fwannes at a lowe water pull it out of the botome of the fea, the which floting vpon the water, ftaies in a certaine place, whereas they goe to gather it. This Ifland of *Wyeringhe* is not farre from that of *Texel*, nor confequently from *Enchuyfen*, *Medenbilck* nor *Horne*, the which befides all other delights which it yeelds, brings forth aboundance of great Skirrit rootes, as delicate a meate as can bee prefented before a King, wherein *Plinie* reports that the Emperor *Tiberius* did fo delight, as hee caufed them to bee brought out of *Germanie* to *Rome*.

ALCMAR.

THis towne is three leagues diftant from *Horne*, where ends the iurifdiction of the *Cannefates*, or *Kennemers* in the countrie language: It is in a manner enuironed round about with diuers great Lakes, the which are made by the brookes which fall from the fandie Downes, fo as in my opinion this name was giuen it by reafon of the multitude of thefe Lakes, the which in the *Cymbrians* tongue they call *Meeren*, as if they would

would fay *Almeer*,and fome in Latin call it *Almeria* . There are tenne of tnefe Lakes , the which by Slufes and Mills to draine out the water , vpon hope of greater profit, haue beene laide drie,partly at the charge of the Lords of *Brederode* , and *Egmont*,as alfo by *Thierry Teyling* a Receyuor and other good Bourgers of *Alcmar* ; the names of which Lakes thus recouered , were *Bergen*, conteyning 1200. *Acres* of ground , *Daele* , *Veronne*, *Suyn*,*Bouckler*,*Heyuluen*,*Grobber*,*Temple*, *Argillar* and the Lake behind . There are yet fiue remayning,that of *Di:pee* Voere, *Scherme*, *Byems* and that of *Waerd* : the which they haue no meaning to lay dry, by reafon of their depth, and the benifit they reape by the frefh water-fifh which they yeelde. They fay that this towne was firft founded by *Adgill* King of *Frifland* a Godly man , nothing refembling his impious father *Radbod*,who mocking at the Saints in Paradife , hauing demanded what was become of his predeceffors which had dyed Infydells , and anfwere being made him.that they were in hell, going to the Font to bee baptized by the Bifhoppe of *Suiffons*,hee retired backe faying, that after his death hee would goe where his Parents were . Of whome thefe rough verfes were made.

O locus,ò *dirum et tibi formidabile femper
Elogium*,Radbode,*tuum poft trifta fata.*

O ieaſt,and diſmall memory withall,
(*Radbode*) for thee , and thy dire funerall.

This *Adgill* , raygned in *Friſland* in the yeare
720.whoſe lymits were very great,he founded the
towne of *Alcmar* but it doth not appere by any
Annales,when it was walled in , yet of late yeares
they haue deſcouered the foundation of a Caſtle,
which *Petrus Nannius* a learned Hiſtoriographer
borne in the ſame towne affirmes that hee hath
ſeene : the queſtion is if this caſtle were built by
King *Adgill* ,and if it were called *Alcmar*, which
town (the *Friſons* hauing ruined ſome 450.yeares
ſince) is now wel fortefied with goodly ditches, &
mighty walles,flanked with nine great Bulwarks,
which haue beene made within theſe 35.yeares,
after that the *Spaniards* had beſieged it , battred it
and giuen maine aſſaults , were in the end forced
to raiſe their ſiege with diſhonour and loſſe, the
Bourgers ,yea the women and children ſhewing
themſelues as courragious and reſolute to defend
their rampars , as any martiall men could haue
done, hauing a late preſident of the Duke of *Aluas* cruelty againſt them of *Harlem* after their
yeelding .It is a faire and pleaſant towne, and ex-
ceedingly well built,furniſhed with fiſh and foule
at an eaſie rate,by reaſon of the Lakes: They haue
great aboundance of butter,cheeſe,beefe,mutton
and conies ,the ayre is holeſome and the ſituation pleaſing,hauing goodly medowes round about
it.

it. Befides the caftle aboue mentioned , there were two others not farre from thence to ftoppe the incurfions of the *Frifons*, who did annoy *Holland* daylie ; which two caftles *Martin van Rof-fen* Marfhall of the campe to *Charles* Duke of *Gueldres* did burne and ruine fome three fcoore and tenne yeares fince . About a thoufand paces from the fayd towne , in olde time was the towne of *Veronna* , the which was faire, fpatious and well peopled; of great welth, and the Metropolitaine of all the bafe *Frifons*, whereof at this day there is nothing to bee feene, but the ruines, the foundations whereof giue good teftymonie what it hath beene.

In the fieds of *Veronna* (which bee verie fertill in corne) is a village called Saint *Pancrat*. Wee muft beleeue that this towne of *Veronna* hath beene the chiefe of all the bafe *Frifons*, the *Fierbrand* of warre and all combuftions againft the *Hollanders*, to whom they were neere neighbours : and for their trecherie and breach of faith were often affayled by the Princes of *Holland*, fo as in the end, *Iohn* Earle of *Holland*, hauing conceiued an irreconciliable hatred againft them, caufed it to bee razed to the grounde, and plowed vppe, forbidding them euer to build it vp againe , for the ruining whereof hee drewe in the *Englifh* , to whom hee gaue it in prey : the fayd towne hauing beene deliuered vnto him by the treafon of *Phobe* Bourguemafter thereof,

H   who

who had fold it for a booetefull of filuer, whofe
fepulcher, (beeing caft aliue into a hole, and couered with dunge) is yet to bee feene in a towre
of thefe ruined caftles, the which is at this daie
called *Phobes* tower. The Hiftorie of the def-
truction of this towne, (the which a certaine
Preeft hath written), hath beene for thefe many
yeares kept in the cloyfter of *Henloo*, but I knowe
not what is become thereof fince it was ruined
in thefe laft troubles. *William Goudan* Schoole-
fellow to *Erafmus* of *Rotterdam* in his Hiftorie
which hee hath written of *Hiero* a *Scottifhman*
who was flaine by the *Danes*, fpeaking of this
towne faith.

Quos prifci Frifios olim dixere minorés
Arctoò a fluvio, pelagióq, venitis ab ora,
Tunc vobis Verona caput, nunc campus et arua &c.

You, whom old writters leffer *Frifons* call
Come from the Northren coafts the firft of al,
Then *Veron* was your head, that now lies wafte &c.

In an other place he faith.

——— *Frifiis, fi quando bella vocabant*
Dux Verona *fuit ac tantæ gloria gentis.*

——— When vnto warres the *Frifons* went
Verona was their guide, and ornament.

Where-

Whereby it doth plainelie appeere that this towne of *Veronna* hath beene verie famous. But whie the *Annales* haue made so base a mention thereof, I can yeelde no other reason, but that it might either bee through the ignorance of writers, or for the great malice and hatred they bare againſt this towne, the memorie whereof they deſired to haue extinct.

This inſcription doth witneſſe the yeare of her deſtruction. *ECCe CadIt Mater frIſIæ* 1303. There are yet two Belles to bee ſcene that were caſt in the ſayd towne of *Veronna*, the one in the village of *Valckenooge*, and the other in the Cittie of London in *England*.

The rights of fiſhing which the ſayd towne hath had, in all the Lakes, the *Rhine* and the *Meuſe*, which at this daie they call Veronna, beeing anexed to the reuenues of the Princes of *Holland*, giue good teſtymonie how ritch and mightie it hath beene: and the accounts which are held of the territorie of the ſayd towne, which they call the accountes of *Veronna*, doe well witneſſe it. The ſeale of the ſayd towne hath beene found within theſe fiftie yeares; in which was grauen an Eagle looking vppe to heauen, with the winges diſplayed, and on the ſide of it a ſworde, with this inſcription. SIGILLVM CIVIVM DE VRO-NELGEYST.

H 2   There

There was about a league and a halfe from *Alcmar*, a good part of the countrie called *La Sype*, twife or thrice drowned, vntill that the well affected Bourgers, with the helpe of manie Noblemen, Gentlemen, and others, both of *Holland* and *Brabant*, had (with their great charge) recouered it, and fortefied it with fo good bankes, as they haue no more caufe to feare any inondation , whereof they haue made a fertill countrie, fit both for tillage and pafture, with many goodlie faimes. Although that *Adrianus Iunius* would make *Horne* the Metropolitaine of *Weft-Frifland*, yet this towne of *Alcmar* hath the firft place and the firft voice , in the Eftates of the fayd Prouince.

MEDENBLIC.

MEdenblic is feated vppon the fea, in the fartheft part of *North-Hollande*, two leagues and a halfe from *Enchuyfen* ; it hath a port made by art, fortefied with that fea graffe aboue mentioned ; a fafe retreate for fhippes in fowle weather , hauing a ftronge caftle. It was quite burnt by the *Frifons* in the yeare of our Lord and Sauiour 1 2 9 0. and the caftle was fo long befieged , as they were forced for to eate horfes.

The ignorant multitude hold an opinion that the *Fabulous* *Medea* gaue the name , and that
her

her Image of braffe guilt, beeing fette vppon an heigh eminent place, did ferue as a fea marke to all faylers : Alfo when as the Sunne did fhine vpon this Image they did call vppe their feruants to worke, crying *Medeeblinckt* (*Medeefhynes*) and that thereof it tooke the name of *Medenblyck*.

They hold that King *Raabode*, who(as wee haue faied) went from the font when hee fhould haue beene baptized, held his Court there. It hath within 34. yeares beene fo fortefied with walles and bulwarkes as it is now held impregnable ; the country about it beeing intrencht with ditches, is full of medowes fit to fat cattell it is well furnifhed with victualls, and good cheape.

EDAM.

THat which at this day is called *Edam*, was in olde time named *Yedam* of a current of water which is called *Ye vry Yde*, the which running about the C nurch, fell by a Slufe, (which they call *Damme*) into the great chanell of the towne, which goes vnto the fea, that is to fay, the Slufe of *Yde*. There is a certaine village in the mideft of this water, called *Middelye*. The towne is at this prefent well walled in, and ditcht, it is famous for the good cheefe which is made there, it hath a long hauen, to the which there belongs many great and goodly fhippes, which are built there
H3   euery

euery yeare, beeing as stately and of as great
charge as any in Holland or Zeeland bee it either
for warre or Marchandise.

In the yeare of our Lord 1 4 0 4. some women
of this towne going in barkes to feed their cattell
in the neere pastures of *Purmermeer*, they did often see at the ebbing of the water, a sea woman
playing in the water, whereat in the beginning
they were afraied, but beeing accustomed to see
it often, they incourraged one an other, and
with their barkes entred into this water, into the
which shee was come at a full sea, and could not
finde the waie out againe: these women hauing
descouered her, made with their boates towardes
her, and the water beeing not deepe ynough for
her to diue vnto the bottome, they tooke her by
force, drewe her into a boate and carried her
to *Edam*, where in time shee grew familiar, ac-
customing her selfe to feede of ordynarie meates:
They of Harlem desired much to haue her, to
whom shee was sent, and liued some fifteene
yeares: shee neuer spake, seeking often to gette
againe into the water, you may reade this discourse at large in the History of the *Netherlands*.
This towne is two leagues equally distant as well
by sea as by land from *Horne.*

MONIC.

MONICKENDAM.

THis towne on the South-ſide lookes towards, the Ile of *Mark*, which is oppoſite vnto it:the ſea therein reaſonably ſtill , for that it lies vnder the *Lee* of the ſayd Iſland : It is not verie ſpatious, and towardes the I and it is walled and ditcht . It takes the name of a Lake neere vnto it called *Mónicker-meere* , the which beeing at this daie defended with bankes , is made a ſea, whereas great ſhippes lie ſafely , beeing couered with that Land . The armes of this towne are a Monke clad in blacke, holding a maſe in his hand whereby wee may conclude that both the Lake and the towne tooke their names from a Monke, but why or what hee was , it is not, knowne. This towne was built in the yeare of our Lord and Sauiour 1 2 9 7. When as the *Friſons* came thether with a fleete of ſhippes to goe and ſuccor the Biſhoppe of *Vtrecht* , it is but a league from *Edam.*

PVRMERENDE.

THis towne ſtands in the mideſt of Moores, lying at the end of the *Purmer* ſea, where is a Sluce, by the which they of the towne ſayle towardes *Edam* , *Monickendam* and other places that border vpon the ſayd ſea, on the other ſide

H 4   there

there is nothing but Lakes, which coaſt the townes of *Ryp*, *Graft*, *Wormer*, euen vnto *Alcmar*. In theſe three Bouroughes, they are ritch men which imploy themſelues moſt at ſea, as well in fiſhing for herring as in trade of marchandiſe. At *Wormer* they make aboundance of good byſcuit, which they carry to ſell in all the townes of *Holland*, *Zeeland* and *Friſland*, for the prouiſion of their ſhippes.

This towne is verie ſmall; it hath beene fortefied during theſe laſt warres, againſt the towne of *Amſterdam*, the which in the beginning of the troubles held the Duke of *Aluas* party, but this was allied to the townes of *Alcmar*, *Horne*, *Enchuyſen*, *Medenblick* *Edam*, *Monickendam*, with other places of *Weſt-Friſland*, againſt whom the *Spaniards* could not preuaile, but loſt many men in this watriſh countrie, the which is rightly called *Waterland* : in the which are the ſayd townes of *Purmerende*, the three Boroughes aboue mentioned, and many other villages.

This towne was fiiſt built by a priuate perſon, but verie ritch, the which came afterwardes with the caſtle to the Earles of *Egmont*, and ioynes vnto his hauen vpon *Alcmar* ſide: It is verie cheape lyuing there, by reaſon of the aboundance of fleſh and fiſh.

MV.

MVDEN.

THe towne of *Muden* is seated at the mouth of the riuer of *Vecte*: some fortie yeares since it was but a poore paltrie village, feeling then the miseries, which it had endured by the burning and spoiles of the Duke of *Guelders*, but within two yeares it was repaired. Since the last troubles (yea within these twelue yeares) it hath beene wholy finished and beautified, with ramparts, goodly bridges and faire houses: It hath a strong castle vpon the gulphe whereas the *Vecte* runnes into the Zuyderzee. This castle is famous by the taking of *Floris* the fift Earle of *Holland*; who hauing forced the wife of a Knight called *Gerard van Vel-sen*, was (by the conspiracie of many noble men of *Holland*) taken, being a Hawking, and carried into this castle, thinking to transport him from thence into *England*, there to end his dayes, and to call home Earle *Iohn*, who had married the Kings daughter: but they found no opportunitie to effect it : besides the commons of the *Water-landers* did rise of all sides to succour him ; the which the conspirators finding, meaning to carry him by land into some other countrie, they ledde him from thence; but as they were egerly pour-sued; *Van Velsen* being loth to abandon his prisoner, whom hee had mounted vpon a paltrie Iade, comming to leape ouer a ditch (as all the country is full of trenches) the horse falling, ouerthrew
the

the Earle into the ditch. *Van Velfen* (feeing that he could no longer keepe him,) with a furious defire of reuenge,gaue him eighteene wounds with his fword, whereof hee died vpon the mount of *Naerden,*whether the pefants carried him.*Van Velfen* and the other confpirators faued themfelues in the caftle of *Croenenburg,*where they were taken and grieuoufly punifhed: The Lords of *Amftel, Woerden ,* and fome others, efcaped, and wandred long vp and downe. The Siegnior of *Nyuelt* is captaine of this caftle of *Muyden,*with a good garrifon well prouided of all things.

NAERDEN.

ALthough that this towne hath fuffered much, being firft ruined by that warlike Prelate the Bifhop of *Vtrecht* , of the houfe of *Arckel*, who changed the place of fituation,and did caufe them to build it where it now ftands, being a faire and a ftrong towne, the which we may iuftly fay is but a fhopp of Weauers ,whereas they make great aboundance of very fine cloath. The houfes of this towne are very faire, being newly built within foure and thirtie yeares. For the Duke of *Alua* meaning to bee reuenged of the *Hollanders ,* (who were for the moft part reuolted, by reafon of his tyrannie,) he fent *Don Frederick* his fonne thether with an armie: who approching neere vnto the towne of *Naerden:*the Bourguemaifter & councell of the towne, went forth to meete him, and to prefent

fent him the Keyes of the towne: when being entred with his troops, the Bourgers feeking to giue
them all the contentment they could deuife : the
Spaniards (contrary to their faith and promife)fell
vpon them, and murthered a great number(whom
they had caufed to retire into a church) in colde
bloud, forced and deflowred the wiues and vir-
gins, fpoiled the towne, and hauing carried away
their bootie, they fet it on fire; the which was a
good prefident for the other townes of *Holland* by
the which the townes of *Harlem* and *Alcmar* tooke
example, the firft being as cruelly intreated after
their yeelding, and the other fo incouraged to defend themfelues, as after a fiege of fixe weekes and
diuerfe affaults, the *Spaniards* were forced to retire
to their difhonor and loffe. This towne of *Naerden*
is the chiefe of the Bayliwicke of *Goeland*, which
the Bifhops of *Vtrecht* haue often pretended to belong vnto them, but fince it is annexed to the reuenewes of *Holland.*

GORRICHOM.

THis towne of *Gorchum* or *Gorrichom*, from a
fmall beginning, is growne to the greatneffe
and ftate wherein you fee it at this day, for it takes
his name from poore Fifherman, who had their
lodgings or cabins along the riuer of *Lingen*, vntill
it ioynes with the *Meufe* and *Wahal*, who by reafon of their pouertie, were in contempt called
Gorrikens: whom *Iohn* of *Arckel* the feuenth Baron

of that race, Lord of the countrie of *Arckel*, caufed to come and dwell behinde and about his caftle, where by degrees hee built a good towne, the which he walled in about the yeare 1230. And to the end they fhould retaine their name of *Gorrikens*, hee called this towne *Gorrichom*, as much to fay (*hom* or *heym*, in old time fignifying a houfe or aboade) as the dwelling of thefe *Gorrikens*. There is in this towne a great market of fifh, fowle, and all other prouifion needfull for the life of man, whereof they make a great trade, as well into *Brabant*, as other places, which doth much inriche the towne : for the Bourgers themfelues are both marchants, marriners and factors, one man alone fupplying the place of three : from the top of the higheft fteeple you may fee in a cleere day two and twenty walled townes, befides bourroughs and villages, which are very many, being a pleafant fight to behold; Neere vnto it is the Champian countrie where (as they fay) *Hercules Alemanicus* did campe. Wherevpon they call all that quarter the country of *Hercules*, the which the common people did afterwards terme *Herkel*, and from that to *Arkel* when the faid towne was obfcured by the houfe of *Arkel*, by reafon of the continuall warres which their Lords made againft the Earles of *Holland*.

Charles Duke of *Bourgongne* caufed a goodly caftle to be built there vpon the riuer, neere vnto the Port of *Dordrect* : the which fince thefe laft
                                                            troubles

troubles hath beene razed and fortified after an other manner, fo as there remaines nothing but a place for the paiment of the cuftome : it is fo fortified with twelue bulwarkes, befides halfe-moones and counterfcarps without it, together with that aboundance of water, as one would fay it were impregnable. It is made halfe bigger then it was twenty yeares fince: the riuer of *Linghen* runnes through the middeft of it, being alwayes full of fhips : it falls into the *Meruve*, and mingles it felfe with the riuers of *Wahal* and *Meufe* : all which together paffe before *Dordrecht*, *Rotterdam*, *Delfs-hauen*, *Schiedam* and the *Briele*, where it falles into the *Brittifh* fea. Maifter *Ihon Harie* Chanoine of the Chapell at the *Hage* in *Holland*, was borne in this towne; hee was fo great a louer of pietie, vertue, and learning, as during his life he fought out (with great care, diligence and coft) all bookes, in all languages and faculties. When he came to refide at the *Hage*, hee brought fo great a number of bookes with him, as the people thought there were not fo many to be found in all *Holland*: wherwith he made a goodly Library, the which he did augment with great care euen to his dying day, which was in the yeare 1532 whereof he made the Emperor *Charles* the fift his heire.

WORCOM.

A Lthough this towne bee out of the limitts of the Countie of *Holland*, beyond the riuer of *Wahal*,

Wahal, on *Brabant* fide, right againft the ftrong caftle of *Loueſtein* hauing a little lower on the other
banke the towne of *Gorchom*, the which in ancient time did belong vnto the Earles of *Horne*,
which the King of *Spaine* did confifcate, and fince
it was quite burnt : but the Eſtates of *Holland* hauing feazed thereon, and fortified it with good
rampars, bulwarkes and ditches, it hath beene
new built, and is made a faire towne, where the
Eſtates doe entertaine an ordinary garrifon, with
a Captaine fuperintendent.

Of late yeares the Eſtates (to cut of all controuerfie touching the iurifdiction of the fayde
Towne) agreed with the Lady *Walburge* Counteſſe of *Moeurs* and *Nyeuwenaert*, widdow to
Philip of *Montmorency* the laſt Earle of *Horne*,
who fold them the proprietie of the faid Towne,
with the caſtle and territorie of *Altena*, not
farre from thence, beeing in ancient time all
drowned, but now it is a countrie full of good
paſtures : So thefe two peeces of *Worcom* and
Altena, are annexed to the reuenewes of the
Countie of *Holland*, where-with it is fo much
augmented. There is an other *Worcum* in Frifland vpon the fea, not farre from *Hindelopen*, the
which hath the title and priuiledge of a towne,
although it bee but a Boroughe without any
walles, but it is great, and almoſt three thoufand
paces long.

HEVS-

HEVSDEN.

IS a reasonable faire towne and well ouilt, situated on *Brab.nt* side, vpon the riuer of *Wahall,* with a goodly caftle, where the Gouernors do refide, the last of which was *Floris* of *Brederode,* Sieg-nior of *Cloetinge,* brother to the Lord ot *Brederode* last deceased, who left one sonne the only heire of all the house of *Brederode.* The Siegnior of *Locren* commands there now for the Estates. It was long vnder a priuate Lord. They of *Brabant* pretended it to be of their iurisdiction, but *Holland* hath held it vnto this day. It hath a large command.

LEERDAM.

THis towne is small, yet walled in standing vpon the bankes of the riuer of *Lingen*; it hath beene so often ruined in the old warres, as they h ie had no great care to repaire it, so as it is of small moment, it belongs to *Philip* of *Naffaw* now Prince of *Orange,* Earle of *Buren,* and hath a castle which is still maintained.

HENCLOM.

HEnclom is a towne seated also vpon the riuer of *Lingen,* opposite to *Leerdam*: it is a little towne and very ancient, but goes to decaye. It hath an olde Castle which they saye was built by *Hercules Alemanicus,* but GOD best knowes how true it is. The Lordes of this
little

little towne are defcended from *Otto*, the yonger fonne to *Iohn* the eight Lord of *Arkel*, who gaue him this Siegneurie in his life time.

ASPEREN.

IS fituated vpon the banke of the fame riuer of *Lingen*, which the Inhabitants call *Lyeuen*, that is as much to fay as Loue, for that the ftreame runs fo gently. In the yeare 1516. it was grieuoufly afflicted by the *Geldrois*, who being accompanied by fome rebells and mutinous *Hollanders*, befieged it, and in the end tooke it by affault, notwithftanding all the valiant refiftance of the befieged, whom they put to the fword, and fet fire of the towne, not fparing the very Churches, into the which the women and children were retired, whom they intreated fo barbaroufly, as *Turkes* in their greateft fury could not haue exceeded them.

OVDE-WATER.

THis word fignifieth Old-waters, which they terme in Latine *Aquas veteres*, it is a reafonable good towne, and hath riche Bourgers in it: it ftands like vnto *Goude*, vpon the riuer of *Yffell*, a league from *Woerden*, betwixt which townes they fowe great aboundance of hempe, wherewith they make ropes, cables and netts for fifhing, which is the chiefe worke of the poorer fort, & the greateft

profit

profit of the richer. This towne was besieged by the Lord of *Hierges* for the Duke of *Alua*, and valiantly defended, but in the end it was taken by assault, whereas the *Spaniards* after they had vsed their accustomed cruelties, set fire of it, so as it is not yet repaired.

ROTTERDAM.

ROtterdam is situated neere vnto the *Meuse*, vpon the mouth of the channell which they call *Rotter*, where-vnto adding *Dam* (which is a Sclufe) it makes *Rotterdam*, the Sclufe of *Rotter*. Of that which *Guicchirdin* and *Sebastian Munster* write of the foundation and antiquitie of this towne, I beleeue no more then Doctor *Adrianus Iunius* doth : for it is a matter without all doubt or controuersie, that the place where-as the towne now stands, was heretofore an arme of the sea, without the riuer of *Meuse*, which the remainder of the bankes doe yet witnesse, the which extended from the castle of *Honingen* (belonging to them of the house of *Asendelfe*) vnto *Croeswicke*, which was a castle vpon the *Rotter*, and so went on vnto the village of *Ouderschye*, and ended at the ditches of *Schiedam*. *Rotterdam* is augmented more then a moitie within these two and twenty yeares, hauing remooued the port of their hauen (which they haue made of goodly Free-stone) from the old seate, at the least a hundred paces neerer vnto the mouth of their hauen,

I and

and to the point : Neere vnto which porte is a
goodly Bourse for Marchants with three galle-
ries , which stand vpon pillers of free-stone. The
towne doth dayly increase in wealth , First by
their fishing with their great shippes, called Buf-
fes , the which are strong and well appointed both
to incounter an enemy, and to resist the violence
of the sea : and of late yeares by their trade to the
East and West Indies, and seeking their fortunes
against the *Spaniards,* from whome they haue many times taken great prizes : The hauen is long,
built all of a blew stone , which doth resist the violence of the water, in which hauen a great number
of shipps may safely lye.

Euery yeare there are goodly great ships built
in this towne for these long voyages , and galleys
where there is any need of them for the warre,
vpon the coast of *Holland* and *Zeland.* Some fiue
and thirty or sixe and thirty yeares since the Earle
of *Boffu* hauing surprized it by the Duke of *Aluas*
command (where some Bourgers were slaine) by
the negligence of some insolent soldiers , it was
fired, the which by the meanes of a great tempe-
stuous winde , did consume aboue nine hundred
houses, and some ships, where there were men lost.
The losse was great, but it was soone repaired, and
the houses built fairer and higher then before, the
most of them being of blew stone. That great light
of learning and knowledge *Desiderius Erasmus Ro-*
terodamus was borne in this towne , almost right
be-

before the Church doore, in a ſtreete which goes
vnto the market place, of which towne hee doth
often ſpeake honorably in his writings. There is
ouer the doore where he was borne being a little
houſe, where I haue ſeene a Taylor dwell, a ſmall
round circle, whereas his face onely is drawne,
with an inſcription in *Latin* and *Spaniſh*, ſaying,
Heere that great Eraſmus *of Rotterdam was borne* :
and in the Market place looking towards the hauen, his picture is planted at length with a booke
in his hand . Hee hath deſerued this honor and
much more for his great knowledge, whereof hee
hath giuen good teſtimonie, by ſo many Bookes
which hee hath put forth to the honor of God,
and the inſtructions of Chriſtians : yet all men
ſpeake not equally of him, but enuie neuer dyes.
Hee had beene an *Auguſtine* Monke, and therefore the Monkes were his greateſt enemies : yet
he was held in good reputation, and had a liuing
from Pope *Leo* the tenth . Hee died at *Baſill* in
Swiſſerland, and is interred in the Cathedrall
Church, where I haue ſeene his Sepulcher entring
into the Quier.

SCHIEDAM.

IS a towne ſituated vpon a current of water,
which comes not farre out of a countrie called
Schie : from whence it takes the name, as if one
would ſay the Sluſe of *Schie.* It hath a good hauen
vpõ the *Meuſe.* It is apparent by the priuiledges of
the

the said towne, that it was made a towne in the yeare 1274. and had their priuiledges granted from the Earle of *Holland*, with power to admini-ster Iuſtice, with many good lawes, wherof menti-on is made in the foundation & of the building of the said towne, which was then called *Nyeuwen-Dam*, that is, the *New Scluſe*, which name it carryed vntill the yeare 1300. and ſince it hath beene al-wayes called *Schiedam*. In this towne there is an hoſpitall, which for antiquitie is equall with the foundation, the which they called the Hoſpitall of the new *Dam*, which hath this priuiledge, that a Bourger or any other dying, eyther within the towne, or in the liberties thereof, the beſt gar-ment hee leaues, doth belong vnto the ſayd hoſ-pitall.

The chiefe trade of this towne is fiſhing for her-ring, to which end they do euery yeare ſend forth a good number of *Buſſes* into the North ſea, and from thence they tranſport and ſell them ſarre and neere. It is a rich marchandize and much deſired in *France* and the Eaſt countries, as at *Danſick*, *Conixbergen*, *Hambourg*, *Lubeck*, *Bremen*, and ge-nerally through-out all *Germanie*. It is a com-mon ſaying, that the herring is a little fiſh, but ſtrong enough to ruine his Maiſter, when hee playes with his tayle, that is to ſay, when hee ſells not, but when the fiſhing and the vent is good, it makes them ritch. Beſides this fiſhing, they commonlie ſend forth euery yeare many great
ſhipps,

fhippes, which traffick through-out all the feas
of the world; fo as there are many good maifters
of fhippes, Pilots, and expert marriners in the
towne. The Marchants and Bourgers of this
towne are fincere and iuft in their dealings, who
imitating the ancient paines of the old *Hollanders*,
hate all pride, pompe, and fuperfluitie, as well in
bankets, apparell, as riche moouables, wherein
they are very moderate, with an honeft parcimo-
nie, fuch as their predeceffors vfed, which is an
honour vnto them.

BRIELE.

IT feemes this towne hath taken his name from
the largeneffe of the gulfe, where as the *Meufe*
and the *Rhine* (ioyned together) fall into the Ocean or Brittifh feas, in which place they fay that
Claudius Ciuilis (iffued from the bloud royall of
the *Battauians* did fight with the *Romaine* fleete,
but with-out any great gaine to eyther parte.
This word of *Briele*, doth well agree with that
of *Hiele* in *Plinie*, which for the largeneffe of the
gulph may bee called *Bre-heile* (which is a large
heele) and by corruption of the tongue *Briele*.
This towne with that of *Ghcervlyet* (a fmall
towne in the fame Ifland of *Vorne*) are reafona-
blie good, the Inhabitants for the moft part
are fea-faring men, which gette their liuing by
fifhing, and that which belongs therevnto. The
ayre of this towne is groffe and heauie, lying fo

I 3 neere

neere vnto the sea, so as it is euery yeare visited
with some disease or other. The countrie about
it is very fertill, and yeelds aboundance of good
wheate, and all other victuals are plentifull and
good cheape there.

SCHOONHOVEN

THis towne takes his name of the goodly and
pleasant gardens, which are both within and
about it, abounding in diuerse sorts of fruites. For
this worde *Schoonhoven*, signifies goodly gardens.
It is situated vpon the left banke of the riuer of
Leck : they hold that it was built of the ruines of
the towne of *Nieuport*, the which at this day is
but a Bourg, on the other side of the sayd riuer,
opposite to *Schoonhouen* : In all this passage euen
vnto the village of *Leckerke*, there is great fishing
for Salmons, which they sell in the said towne, and
the villages there-abouts.

　　Christopher Longolius that excellent Orator,
was borne in this Towne, although that some
would haue him a *French-man*, or a *Wallon*. The
which *Peter Longolius* his Vncle, a very learned
man did witnesse, whose testimonie is sufficient to
confute all other opinions. There passeth a channell through this towne which comes out of the
riuer of *Yssell*, very commodious to passe from one
riuer vnto the other.

ISELSTEYN.

ISELSTEYN.

IT is a fmall towne but very ftrong, beeing fo fortified by reafon of their great warres. It is fo called of a little channell which paffeth, comming out of the riuer of *Yffell*. There had beene a long controuerfie betwixt the *Hollanders* and them of *Vtrecht* for the iurifdiction of this towne, either partie pretending an intereft. Some foure and thirtie yeares fince, the Church fteeple was burnt by lightning from heauen, but did no other harme vnto the towne. It is of the patrimonie of the houfe of *Egmont*, whereof the laft Lord was *Maximilian* of *Egmont*, Earle of *Buren* and *Ifeifteyn*, who left one daughter, fole heyre to the Lord of *Launoy*, whom *William* Prince of *Orange* did marry, being his firft wife, fo as all the inheritance of thefe houfes of *Buren* and *Launoy* came to *Phillip William*, and to the Lady *Mary* of *Naffau* Counteffe of *Hohenloo* his fifter.

WOERDEN.

IS a reafonable good towne and well built, with a market place, whereas all prouifions are to bee folde once a weeke: it ftands in a moore hauing a ftrong caftle, whereas they keepe prifoners of importance: as of late dayes the Admirall of *Arragen*, the Earle of *Bufquoy* and others. The Lord of *Hierges* hauing taken *Oudewater* (as wee haue faid) for the Duke of *Alua*, & the towne of *Schoon-*

houen

hoven, he went to befiege *Woerden*, where hauing begun to make his approches, and to plant boates for his batterie, they of the towne let goe all their Slufes, the which in one night drowned the countrie about, fo as hee was forced to rife and leaue two peeces of ordinance. This towne was built by *Godfrey* Bifhop of *Vtrecht*, a man giuen to armes, to fuppreffe the courfes of the *Hollanders*. And therefore the fuperioritie thereof was for a long time queftionable betwixt the Earles of *Holland* and the Bifhops of *Vtrecht*. It hath for long time had a particular Lord, among others a brother to the Lord of *Amftel*, who being one of the confpirators of the death of *Cont Floris* the fift, fled and continued a vagabond; fince by the law of Armes the *Hollanders* haue enioyed it.

VIANE.

IT is a little fquare towne feated vppon the left banke of the riuer of *Leck*, a free Baronie belonging to the houfe of *Brederode*, which would neither be fubiect to the King of *Spaine*, nor to the Earles of *Holland*, whereof there hath bin fome queftion, (yet it is held of the dependances of *Holland*) but it is not yet decided. It hath a faire Caftle, which is the ordinarie aboade of *Walrard* Lord of *Brederode*, Baron of V*iane*, *Ameide*, &c. hauing a large iurifdiction. It hath endured much after the retreate of *Henry* Lord of *Brederode*, in the yeare 1567.

SAINT

SAINT GERTRVTDENBERGHE.

THis word signifieth the mount of *Saint Geertruyde*, it may be, for that the place had beene dedicated to that Saint. It is a strong towne both by nature and art, situated vpon the left banke of the riuer of *Meruve*: more famous for the taking of great *Salmons* then any part of all the Netherlands;and such aboundance of *Aloses* or troutes, as on a market day you may see aboue 18000. great and small, and many great sturgions , which in a conuenient season are transported to *Antwerp*,*Brusselles*, *Gand* , *Bruges* and other places,besides that which is distributed into *Holland* , *Zeeland* and the rest of the vnited Prouinces. The like is found in the riuer of *Yssel* nere vnto the towne of *Campen* in the country of *Oueryssel* . In former times there hath beene great controuersie for the proprietie of the sayd towne , the *Brabansons* pretending a title therevnto for that it stands on their side ,'and the *Hollanders* making claime also vnto it , by reason of their ancient possession. Which question proceeded so farre, (there beeing no meanes to reconcile it) as the Estates of *Holland* (when they did receiue their Earles) bound them by a sollemne oth to keepe it vnder the sayd Earldome , and they of *Brabant* on the other side did binde their Dukes to recouer it : Yet it appeeres plainely by the Chronicle of *Holland*, that when as their Earle (who was also Earle of *Henault*)

Henault)intended to goe to *Mons*, *Valenciennes* or any other place of the fayd Earldome, the Nobility of *Holland* came to accompanie him to this towne, whether they of *Henault* came to attend him, and did conduct him whether he would goe, as alfo in his returne they brought him thether, where as they of *Holland* did incounter him to conuoie him into *Holland*. This towne is of the inheritance of the house of *Naffau*, in whose name it was cunningly furprized in the yeare 1 5 7 3. and fo continued vnder the vnion of the vnited Eftates, vntill that fome leud perfons (vnder collour of an ill grounded mutynie,) fold it in the yeare 1588. to the Duke of *Parma*, for readie money. But fince in the yeare 1 5 9 3. it was recouered by fiege in viewe of the old Earle of *Manffeldt*, who was generall of the King of *Spaines* armie, and gouernor by prouifion after the death of the Duke of *Parma*: It is at this day vnder the vnited Eftates, better fortefied then euer, and alwaies manned with a good garrifon, and furnifhed with all other neceffarie prouifions.

THE HAGE.

BEfides Citties and walled townes which they account to eight and twenty in number, there are in *Holland* manie great Bourroughs, which their Princes haue inricht with goodly priuiledges being nothing inferior to fome walled towns, both

both in greatneffe, buildings and beautie. Among
the which no man can denie but the *Hage* holds
the firft place, which they doe commonly call the
Earles *Hage*: which place the old Earles and Princes did choofe for their Court, and for the feate
of their great councell, whereas all caufes are ended as well vpon the firft inftance, as by appeale
to the Earles of *Holland, Zeeland* and *Weft-Frifland*.
This place is as ftately, and pleafing, as well in
buildings and houfes of Princes, great perfonages and of the meaner fort, as in gardins and o-
ther delights, as any other in Chriftendome. The
Pallace is great and dicht about, whereas all the
councellors both for iuftice, gouernment, warre
and treafure affemble. It was built by *William*
King of *Romaines* and Earle of *Holland*, who caufed the councellors to bee tranfported from *Gra-
uefandt* (which is neere vnto the fea) to the
Hage. The great hall of the Pallace is built wi h
wonderfull art; beeing not ftrengthened with
any great beames a croffe, but onely with a
roofe in forme of an Arch, which binds the whole
building; the timber was brought out of *Ireland*,
which hath a propertie not to endure any poifon,
and therefore you fhall not at any time fee a cob-
web there. On the North fide it hath a great
poole, and aboue it a little hill planted with
great trees, where as there are pleafant fhadie
walkes for Summer, and feats to reft themfelues on.

Along

Along thefe walkes are many houfes of Noblemen, Prefidents, Gentlemen, Councellors and
other men of quality. Going out of the Court-
gate on the North-fide alfo, you come vnto another
ther goodly place, which is appointed for the execution of Iuftice, all fo neatly paued, as the more
it raynes the cleaner it is, the ftreetes clenfing
themfelues with the rayne: Paffing on they come
to an other great walke full of trees, one ioyning
to an other, the which in the fpring time yeeld a
fweete and pleafant fmell; this walke comming
behind the houfes and a ftreet betwixt both, it
goes to the gardins of the Harguebuziers and
Crosbow-men, whereby they enter into the court
on the backe-fide. This Pallace is the ordynarie refidence of the Gouernors of *Holland, Zeeland* and
weft-frifland, who at this day is that great captaine
Prince *Maurice* of *Naffau, Marquis* of *Campvere
Fluffing &c.* High Admirall for the vntied Prouinces, fecond fonne to that valiant and wife
Prince of *Orange, william* Earle of *Naffau.* It is
halfe an houres paffage to goe from the South
which comes from *Delfe,* vnto the end of the
North, (which goes to *Scheueling* vpon the fea-
fhoare) it is not muchleffe from the Eaft to the
Weft, which are the two bredthes compaffing in
the Bourrogh: going out on the Eaft-fide towards *Leyden,* you enter into a pleafant little wood
fome 1500. paces long, but not fo broade, well
planted with oakes and all other forts of trees, and
full

full of Deere and Conies, a very pleafant place,
the which in the Somer time is much frequented;
whether the Aduocats and Proctors goe often to
walke when as they come from pleading, before
they goe to dinner. The Prouinciall councell
confifts of a Prefident and foureteene councelors,
(among the which is numbred the Aduocate *Fif-
call*) an Attorney generall, a Regifter and other
Officers. There alfo doth the Receiuor generall of
the fayd country and of *weft-frifland* remaine. The
Chamber of accounts which was wont to be there
for *Holland, Frifland, Groning, Oueryffel, Vtrecht* and
Zeeland, is now reftrained to *Holland* and *Weft-
Frifland* alone: the other Prouinces hauing with-
drawne themfelues, euery one hauing his Receiuor and chamber of accounts apart : True it is
they haue fubiected themfelues to bring the money which ri eth of contributions and taxations
thether, and to deliuer it vnto the Receiuer generall, and to be accountable vnto the Treaforer generall of the vnited Prouinces, and to the Exche-
quer of the generall Eftates. In this Pallace is yet
remayning that great and royall Library, which
was gathered together by that famous Chanoine
Iohn Harrie aboue mentioned. About three fcore
ard ten yeares fince *Martin van Roffen* came with
his *Geldrois* of the garrifon of *Vtrecht*, at noone
day to fpoile this goodly Bourg, all the councel-
lers and Aduocates flying away and abandoning
their houfes to thefe infolent fouldiars, who carryed

ryed away their ſpoile in boates to *Vtrecht*, without any oppoſition. They ſaid that if this goodly Bourg had beene walled in, they had not beene
ſubieċt to calamitie . Within theſe ſix and thirty
yeares they had attempted it,but by reaſon of the
furie of the *Spaniards* it was not held fit : for ſuch
as were oppoſite vnto it , ſayed, that comming to
bee beſieged it ſhould bee quite ſpoiled and ruined : whereas finding it open and the people fled,
they did but lodge there ſometimes as they paſt,
and ſometimes they ſtayed there, whileſt they did
ouer-runne the villages of *Weſt-holland* . In this
place was borne that learned Prelat *Iohn Iugenhage*
being of a Noble family, of whom the Abbot *Tri-
temius* and *William Vuytenhage* make mention,bee-
ing the firſt comicall Poet of the Lower *Germaine.*
Of the ſame place was *Gerard* Signior of *Aſſen-
delf*, who was Preſident of Holland, of an honorable houſe, very learned in Greeke and Latin, and
an excellent Poet,and his ſonne *Nicholas* of *Aſſen-
delf* very learned alſo. In like ſort *Hippolitus* of
Perſin Preſident of the Prouince of *Vtrecht* was
borne there, with *Splinter* *Hargene* Siegnior of
Ooſterwyck,and *Arnold Knebel*, who was treaſurer
for the Eſtates of Holland, and his brother *Philip*
councellor of the priuy councell at *Breſſelles*, all
men of great knowledge.

Halfe a league from the *Hage* in our time was a
goodly Abbay of Relligious Noblewomen of the
order of Saint *Bernard*, called *Loſdune*, whereas is
yet

yet to bee scene in the Church of the sayd Abbay which hath beene quite ruined by these last furious warres)the tombe of the Lady *Marguerite* of *Holland* Countesse of *Hausberge*,with her Epitaph both in Latin & Dutch, set there by reason of her strange & miraculous deliuerie of three hundred sixtie and foure children at one birth,whereof *Erasmus Roterodamus* ,*Iohannes Lodouicus Viues* and many other famous Authors make mention in their writings , the which I forbeare to relate being set downe at large in the History of the Netherlands.

An example of the like child-birth is to bee found in the *Annales* of *Brunswyck* : with whom *Albertus Crantzius* , Historiographer to *Ernestus* Prince of *Anhalt* doth accord in his Comentaries of *Vandalia* , who writes that seauen and thirtie yeares after the sayd child-birth,the like happened to the Lady *Marguerite* daughter to the Earle of *Holstein*,the which were all baptized. *Martin Cromer* in his Chronicle of *Poland* writes that in *Cracouia* in the yeare 1269. the wife of the Earle *Buboslas* was deliuered of sixe and thirty children all liuing, the which is against all the rules of Phisick and naturall Philosophy ; yea against the course of nature it selfe,yet there is no rule but hath some exception , whereas the grace or diuine vengeance interposeth it selfe, the which ouer-rules Nature and the force of the Elements.

V L A E R-

VLAERDINGHE.

ALthough this bee but a Borroughe at this day yet it is put in the firſt ranke of all the walled townes of Holland, the riuer of *Meuſe* vpon whoſe bankes it ſtands) laning in a manner eaten it vp with the caſtle, and by great tempeſts driuen it into the ſea. *Thierry* of *Waſinare* doth maintaine that it ought be called *Verdinge*, by reaſon of the tolle which doth yet belong vnto the Lords of *Waſſenare*, where they did bargaine as well as they could, it is two leagues diſtant as well from *Delfe* as *Rotterdam*.

SEVENBERGHE.

THis towne is ſeated vpon the riuer of *Merve*, three leagues beneath *Gheertruydenberghe*, and as much from *Breda*. The towne lies open; it is ſmall, but reaſonable good, where there was a mighty fort during all the time of the laſt troubles, the which was held by a garriſon for the vnited Eſtates: It belongs now to the Earle of *Aremberghe*, who hath liberty from the Eſtates, that paying contribution, it ſhall remaine neuter, as it hath done.

All the aboue named townes although they bee not ſo great as thoſe of *Brabant* and *Flanders*, yet they are not much inferior, beeing for the moſt part greater by the halfe, ſtronger and better peopled then they were thirty yeares ſince: ſo as they

they which haue not beene there since, especially in *Amsterdam*, will not know it . Of all these townes there are fiue which should bee held for Bourroughs, whereof wee will presently speake some thing : that is to say, the *Hage*, (which deserues well the name of a towne) *Vlaerdinghe*, *Seuenbergh*, *Muyden* and *Voorn* : yet there is an other towne not walled in, called.

GOEREE.

WHich I finde to bee the last of the townes of *Holland*, it is situated in a little Iland inhabited for the most part by fishermen, and makers of nets, which is their greatest labour and trafficke : it hath as good and as deepe a roade as any is in *Holland*, where as great shippes which go long voiages cast anchor, attending their last prouision , and a good winde. This place hath of late yeares beene spoiled by the garrisons of *Woude* and *Hulst*, as also *Hellevooet sluys*, opposite vnto it, which is the Sluse of the Iland of *Voorn* on that side towards the sea, whereas *Bryle* lies on the other side vpon the gulphe of the riuer, which they call the old *Meuse*.

BEVERWYCK

THis word is as much to say as a retreate for *Bauarians* for it seemeth that the Kings of *France* hauing subdued *Holland*, did diuide the

K   inheri-

inheritances of the countrie amongſt their olde
fouldiars, whether they ſhould retire themſelues
and inhabit , the which they did diſtribute by
nations . This Bourg is two leagues from
Harlem , vpon the riuer of *Tye* , not aboue two
thouſand paces diſtant from the ſea ; it is well
built and hath goodly farmes about it . The No-
bleſt of all Borroughes and Villages ending in
wyck , is *Calwyck* , whereof there are two , the one
vppon the ſea , and the other farther vppe into
the countrie : which haue beene built by the
Cattes,fathers to the *Battauians* or *Hollanders*,who
following their Prince , *Batto* , went and ſeated
themſelues neere vnto the gulphe whereas the
Rhine diſchargeth it ſelfe into the ſea : which
place by reaſon of the commodity of the ſituation,hath beene heretofore ample , ſpatious and verie fit to receiue ſhippes and marchandiſe,but diuers times deſtroyed and ruined by the incurſions
of *Barbarians* and Pirats.

Beſides there is *Suydwyck* neere to *Waſſenare*,
where there is a Mil vpō the South ſide, the which
by a breuiation they call *Suyck* : then there is
Noortwyck on the North ſide , to the which it
ſeemes that the *Normans* which came out of *Denmarke* and *Suedland* gaue the name , whereof that
worthy man *Ianus Douza* was Lord, and left it to
his children. Then haue you *Oſterwyck* , which
ſome hold was inhabited by the *Vandales* or *Eſter-
lings*,vnleſſe that *Foppo* Lord of *Arckel* gaue it the
name

name of *Eſterwyck*. Then is there *Naeldwycke*, wherof the Lords of the direct line are dead, and now it
belongs vnto the Earle of *Arembergh* , where
there is a Chanonry; *Martin van Dorp* a great diuine and a Poet was borne there. After it is *Riſ-
wyck* nere vnto the *Hage*; *Stolwyck* famous for the
good cheeſe which is made there nere vnto *Goude*:
Blcuſwyck belonging vnto the Siegnior of *Bronck-
hurſt* : *Brerdwyck*, beeing ſo called of the Bardes,
Gaules , or of the *Lombards* a people of *Germanie* :
Brandwyck , *Schalcwyck* and *Hontwyck* , whereof it
were hard to write the etimologies & beginnings.

NIEVPORT.

IS on the other bancke of the riuer of *Leck*, right
againſt *Schoonhoven* : It hath beene in former
times a good towne , but as the condition of hu-
maine things is frayle and tranſitorie , it ſeemes
that the ſpoyles of Barbarous nations,& the inteſ-
tine warres which they haue had in *Hol and* hath
brought it to decay , yet it is ſtill a good Borrough.

SCAGE.

IT is a good Bourg, well built like vnto a towne
the market place is made of a triangle forme,and
goes into three ſtreetes, where there are little paſ-
ſages from the one to the other. It hath the beſt &
moſt frutfull ſoyle of all *Holland*, both for tillage
and paſture; the Bourgers are verie rich.

There is a goodly castle, all which belongs vnto the Siegnior of *Scagen* and B*.rchom*, who descends from Duke *Albertus* of *Bauaria* Earle of *Holland*.

It were an infinite thing to describe the other Bourgs and Villages of the fayd county, the which we will omit and speake something of the castles; as well of those which haue beene ruined during the factions of the *Hoocs* & *Cabillaux*, as of the rest which are yet standing. Among those which are ruined are the castles of *Brederode*, halfe a league from *Harlem*, and of *Egmont*, being 5 0 0 0. paces from *Alcmar*: It was first ruined long since, and afterwards in the last troubles, in reuenge that the Earle of *Egmont* the father, left the Noblemen of the *Netherlands*, who had entred into league against the Duke of *Alua*, the which cost him his head, and for that the sonnes (in steede of reuenging the ignominious death of their father) followed the *Spaniards* party. Then is the castle of *Teylingen*, where as the Countesse *Iaqueline* tooke great delight, betwixt *Leyden* and *Harlem*, ruined also nere vnto the walls, but it might be easily repaired. On the other side of the town of *Schoonhouen*, is the great and mighty castle of *Lyffeldt*, nere vnto the bankes of the riuer of *Leck*, belonging vnto the Duke of *Brunswyck*, if of late yeares hee had not exchanged it together with the towne of *Woerden*, with *Philippe* Earle of *Hohenlo*. At *Vianen* there is also a faire castle belonging to the

Lord

Lord of *Brederode* as wee haue sayd, with that of *Ameden*, which is betwixt *Viane* and *Nieuport*, on the same side.

Wee haue heretofore made mention of the castles of *Woerden*, *Goude*, *Gorchom*, *Medenblyke* and *Muyden*. There is neere vnto the towne of *Alemar* the castle *of Assenburg*, which is the place of the Lord of *Assendelf*, who hath an other castle nere vnto *Rotterdam*, called *Hemingen*. The castle of *Abcoude* is one of the Noblest and most antient, betwixt *Leyden* and *Vtrecht*; there is a remainder of a little castle neere vnto *Hemskerke*, seated vpon a hill, with foure towers, the which for the hight doth some times serue as a sea marke vnto Mariners. Those of the house of *Adrichom* had a castle neere vnto *Beuerwyke*, which the *Frisons* did raze and ruine; with the ruines whereof the Siegnior *Antony Vander Burcht* heire of that place by his mother, hath caused a house and a farme to bee built there, all walled about. The old castle of *Riuiere* nere vnto *Schiedam*, as wee haue sayd, doth belong vnto the Siegniors of *Matenesse*. After it is *Kenebourg* belonging vnto *Iames* of *Egmont van Merensteyn*, or to his heires. Then *Mereburg* to the Siegnior of *Lochorst*: and the castle of *Duyuen* nere vnto *Seuenhuysen* to the Siegnior of *Sprangen*. There was nere vnto the *Hage* not farre from *Voorburg* a castle called *Elin*, at this present wholie ruined. The ruines of the castle and temple of *Hildegarde*, within a league

K 3   of

of *Rotterdam* are yet to bee feene vpon a high e-
mineut place, whereas in old time there kept one
Hildegarde a kinde of *Sibille* or diuine, whofe O-
racles did reprefent the times which wee haue
now feene in *Holland* There yet remaines a tower
all tattered, the ground of which caftle is the
inheritance of the houfe of *Matcneffe*. Within
the compaffe of the walles of *Rotterdam* there is
to be feene the ruines of *Bulgeftein*, and of the caftle of Veen which they call *Thoff*, that is to fay the
Court, fo as the gate which is fet in that place, is
called the H*off*-port. You may fee vpon the riuer of *Schye* the remainders of the caftle of *Ster-
rcburg* the which belongs vnto the Siegnorie of
Duyvenvorde, there was alfo in former times an
old caftle in the village of *Capelle*, whereof the
ruines are yet to bee feene; it comes from the
houfe of *Naeldwycke*, and doth now belong to the
Earles of *Aremberghe*. The caftle of *Hodenpyle* in
the iurifdiction of V*laerdinghe*, is quite downe.
The like hath happened to the caftle of *Polanen*, the
which did belong vnto one of the noblest families
of *Holland* : All thefe ruines happened during
their curfed factions of H*oecks* & *Cabillaux*, wherof thefe Noblemen were the chiefe fupporters,
taking a diuilifh delight to ruine one an others
houfes, yea in townes the ftrongeft factions
of the Bourgers chafing awaie the others, which
factions continued not much leffe then two hundred yeares.

                                                    The

The castle of Velsen, for that *Gerarde van Velsen* Knight had murthered *Floris* the fift Earle of *Holland* was in like manner ruined, nothing remayning but certaine old peeces of walles, the ground whereof belongs vnto the heires of *Ianus Douza* Siegnior of *Nortwyck*: nere vnto which ruines *Adrian Groeneveen* a rich Bourger of *Harlem* hath built a faire house with large ditches, almost like vnto a castle. *Sandenbu g* which was a castle of the Earles of *Holland*, (after that the Court had beene transported from *Grauesandt* to the Hage, by Count *William* King of *Romaines*) was also ruined, and so remaines. The like happened to the castle of *Zyle*, in old time called *Thoff van Zyle*.

The castle *Ter Does* had beene also ruined, but within these foureteene or fifteene yeares it hath beene repaired. *Altena* (that is to say, to nere) so called for that it was feared by them of *Delfe*, by reason of the fort, beeing neighbour vnto them, belongs to them of *Almonde*: *Croeswyck* on the other side of the riuer of *Rotter*; and *Croelinghen* halfe a quarter of a league from *Rotterdam* are also ruined, but if the Signior of *Croelinghen* had a good purse, it should bee soone repaired. *Louestin* right against *Worcom*, and *Henselaers-Dyck* neere vnto *Naeld-Wyck* are yet in being.

K 4 *Of*

Of the Nobility of Holland.

I Will content my felfe with that which diuers
Authors haue written touching Nobilitie, how
it is pourchafed and maintained, what the dutie
is, and wherein true Nobilitie confifts: who de-
firs to be inftructed, let him read *Adrianus Iunius* in his *Battauia*, in the chapter *De Nobilitate Ba-
tauica*, But I will here relate fuccinctly what the
ancient Nobilitie of *Holland* was, how it came
to decline, and what hath remained. The ancient Nobilitie of *Battauia* or *Holland*, tooke their
greateft exercifes in Armes, by the which they
fought the degrees of honour, for as *Tacitus*
faith . *Vt Gallos pro libertate, Germanos pro præda,
ita Batauos pro gloria ad capeffendam pugnam olim
fuiffe inftigatos*. As the *Gaules* for libertie, the
Germaines for prey, fo the *Battauians* were in old
time prouoked to enter battaile for the defire of
glorie . They were moft commonly the beft
mounted, and had the faireft and moft refolute
troupes of horfe, that ferued vnder the *Romaine*
Emperors.

After that *Holland* had a particular Prince, beginning with *Thierry* of *Aquitane* their firft
Earle, the Nobility of *Holland* began to fhew them
felues, fo they grew to haue many great and worthy families, & a great number of gentlemen, who
had pourchafed their nobility, either from their
Anceftors, or by their own vertues and proweffe.
But

But I cannot but lament, that so many great, noble, riche and mightie families, are now extinct, as well by their intestine warres against the *Frisons*, as against strangers; for which consideration the heyres males fayling, the successions fell to the women, and so came to other families: besides the furie of *Gerard van Velsen* had many companions, all which were put to death, and their neerest kinsmen pursued to the death, euen vnto the ninth degree (a most crueil reuenge) and such as could escape, were forced to become vagabonds in forraine countries, such as had hidden themselues vntill this furious reuenge was past, were afterwards forced to take borrowed names of other families, and to leaue their owne. To come then to that which remaines, and to those which are past. We will say that the house of *Wassenare* (as wee haue said elsewhere) was the most ancient of *Holland*: as it appeares by this common prouerbe. *Vassenare the most ancient*; Brederode *the most noble* (for that they descend from the first Earles) *and* Eg nond *the most rich*. Wee haue scene in this last age, *Iohn* of *Wasenare*, the subduer of the *Frisons*, a braue and valiant Knight, who was slaine in those warres leauing one onely daughter and heire, married to the Earle of *Lingue*, whereby this familie and surname is extinct.

The memorie of the house of *Brederode* may easily be found in the Annales of *Holland*, being come from *Ziphard* the second sonne of *Arnulph* the

the third Earle of *Holland* and *Zealand*, who to a-
noyd his fathers wrath, retyred into *Freezeland*,
and there without his priuity he marryed the Po-
teſtats.daughter of the country, by whome hee had
two ſonnes, *Thierry* and *Simon*: Being afterwards
reconciled to his Father, he had certaine land alot-
ted him for his portion, which was meaſured by
the great rod, the which in the coun¹ry language
is *Brederode*, from whence they tooke their name:
His father gaue him alſo the Caſtle and Territory
of *Theylingen*; the which *Zyphard* at his death dif-
poſed to his two ſons; to *Thierry* he gaue *Brederoʒe.*
and to *Simon Teylingen*, from whence are iſſued the
two families of *Brederode* and *Teylinge*, the which
ended by the death of two bretheren, who were
ſlaine with their Prince *VVilliam* King of *Romans*
in the warre againſt the *Friſons*. As for that of *Brederode* we haue ſeene foure bretheren of the right
lyne dye alſo in the warres againſt the *French* in
few yeares, ſo as it fell by a collaterall line vnto
VVairauen Lord of the ſaid *Brederod·*, *Vianen*,
Ameyden,&c. who hauing not any children, and not
likely to haue any by reaſon of his age and his
wiues; all muſt returne to *Floris* of *Brederode* his
Brothers ſonne, who may raiſe vp the houſe being
now halfe extinct.

The beginning of the houſe of *Egmont* is
doubtfull, for the Lordes thereof cannot truly
ſhewe a continuance of their deſcent for three
hundred yeares: yet they ſay they are iſſued from
Radbod

Radbod (I know not which) King of the *Frisons*, but I thinke it would bee a tedious thing to finde out this pedigree. Such as contradict it say, that they are descended from a Receiuer of the Abbay of *Egmond* , which Office had beene called *Aduoe*, and vnder this title hauing inrich-ed them-selues with the goods of this Abbaie, by little and little they attained to great wealth, and thereby to great allyances, which haue aug-mented their house , as well in possessions , as degrees of honour , so as in the end they marry-ed a daughter of the famous house of *Arckel* , the which was heire to the Dutchie of *Geldres:* Whereas *Arnold* of *Egmond* the first Duke of that house , had one sonne called *Adolph* , who did much trouble his father, yea hee detained him in prison , vntill that *Charles* Duke of *Bur-gongne* sette him free. *Adolph* retyring into *France*, married a Lady of the house of *Bourbon*, who hauing one son named *Charles*, hee was after-terwards slaine being Generall of the *Ganthois* be-fore *Tournay* : After whose death the Emperour *Charles* the fift vnder coullor of some transport which hee pretended, that Duke *Arnold* had made vnto duke *Charles* of *Burgongne* beeing in dislike with his son, hee seazed vppon the whole Duchy: but *Charles* of *Egmond* , sonne to Prince *Adolph* (for he was neuer Duke) with the helpe of the Princes of the house of *Bourbon* , who stirred vp the *French* King , returning into his Countrie
he

hee was receiued and acknowledged for Duke in
many townes, & the Emperors men chased away.
Afterwards (being of a turbulent spirit) hee had
great warres, so as in the end hee dyed, about the
yeare 1 5 3 6. without any children, and in him fai-
led the distrect lyne of this house of *Egmond* The
Seigniory of *Egmond* falling to the yonger house
who was father to *Iohn* the first Earle of *Egmond*,
which *Iohn* had one brother *Maximliā* of *Egmond*,
Earle of *Buren*, Lord of *Iselsteine*, whose daughter
being issued of a Lady of the house of *Launoy* and
the onely heire, marryed with *William* of *Nassau*
Prince of *Oranze*, so as the possessions of these two
houses of *Buren* and *Launoy* are discended to
Prince *Philip* eldest son to the deceased Prince of
Orange, as wel by his grandfather, as by his father.

Some do account next among the mo t ancient
and Noble families, that of *Vander* Merwue as descended from *Merouee* King of *France* in honour of
whome some beleeue that in that place the riuer of
Wahall was changed into *Meruwe*: but this Original
is farre fetcht: There is yet some remainder of a
Tower in the midst of *Meruve*, which in old time
was the place where they payed toll, the which is
now receiued in *Dordrect*, whereas the Baron of
Meruve, who is also Lord of *Aspren*, hath one day
in the yeare all right of superiority and power to
pardon murthers and al other offences. The house
of *Arckel* did for a long time command insolently
in the Earldome of *Teysterbandt*, betwixt the *Wahal*

hal and the *Leck*,the which the riuer of *Linge* doth
croffe, and paffing through *Gorichom* it fals into
the *Meruve*. In this County there are many other
Townes then *Gorchom* with the Caftle;as *Leerdam*,
Henkelom,*Haerftricht*, *Afpren*,*Euerfteyn*, *Hagefteyn*,
and *Gafprien*, wherof the three laft and *Haarftrecht*
haue beene burnt and ruined : It feemes that all
the neighbour Princes haue confpired againft this
houfe for their great pride : For *Frederick* Bifhop
of *Vtrecht* hauing taken *Gafpren*,*Hageftein* and *Euerfteyn*, he ruined them quite. The Lord of *Vianen*
wrefted *Rhynftein* from him. *Arnold* Duke of *Geldres* tooke *Leerdam* and *Steenvoerd*. *Albert* Duke
Bauaria Earle of *Holland* took *Haeftrecht* from him
and ruined it Afterwards the faid Duke bought of
Iohn the laft Lord of fo many townes, and Seigieu-
ries,that of *Gorichom*, with confent of his fonne,
and vnder his hand writing, who notwithftanding
foone after difavowed the contract,the which hee
brake after his fathers death, and found meanes to
furprize the faid towne. The Counteffe *Iaqueline*
went thether with an armie,befieged it,and took it
by affault, whereas the faid young Lord receiued
the reward of his difloyalty for he was flain there:
Thefe Lords of *Arckel* were fo mighty,as befides
the County of *Teyfterband* (in the which are the
townes aboue mentioned) they had liuing in *Brabant*,*Lembourg*,*Bar*,*Vtrecht*,*Geldre*,*Holland* and *Zeland*, which poffeffions made them proud , arro-
gant & hatefull vnto their neighbours,ouer whom
they

they did infult, vntill they came to the end which we haue fpoken of.

The houfe of *Batenbourg* is without al queftion one of the moft ancient : taking their name from Prince *Batto* , from whome *Battauia* is come whereof there were of great fame for their vertue fome fiue hundred yeares fince, *Albert*, *Rodolphus* and *Thierry* Lordes of *Battenbourg*, as of late *Thierry*, *Gifbercht*, and *VVilliam* , who beeing Lieutenant to the Prince of *Orange* , leading an army to victuall *Harlem* , befeeged by the Duke of *Alua*, was defeated by the Spaniards : This Towne of *Battenbourg* was afterwards burnt, and the Caftell held long by the *Spaniardes*. The fayd *Ghifbrecht* had befides *William* three other fons, wherof one was traiteroufly flavne at *Collegne*, *Ghifbrecht* and *Thierry* beeing taken prifoners in the VVarre by the Earle of *Arembergh*, hee deliuered them to the Duke of *Alua* , who caufed their heades to bee cutte off at *Bruffelles*, with other Gentlemen of their religion : But it was not long before this Earle receiued his due punifhment , for before a yeare paft hee was flayne in Battaile in the fame Countrie where hee falfified his faith to thefe two young Barons.

The race of the Lordes of *Harlem* is alfo very ancient, and noble , who they fay tooke their beginning from the Kinges of *Freezeland* , which had built the Caftell of *Harlem* according to their

their name in the yeare a thoufand fixe hundred.
The ruines of this Caftell are yet to bee feene
not farre from *Hemfkerke*. It appeares by the
Annales of *Holland* that one *Ijbrandt* of the
houfe of *Harlem*, did accompany the Ladie *So-
phia* Princeffe of *Holland*, and Prince *Otto* her yongeft fonne in a Pilgrimage which they made
through deuotion vnto *Ierufalem*. Some Knights
of this houfe vnfortunate in the warre againft the
Frifons, haue loft their liues there. Of this houfe
was *Simon* of *Harlem* knight, who conuerted a faire
houfe which he had within the wals of the towne,
into a Cloyfter of *Carmelites*, in the yeare 1 2 4 9.

Of which houfe by changing of the name,
they of the houfe of *Affendelfe* haue obtained
the inheritance and the Armes vnto this daie.
Nicholas Lord of *Affendelfe* was wont to fay, that
his father hauing built the Caftell of *Affenburch*,
had repented him a hundred times that hee had
not fet it vppon the ruines of the Caftell of *Harlem*, to preferue the honour of antiquitie. This
houfe of *Affendelfe* takes his name from the Village which is richer, the which in ancient time
(as at appeares by old Charters) was called *Afo-
maundelfe*.

Cralinghen or rather *Carolinghen*, is faid to
haue had their beginning from the Emperour
Charl maigne: for the *French* had for a long time
caufed a part of *Germanie* and *Gaule* to be gouerned by them of *Meruwe* and *Craelingen*, which
are

are two noble families , and very famous in Holland .

We read that t⟨h⟩e houſe of Heuſden (where there is
a towne and Caſtle) is iſſued ſome eight hundred
yeares ſince from the Earles of *Cleues*, hauing carryed the armes as well of *Edmond* King of *England*
whoſe daughter *Baldwin* Lord of *Heuſden* ſtole a-
way and marryed her , who hauing many children
by her, would haue his nephewes to carry a wheele
of *Geules* in a field *Or*. The reaſon was that when
as the King of *Englands* ſeruants ſent to ſeeke his
daughter, came to the Lord of *Heuſdins*, they ſoud
her ſpinning at the wheele, with ſome pretty children about her , which brought her into fauour
againe. Since the yeare 1 2 9 0. the Earle of *Cleues*
reſigned all the intereſt he had to the Lordſhips of
Heuſden and *Altena* , to *Floris* the ſixt Earle of *Holland* to hold them of him in fee; but this reſignati-
on did not hold long ; for the Duke of *Brabant*
came and fell vppon *Heuſden*, and became maiſter
of it, but he held it as little, for Count *VVilliam* of
Bauaria) being a mediator betwixt the duke of *Bra-
bāt* & the Earle of *Flanders*) dealt firſt for himſelfe
in ſuch ſort, as hee ſhould haue *Heuſdē*, the which
hath bin annexed to this day to ẙ conty of *Hollād*.

Thoſe of *Duyvenuoorde* are iſſued from the houſe
of *VVaſſenare*. This word hauing taking his beginning, for that two Bretheren of the houſe of
VVaſſenare being a fiſhing , the elder to cauſe the
boate to aduance , ſaid to his younger Brother
Dele voort

Dole Voort, that is to fay, aduance, which word as a good prefage, remained to the younger houfe, whereof are come by corruption of the word, the Siegnior of *Duyuenvoort* . This name was firft giuen to *Philippe* the fecond fonne of *Aldewyn* Vicont of *Leyden* Lord of *Waffenare* and of *Rhinlandt*, who alfo gaue him libertie to carrie his armes, which were three *Croifants* . Or in a field *Sables*. *Philippe* Curat of *waffenare* doth report it fomewhat otherwife: hee fayth this *Philippe* had fiue fonnes, whereof the eldeft being heire of the name and armes, was called *Thierry*, the fecond *Philippe* Signior of *Duyuen-Voorde* : the third *Iohn* Lord of *Polanen*, who carried in a field *Argent* three Croiffants *Sables* : the fourth called *Sandthorft* who remained vnknowne, and the fifth *Arnold* of *Groenevelt*, who carried *Sinople*, and the *Croifants* filuer: of which houfe the Signior *Arnold* of *Groenevelt* is yet lyuing, beeing Collonel and Gouernor of *Nymegen* for the vnited Eftates. In the yere 1353. *William* of *Duyuenvoorde* Signior of *Ofterhout* was fo ritch as hee knew no end of his welth, who hauing no children, he would not make his kinffolks partakers thereof, but did build two Monafteries or Cloifters , neere vnto *Gheertruydenberghe*, the one of *Chartreux Monks*, the other of Saint *Clare*. And not content with this prodigality of his welth, he caufed a caftle to be built at *Ofterhout*, & made the towne of *Viane* to be walled in and dicht, as appeeres by his Epitaphe at *Bruffelles*.

L   The

The houfe of *Polanen* (as wee haue euen now fayd) is iffued from that of *Duyuenvoorde*, but it was of fmall continuance : for *Iohn* Lord of *Polanen* hauing left one onely fonne called alfo *Iohn*, hee dyed without any heires male', leauing one daughter, the fole heire of *Polanen*, of *Lecce* and of *Breda*, the which fhee brought in marriage to *Engelbert* Earle of *Naffau*, who was the firft Gouernor of the *Netherlands* for the Ladie *Mary* Dutcheffe of Bourgogne, fo as the fayd Siegneuries doe at this day belong vnto the children of *William* of *Naffau* Prince of *Orange*.

That of *Naeldwyck* was not of much longer contynuance, whereof wee finde that one *Baldwin* a Knight, Gouernor of the caftle of *Windeneffe* in *Weftfrifland*, a league from *Horne*, carried himfelfe valiantlie, vntill that for want of victualls and all other neceffarie prouifion, hee was forced to yeelde vppe the place. Thofe of that houfe conuerted their goodly caftle of *Wateringhe* into a Monafterie, which was ruined in thefe laft warres.

I will make but one houfe of thofe of *Woude* and of *Warmont*, for that the Siegnor of *Woude* tooke more delight at *Warmont*, which ftands in a good ayre and in a goodly country, then in the caftle of *Woude* which ftands in a Moore, fo as the caftle of *Woude* being neglected it fell to decay, and that of *Warmont* florifhed.

This houfe of *Warmont* was wont to beare in a field

Or three *Lozenges Geules ,* vntill that *Thierry* of *Waſſenare,* Vicont of *Leyden ,* giuing the poſſeſſion of certaine Lands in the yeare of our Lord 1359. to *Iames* the foureteenth Lord of W*armont ,* hee ſuffred him to carrie his owne Armes , which is a band *Or* vpon a field *Azure* betwixt three Croiſants *Argent ,* which that houſe carries vnto this daie . But thoſe of that houſe beeing partakers of the furie of *Gerard van Velſen ,* the murtherer of Count *Floris* the fifth, they were for the ſafe-gard of their liues forced to abandon the countrie. But ſome fiue yeares after the death of Cont *Iohn* the ſonne of *Floris ,* *Iohn* of *Henaut* beeing Earle of *Holland ,* to whom *Iames* Lord of W*armont* did great ſeruice at the defeate of the Biſhoppe of *Vtrecht ,* all iniuries beeing troden vnder foote, this houſe was reconciled to their Prince, and ſo haue continued in good Eſtate vnto this daie.

Thoſe of *Poelgeeſt* are alſo of a famous race the which in olde time had a caſtle of the ſame name in the quarter of *Oeſtgeeſt ,* the village whereof was called *Kerkwerve ,* the which by changing of the name, is now called *Alcmada ,* I know not by what title. Cont *William* King of *Romaines* gaue the Lordſhippe of *Hoochmade* to this houſe : as alſo an other *William* Earle of *Holland* and *Henaut ,* gaue them the village of *Coudekerke* vppon the *Rhine ,* a League from *Leyden ,* where there was a mightie

L 2 caſtle

caftle, the which was razed by the factions in the yeare 1489. It was before called *Horne*, whereof the proprietaries were called Lords of *Horne*; whofe memory lies buried with their perfons; *Gerard* of *Poelgeft* a Knight did afterwards caufe this ruined caftle to be repaired,(with the confent of the Emperor *Charles* the fift) as faire as euer: who died to foone for his children.

The caftle of *Alcmada*, from the which they of the houfe take their name, is fituated in the iurif-diction of *Warmond*, whereof the ruines are yet to bee feene: for that which is now called *Alcmada* ftanding vpon the current of *Marne*, was wont to bee called *Poelgeeft*, as appeeres by the letters of *Thierry* Vicont of *Leyden*, faying that hee had giuen the inheritance thereof to *Ifbrandt* of *Poelgeeft*. We finde that *Henrie* of *Poelgeeft* and *Floris* of *Alcmada* bretheren by the mother, liued in the yeare 1320.

Thofe of *Culembourg* are defcended from that Noble and famous Lord *Ralfe* of *Bofitom*, of the race of the Earles of *Teyfterbandt*: The towne of *Culembourg* is reafonable good, ftanding vpon the riuer of *Leck*, two leagues from *Viane*, and one from *Buren*, it is now erected to an Earldome, belonging to the Lord of *Palant*.

Abcoude was wont to bee a famous and mightie family, the which had great poffeffions in the dio-cefe of *Vtrecht*: the towne and caftle of *Wyckter Duerftede*, did alfo belong vnto them, the Lord where-

whereof did build the caftle of *Abcoude* in the *Moores*, midde-way betwixt *Vtrecht* and *Amfter-dam*. One *Ghifbert* of *Abcoude* did purchafe the Lordfhip of *Gaefbecke*, who gaue it to his yongeft fonne *Afueres*, who married a daughter of the Earle of *Lygnes*, by whom hee had one fonne called *Iames*, verie rich and mighty in poffeffions, for beeing Lord of *Gaefbeck*, hee was Siegnicr of *Abcoude*, *Putten* and *Streuen*, all which are goodly Signeuries, hauing iurifdi&ions. It was he which foūded the *Chartreux* nere vnto *Vtrecht*, who fince, after the death of his fonne & only heire, being taken prifoner in battaile by the Bifhop of *Vtrecht*, was to redeeme his liberty forced to yeeld him the Lordfhip, towne and caftle of *Wyck* (where fince the bifhoppes haue kept their ordynarie refidence,) and the caftle of *Abcoude* : which fince hath beene the aboad of one of the Marfhalls of the Diocefe of *Vtrecht*, and of his gard, which is there in garrifon. The houfe of *Perfin* is alfo an honorable family from the which are iffued manie Knights & gentlemen of *Waterlandt* and the Ile of *Marke*, right againft *Monikendam*. It is at this time wholy extin&. The caftle of *Perfin* is yet ftanding without the wood at the *Hage*.

The houfe of *Raphorft* is noble and very ancient whereof it appeeres that two bretheren had been flaine with their Prince Cont *Floris*, in the warre againft the *Frifons*.

That of *Mateneffe* hath in like manner with many
L 3   others

others taken their beginning from the Lord of *Waffenare*, Vicont of *Leyden*.

The houfe of *Vlyet* was in old time banifhed not as guilty of the murther of Cont *Floris*, but in hatred of his brother the Siegnior of *Woerden*, one of the cheefe confpirators, fo as *Gerard van Vlyet* going into exile was difpoffeft of his lands & degraded of his armes. But afterwards by the interceffion of the Lords of *Duyuenvoorde* and *Lithtenberg* (for his valour fhewed in battaile for the Earle of *Holland*, where the bifhop of Vtrecht was flaine)he was receiued into grace, and reftored to the poffeffion of all his goods.

The honors which the houfes of *Woerden* & *Weffon* were accuftomed to haue, were loft in the perfons, of *Herman van Woerden* for the murther of Cont *Floris*, whereof *Gerard* being the firft author & executioner, was cruelly executed, beeing rowled vp & down in a pipe ful of nailes in the town of *Leyden*, where hee died miferably; *Herman* his father in law, being brother to the Lord of *Amftel*, efcaped, and died poore in exile.

The houfe of *Amftel* was alfo blemifhed with this murther, namely *Ghyfbrecht* of *Amftel*, Lord of *Amfterdam*, *Amfterweel* and *Ijelfteyn*, who died in exile, poore and miferable, beeing difpoffeft of halfe his goods, and the reft remayning to his wife & fonne *Arnold*, who were befieged a whole yeare in the towne of *Amfterdam*, and were in the end forced to yeeld it, vpon condition that for all their goods they

they fhould content themfelues with the towne &
caftle of *Ifelfteyn*,which fince came vnto the houfe
of *Egmond*, whereof the Emperor *Maximilian* the
firft created *Frederic* of *Egmond* firft Earle of *Ifelfteyn* & of *Leerdam*. *Iohn* of *Henaut* Earle of *Hollād*
had giuen the figneuries of *Amftell* & *Woerden* to
his brother *Guy* then Prouoft & afterwards bifhop
of *Vtrecht*,during his life, the which hee caufed to
bee built, but after his death they were anexed a-
gaine to the reuenues of the Earle of *Holland*,
which then was Cont *William* furnamed the good.
The figniors of *Schagen* are defcended from a
baftard of Duke *Albert* of *Bauaria* Earle of *Holland* and *Henaut*, who gaue this goodly Siegneury with that of *Burchorne* to *William* the firft Lord
of *Schagen*, and from him fucceffiuely to him
that is now vnder the Eftates of *Holland*. So
the Signiory of *Hoocht-wood*, came from Duke
William of *Bauaria*, called the mad Earle (for that
after two battailes which hee had againft the Em-
preffe *Marguerite* his mother, whereof hee loft
one with eight thoufand men nere to V*laerdingen*,
and the other he wonne, hee was diftracted of his
wittes fifteene yeares, and as a madde man was
kept clofe vnto his death) to whom Duke A*lbert*
his brother fucceeded. This *William* gaue vnto his bafe Sonne the poffeffion of *Hocht-Woude*
and A*ertfwoude*, which are two goodlie villages. But this line fayling, thefe two places
haue paft from one to an other; *Hochtwoude*
belong-

belonging at this day to _Cornellis Mirop_ Receiuer generall of _Holland_ and _Westfrisland_ , signior of _Caelslagen_, _Sweiten_ &c.

The houfe of _Hamstede_ did begin at _Witte_ who was the firft Lord , and baftard to Cont _Floris_. That of _Horst_ is of great antiquity , the which feemes to haue had many branches , as that of _Bronckhorst_ in _Gelders_; that of _Lochorst_ in the countrie of _Vtrecht_ , and that of _Raphorst_ , whereof the old caftle is yet ftanding betwixt the _Hage_ and _Leyden_ : then _Bockhorst_ twife or thrife ruined, being a league from _Nortwyck_ , but not in that eftate it hath beene.

The family of _Dune_ is alfo very ancient, the only daughter and heire whereof, married fome thirty yeares fince to _Thierry_ the fecond fonne of the Lord of _Brederode_, who left the title thereof to his children , yet carrying the armes of _Brederode_ and not their mothers : It continues ftill in that race, who hoe alfo enioy the Siegniorie of _Sprangen_ which came by mariage from them of _Wcifteyn_.

The houfe of _Zyle_ haue taken their name from a caftle ftanding vpon the banke of the current _Zyle_ , which falls into a Lake thereby, fo as there is yet in the towne of _Leyden_ the Court of _Zyle_, the port and bridge of _Zyle_ : _Gerard van Zyle_ a Knight , Siegnior of _Purmerende_ and of _Purmerlanat_ , hath made this houfe verie famous by his vertues.

That

That of *Hattinghen* is one of the moft ancient races in *Holland*, whereof hiftories make mention aboue feauen hundred yeares paft. Among others they make mention of one *Hafting* a Duke or Captaine Generall of the *Normans* who in the yeare eight hundred fixty eight fhould haue entred into the mouth of the Riuer of *Loire*, and ouer-run a part of *Brittaine*, *Aniou*, *Turene*, and *Poittou*, who hauing defeated *Robert* and *Ranulphe*, *French* Captains that purfued him, and were flaine in battaile, he brought his army (being laden with fpoyles) brauely back vnto his fhips.

There haue bene in *Holland* many Abbaies, and Monafteries, both of men and women, founded by the Nobilitie of the country, befides Couents of begging Fryars or Bribers, which wee will omit; and treat fuccinctly of thofe which were appointed for Noble perfons. Firft *Thierry* of *Acquitane*, the firft Earle of *Holland* founded one all of wood for women: the which his fon caufed to be built of ftone for Monkes, and bee made an Abbaie neere vnto the Village of *Egmond* (whereof the Abbot did afterwards weare a Miter) inricht with great reuenues, which made both the Abbot and his Monkes too idle. And feeing wee are difcourfing of this Abbaie, I muft by the way deliuer a tricke which this Abbot plaid in the yeare 1 5 6 5. with the Earle of *Egmond*: The Prince of *Orange*, the Earle of *Horne* and the Baron of *Brederode* went with the Earle of *Egmont* to dine in this Abbaie, where

where they were very honourablie entertained,
when as they fhoulde wafh , my Lord Abbot
(who was but a Monke) tooke thefe three Noble
men by the handes to wafh : The Earle of *Egmond*
comming to prefent him-felfe , the Abbot fayd
vnto him ; No , for you are my Vaffall,it becomes
you not to wafh with your better ,yea he offred to
put the towell vppon his fhoulder , to giue it
vnto the other Noblemen , when they had wafht,
whereat the Earle of *Egmond* was much difcon-
tented , and went away curfing the Monke . One
of the Abbots feruantes , who was then prefent,
reported it vnto mee for a very truth. VVithout
doubt it was a great affront vnto this Earle , who
was proude and high minded , valuing him-felfe
more then the Prince of *Orange* , who was iffued
from the race of the Emperours, by the Emperor
Adolph of *Naffau*.

There were foure Abbaies for women , into the
which not any one might be receiued,that was not
Nobly borne,or at the leaft ỷ had not their Armes
quartered. Thefe were *Rhinfburg*; *Conninxffieldt*,
Leuenhorft and *Lofdunen* : this laft in the end had
little refpeƈt of Nobilitie , receiuing as well the
children of Marchants as of Gentlemen ,for that
it was none of the richeft : *Rhinfburg* tooke the
name of a Caftell which was fituated vppon the
Rhyne neere vnto the *Gulph* : It was pleafantly feated,& a very commodious building. There is this
thing memorable , that the Ladie *Elburg* the Ab-
befle

beſſe, cauſed a quarter of a lodging to be built for ſtrangers that ſhoulde come to ſee it. Vppon the Front whereof there were two Latin verſes, made by Doctor *Adrianus Iuntus,* ſhewing the date of the time.

NoBILItas probItaſqVe IſthVC ſIbI IVre LegVnto HoſpItIV M ElbVrgIs dVLCES qVod feCIt ał VſVs.

NObILItle & Worth MaDe ChoICe to reſt, In *ELburg* as a place for pLeaſure beſt.

THis Abbay was founded by the Ladie *Petronel,* Siſter to the Emperor *Lothaire* ; wife to *Floris* the ſecond Earle of *Holland,* the which was quite ruined by the ſoldiars in the firſt troubles.

Leuenhorſt was but a League from *Rhynſbourg,* and fifteene hundred paces from *Noortwick,* in a very pleaſant ſeate : whereof *Arnold* of *Saſſenheim* was founder, who ſpent largely as well in the foundation of this Cloyſter as in an other religious houſe in *Harlem,* which was about the yeare 1262.

Coninx-Feldt, ſignifies a royall field, founded by the Lady *Richlandt,* Siſter to *William* King of *Romaines,* in the ſuburbs of *Delph*: But in the beginning of theſe warres, for that it was too neere the Towne, fearing ſome ſurprize, it was purpoſely ſette on fire, which did conſume it vnto the foundation. *Loſdunen* is two myles from the *Hage*, whereas there are yet to bee ſeene the two Baſins in the which the three hundred
sixty

sixtie foure children of the Lady *Marguerits* Conteſſe of *Heneſberg* were baptized, with her Tombe
and Epitaph. This Abbaie hath felt the fruites of
warre with the reſt, whreof we haue made mention in the deſcription of the *Hage*.

Behold what wee could ſay briefly of theſe Abbaies, omitting ſo many other Cloyſters, Monaſteries and relligious houſes, who haue all tryed
the like fortune. : And ſo wee will make an end of
the deſcription of *Holland* (in the which is alſo
comprehended *Weſt-Freezeland*, which they call
Nort-hotland) to come vnto *Zealand*. But firſt
I may not forget that remarkeable Antiquitie,
which is neere vnto *Catwieke* the Arcenall of the
Romaines, which ſome ſay had beene built by the
Emperour *Caligula*, whereas hee prepared to paſſe
into great *Brittaine* with his armie. But hauing
aduanced nothing but on-ly put forth to ſea, hee
returned ſodainely, and went to land, commaun-
ding al his Soldiers by the ſound of Trumpets and
Drummes, to fill al their head-peeces with cockle-
ſhelles which they gathered vppon the ſandes, and
to carry them vnto the Capitoll, in ſigne of try-
umphe, and as a trophee that hee had beaten the
Sea. VVhich Arcenall, (whether that he built it
or not) was afterwards called the *Brittiſh* fort
or *Caſtell*, from whence there was a ſhort cut into
England : And this it was.

A deſcription

A Defcription of the Brittifh *Fort*
called *T'huis te Britten.*

THis fort in the beginning did ferue as a Bea-
con to fet a Fyar in the night for the directi-
on of Marriners that fhould faile vpponthe coaft,
as we fee at this day the Tower *D'ordre* or old man
neere vnto *Bologne* in *Picardie*, very old alfo, the
which the Emperour *Charlemaigne* caufed to bee
repaired, & fo did the Emperor *L. Septimius Seue-*
rus this Arcenal or *Britten* fort, whreof the memory remaines yet grauen in a ftone, brought to the
houfe of the Lord of *Waſſenare* at the Hage vppon
whofe Territory before the Inondation this fort
was built, beeing now fwallowed a good league into the fea, which is fometimes feen, when as the
wind driues back the fea at their loweſt ebbs, as it
hapned in the yeare, 1520. when as this ftone was
found with this Infcription. *Imp. Cæſ. L. Septimius*
Seuerus Aug. Et M. Aurelius. Antoninus Cæſ. Coh.
XV. Vol. Armamentarium Vetuſtate collapſum, reſti-
tuerunt ſub. Val. Pudente, Lec. Au. Pr. curante. Cæcil.
Batone Præ. This Arcenall was built of a fquare
forme, euery corner of equall diſtance, that is,
foure hundred feete ; each corner had two Towers ioyning together, and in the middeſt from one
corner to another a Tower all flanked with great
broad ftone, to refiſt the flowing of the *Rhyne*, vppon whofe banke it was feated : fome fortie of
thefe ftones were digged vp in the yeare 1552.
the

the which were foure foote long and three broad.
There was alſo peeces of bricke found a foote
ſquare , on the which were theſe letters *X. G. I.*
which ſeemes to ſignifie E*x Germania inferiori:*
Moreouer an other ſtone broken at both the end*s*,
in which there did yet remaine theſe imperfect
wordes , *euer. Pius. An. max. Trib. Pot. XIII. ₆nto-*
nin. Pius. ec. Milit. Leg. I. me. Euidiorum. There
were alſo Peeces of ſiluer with this inſcription, *L.*
Septimius Seuerus. Pertinax. Aug.Imp. Beſides there
was an other ſtone all eaten with the waues of the
ſea , and windes,repreſenting victory with wings,
and on the left hand an Eagle , with theſe letters,
Imp.Caſ. Ant. ne. Aug. Coh. M. To. Ru.Pe. There
were other ſtones , one with a ſhippe, ſuch as the
Saxons vſed in thoſe times., an other with a mans
face, hauing a beard and long hayre : an other hauing the figure of *Hercules* with his mace. Beſides
an other long ſtone brokē at one end, wheras theſe
wordes were comprehended. *Brittanic. Germanic.*
Pius. Fælix. Auguſtus. Pont. Max. Trib. Pot. XVIII.
IIII. P. P. *Imp.III.* A*ram. a* Diuo. C*laudio. et. poſtea*
a diuo Seuero Patre *ſuo reſtitutam:* In the ſame yeare
1 5 2 0. there was a Key found which they did ſup-
poſe was that of the Arcenall. There were alſo
found many figures, veſſels, pottes, lampes and o-
ther ſquare ſtones,where there was grauen X. *Ger.*
Inf. There haue bene alſo found peeces of gold,
ſiluer and Copper of *Iulius* C*æſar* and others. In
the yeare one thouſand ,ſiue hundred ſixtie two,
the

the foundations of this *Arcenall* were defcouered aboue twenty daies together, from whence the people there-about drewe many thoufands of ftones. It hath beene defcouered againe of late yeares, but the fand of the fea hath buried much.

Zeeland, with the Iflands, Townes and
Bourroughes.

NO man can denie; but the *Danes* and *Normans* haue ouerrunne thefe Iflands, as well as *Holland* and other farther Regions, who (as it is the cuftome of conquerers to impofe new names to places which they haue conquered, efpecially the names of countries and townes from whence they are come) fome thinke haue giuen this name of *Zeelandt* of one of their chiefe Iflands fo called, in the which is the royall towne of *Coppenhagen.* But admit it were not fo: and let vs drawe their beginning from the fignification of the worde it felfe. *Zee* fignifying the fea, and *Landt* countrie, which is, a countrie of the fea, as in truth it is.

There is no neede then to make anie further fearch for the *Etimologie*, but wee will content our felues with it. The countie of *Zeelande* which hath now more power and authoritie then it euer had, is for the moft part comprehended in feauen principall Iflands, the which are *Walchren* where *Middlebourg* ftands; *Schoven* and there is *Ziricxee*: *Zuytbeuelandt* where *Ter Goes* is; *Tertolen*, where there is the towne of *Tolen*; *Noortbeuelandt*

beuelandt recouered from the Sea within thefe ten yeares: *Duyuelandt* and *Wolferfdick*:there are other fmall ones , whereof we make no mention.

Thofe of *Walchren* and *Schouen* lye moft open to the fea on the Weft part, on which fide they be na-turally defended with thefe fandie hils which they call Downes ; and where there are not any , they haue made good and high bankes , ftrengthned with thicke turffes and wads of ftraw,which binde them firmely together , the which they call dikes: True it is that the ordinary charge to repaire and entertaine them,is very great , and the time and toyle they imploy greater. But they obferue a good order , with fuch proportion,as fuch as haue the propriety of the land adioyning , beare the charge for the entertaining of thefe dikes , euery one according to his portion. All the country of *Zealand* is fatte and fertile , for all kind of Tillage, but efpecially for faire white wheat,and of a grain to die red,which is a rich commodity , and diftri-buted through all Europe: There is alfo a certen kinde of turffe for fyring , which they call Dary, the which they are forbidden to cutte neere vnto the dikes,for that it is their foundation and defece.

Ther are none but the poorer fort that vfe it, for that it yeelds a ftinking fmoake. There is generally as pleafant and fat paftures for cattel,as in *Holland*: But the better toknow the whole country,we muft begin to defcribe the Ilands , and the particular townes of euery of them.

VValachrie.

Walachrie.

IS in the country language called *Walchren* , the
most famous and most rich of all the Ilands of *Zeland* , not for the greatnesse , for it hath not tenne
leagues circuit, but for the strength and safetie of
the Seat and the quallitie of the soyle , the infinite
number of people that inhabit it , their great co-
merce and the great riches , which the Sea bringes
vnto them by their nauigations : This Iland hath
foure walled townes , *Middelbourg* which is the
Metropolitaine of all *Zealand,*where the Court remaines, *Flissing*, *La Vere* , *Teruere* , or *Camp Vere*,
which are all one , and *Arnemuyden: Doubourg* is
the most ancient town of *Zealand,*but now it is but
a Bourg beeing couered with the sandes of the sea
where it is situated , yet it retaines still the municipall priuiledge of a towne,we will then begin with
Middelbourg.

Middelbourg.

SOme attribute the beginning of this towne to
one *Metellus* a *Romaine* Captaine,who first built
the Bourg,that is to say the Castle. the which is in
the middest of the towne,whereas now the prisons
are. Of which *Mettellus*, by this Castle, it hath bin
called *Metelli Burgam;*and so *Middelbourg* in Ductb.
But let vs leaue this definition, and say that it hath
taken his name of these two wordes; *Middel*,which
signifies the middest , and *Vourg* a Castell , as
M much

much to fay as a Caftle in the middeft , as beeing
fituated (before the Sea had gotten fo much on
that fide)in the very center of the Iland. It ftands
in 50. degrees ½ of Latitude: It is but a quarter of
a league from *Arnemuyden* , vnto which it was
wont to haue a narrow and crooked hauen, which
went vnto their falt pits : But within thefe fiftie
yeares they of *Middelbourg* haue made a new
ftraight hauen from their port of *Dam* vnto the
Sea,the which is good and deepe, able at a full fea
to carry fhippes of 4. or 500. tunnes.] Within
thefe twelue yeares they haue augmented their
Towne more then halfe round about , wherin they
haue done preiudice without any recompence to
them that had gardens and poffeffions in the
Suburbs : yet all this great increafe ferues for no
other vfe but for houfes of pleafure and gardens for
Marchants , although there were place to haue
built aboue 3000. good houfes,for the cõmoditie
whereof they might make many chanels to paffe
frõ the one to the other:but God knowes when al
this voide place fhall bee filled with buildings.

The rampars of thefe new workes are but of
earth , with mightie bulwarks flanking one another , where there is alwaies fomething to repaire.
At the fame time when as thefe workes were made
the Magiftrate caufed the Steeple of the Abbaie
Church to bee new built vp , whereas they now
keepe the Court of *Zealand*, they haue drawne a
bell vppe into this fteeple of eighteene thoufand
waight

waight to ftrike the houres on, and fome 24. fmall ones, which ferue for the chyme; but this fteeple is fallen crooked, elfe it were one of the goodly-eft peeces in the whole country.

The Court which was wont to bee an Abbaie is faire and fpatious, and is the lodging of Princes when they come into *Zealand.* There the Councel-lors of Eftate for the Countie are eftablifhed, as al-fo for the Admiralty, the Chamber of account and the Treafor. The Admirall and in a manner all the Councellors are well lodged there. This houfe was founded by *Goudebault* the three and twentith Bifhoppe of *Vtrecht,* and afterwardes am-plyfied and in a manner built a new by Cont *Wili-am* King of the *Romaines*, who lyes there interred with Queene *Elizabeth* his wife: the foundation was made in the yeare one thoufand two hundred fifty fixe. The towne is good of it felfe, faire and neate and of great trafficke, which the Gallies of *Spaine* which came to *Sclufe* vnder the commaund of *Dom Frederic Spinola* reftrained for a time: But fince they haue vndertakē long voiages to the Eaft & Weft Indies as wel as the *Hollanders,* frō whence they draw great commodities, & withal fince the taking of the *Sclufe,* the faid galleis being falne into the Eftates handsthey are no more anoied, neither haue they any more feare on y fide: this town alone hath the right of the ftaple for all wines ȳ come frō *Frāce, Spain, Portugal, Candy,* ỹ *Canaries,* & other pla-ces by fea: not many years fince they purchafed the

M 2   Towne

Towne of *Arnemuyden*(being then but a Bourg) in
regard of their roades and the Salt-pits, the which
they had good cheap from the Proprietary. But
this sale was afterwards changed, as we wil shew in
the description of the towne of *Arnemuyden*. In
this towne the ordinary Soueraigne Iudge doth
commonly remaine, they call him the Receiuer of
Beuerstersheldt, to whom all commandements come
from the higher powers for the execution of iuftice by the sword in his precinct. Many learned &
excellent men were borne in this towne. Among
others *Paul* surnamed of *Middelbourg* a famous Mathematician, who for his great knowledge was called to *Rome* and presently made a Bishop. Then *Nicholas Euerardi* a great Lawyer, and well seene in
matters of State, President of the Prouincial Councel of *Holland*, and afterwards of the Parliament or
great Councell of *Macklin*, where he died in the
yeare 1 5 3 2. leauing many children, all men of
qualitie, & worthy of such a Father. The first was
Peter Nicholai, Doctor of Diuinity and Ciuill Law,
Prelat of the Abbay of *Middelbourg*. The second
was *Euerardi Nicholai*, a Licentiat in the lawes, who
was President of the Councel in *Friesland*, & after-
terwardes (as the father) of the great Councel at
Macklin, wher he died in the yeare 1 5 6 0. The third
was *Nicholas Nicolai*, Licentiat in the lawes, & very
learned in al faculties, a good Poet, & Histriogra-
pher, which aduanced him to be Councellor to the
King of *Spaine*, and Register of the order of the golden

den fleece. The fourth was *Adrian Nicolai*, who was Chancellor of *Geldres*. The fift was *Iohn Nicolai*, (surnamed the second) who was an excel‑lent Poet, giuing great hope of him, but death pre‑uented him in his course.

Veere or Camp-veere.

V*Eere or Camp-veere* is a good Sea-towne, one of the foure of the Iland of *Walchren*, it retaines this name of the passage it was wont to haue vnto the Village of *Campe* in the Iland of *Northbeuelandt* right against it : Which Village within these ten yeares with the whole Iland hath beene recouered from the Inondation which happened in the yeare one thousand fiue hundred twentie foure. This town was in the yeare one thousand three hundred sixtie eight walled in by the Lord of *Borsell* : Being since made greater, it was endowed with goodly priuiledges, so as in the time of *Maximillian* of *Bourgongne* their Lord, it was made a Marquisate. And for the commoditie of the seat, the goodnesse of the hauen and of the road; it was frequented by many nations. They were the first that sent vnto the *Canaries*, from whence they brought in the yeare 1508 a shippe laden with sugar.

They haue trade into *France*, where they haue priuiledge of *Franche Grue*, that is to say, free lading and vnlading: In like manner into the *East-countries* they had liberty to traffick, before that the townes of *Antwerp* and *Amsterdam* had any trade

M 3 thether

thether: As alfo into *Scotland*; the *Scotifhmen* hauing many yeares fince held their ftaple there, for
diuers forts of Marchandize, as they do at this day
for their cloth and frizes, and for their Salt-fifh.
This towne hath alfo the fifhing for herring wherof there is a ftaple, and the marke is well knowne in
diuers Kingdomes, where the *Bourgers* trafficke
moft, as to *Spaine*, *France* and other countries, and
of late yeares they haue trade to the *Eaft* & *VVeft-
Indies*. This towne was in the old time honoured
with the Refidence of the Admirall Generall and
the Admiraltie of the *Netherlands*. To which end
the King of *Spaine*, as Prince of the faid countries,
caufed a goodly Arcenall or Magafin for munition
to bee built in the yeare 1 5 6 8. wherein they laid
all their prouifion and furniture belonging to the
fea. The Inhabitants of this towne are growne
ciuill and curteous by the daily frequentation of
their Lordes and their Attendants, keeping their
Court within an arrow fhotte of the Towne at the
goodly caftle of *Sanderburg*, which is quite ruined
in thefe laft troubles, as being too neere a neighbor
vnto the towne. This Marquifat was fold by decree for the debts of the faid Marquis *Mazimillian*,
which *Philip* King of *Spaine* caufed to be bought in
his name: But when the creditors were not paid, it
was fold again and bought by the Prince of *Orange*:
who to the great contentment of the *Burgers* and
all the fubiectes, receiued the poffeffion in the
yeare one thoufand fiue hundred eighty one,
giuing

giuing them goodly priuiledges, with high and bafe luftice in nine Villages depending thereon: whereof *Oeft capel* is one. By the death of which Prince, and by his Teftament the moft worthie Prince *Maurice* of *Naffau* Gouernor, Captaine & Admiral general of the vnited Prouinces his fon, was left heire of the faid Marquifat, and put in pof-ffion in the yeare one thoufand fiue hundred eighty eight, and in the yeare after of that of *Fliffinghe*. Be-fides other particularities, one thing is fpecially to be noted, that the Magiftrate of this towne neuer fhewed any rigor againft them of the refor-med religion, yea hath alwaies fauoured and fup-ported them as much as he might, fo as in the be-ginning of the wars and troubles fince, the yeare one thoufand fiue hundred feauenty two, they haue with all their meanes both of bodies and goodes, with them of *Fliffinghe* more then any other of their neighbours, repulft the tyrannie of the Inqui-fition of *Spaine* in diuers exploits and enterprizes of warre both by Land and Sea: And efpecially with their braue Captaines at Sea, in the begin-ning of the yeare 1578. they did before *Bergen vp Zoom*, aid, to defeate that mightie *Spanifh* Fleete in view of the great Commander of *Caf-tille*, which went to victuall *Middelbourg*, beeing ftraightly befeeged by the Prince of *Orange*, fo as this victualling fayling them, they were forced to yeelde vnto the Prince. Afterwardes their Captaines did in the like manner helpe to

M 4 confound

confound that feareful and inuincible fea-armie(as
they did write it) which the King of *Spaine* fent in
the yeare one thoufand fiue hundred eighty eight,
to inuade *England.*

Flifinghee.

OR *Vliffinghen* is the third town of the Iland of
Walchren, right againſt *Flanders*, and a league
from *Middelbourg.* It is alſo a Marquiſate, belonging to Prince *Maurice* of *Naffau*, as *La Vere*, not that
they are two Marquiſats, but one onely, euery one
apart carrying diuers armes. *Fliffinghe* was in old
time but a country village, and did ſerue onely for
a paſſage into *Flanders.* But within theſe hundred
yeares, *Adolph* of *Bourgongne*, Lord of *La Vere* and
Fliffinghe, cauſed it to be walled in, and then it began to take the forme of a good towne. So as in the
yeare one thoufand fiue hundred feauenty one, the
Duke of *Alua* pretending to build a Caſtell on the
ditch ſide towards *Ramekins*, which ſhould alſo
command the hauen : After that the Prince of O-
range Gouernor of *Holland* and *Zealand*, had by the
Earle of *Marche* Lord of *Lumay* his Lieutenant
ſurprized the Iland and towne of *Bryel*, when as the
Seignior of *Wakenes*, the Vice-admirall pretended
to put a *Spanish* garriſon into the towne, beeing
fauored by the Magiſtrate, the people diſcouering
it, fell to armes, forced the Arcenall, and chaſed a-
way the Burguemaiſters and Aldermen, and being
maiſter of the Ordinance and of the towne-gates,
they

they fhotte at fiue or fixe fhippes full of *Spaniards*,
which thought to enter into the Towne , who by
reafon of the contrary tide , fent a man fwimming to land, to intreat them that they would not
finke them,promifing them to retire ypon the firft
floud,as they did,going towards *Berghen vp Zoom*,
whereas they could not be entertained. This town
being thus freed from the *Spanifh* yoake ¸ it was in
a fhort time fortified, and in a fhort time with the
helpe of the Prince of *Orange* (who prefently fent
them a garrifon of *Wallons*) they made fharpe wars
with them of *La Vere* againft *Middelbourg* and *Arnemuyden*,which were held by the *Spaniards:* going
to Sea with their fhips of warre,they brought in
good prizes , and many good prifoners,among o-
thers the Duke of *Aluas* Coufin,who notwithftanding any ranfom that he offered, could not redeem
him-felfe from the gallowes , fo hatefull the *Spaniards* were vnto the *Fleffingers* in the firft warres,as
al that they took,they either caft them ouer-boord
or hung them at land,wherein the women and children tooke great delight. They had an Admirall
called Captaine *Worft*, who did continually annoy
them of *Antwerp* and *Scluſe* , and did fet vppon all
fhips going vp to *Antwerp:* one day he incountred
a *Spanifh* Fleete , in the which was the Duke of *Me-
dina Celi* ¸ who came to gouerne the *Netherlands* in
the Duke of *Aluas* place. The combat was very furious neere vnto *Scluſe* , but in the end the Duke
was forced to leap into a boat and to faue him-felfe

in

in *Sluse*. It is infinit to tell what the captaines both by sea and land, that were at time in *Fliſſinghe*, did againſt the *Spaniards*. They beſieged the ſtrong caſtle of *Ramekin*, (called *Zeebourg*) both by sea and land, ſtanding vpon the *Dyke* betwixt *Fliſſinghe* and the head of *Middelbourg*, the which they tooke in leſſe then ten daies. At the battaile of *Berghen* and in all other incounters the *Fliſſinghers* were alwaies the formoſt. Snce they haue much inlarged their towne, eſpecially on that ſide where as the Duke of *Alua* had begun to build the caſtle, where there are three goodly Bulwarkes, two towardes the land, and one to the sea, which defends the hauen on that ſide, flanking it at the port. In this inlargement they haue drawne in a new hauen and a Sluſe, capable for many great ſhippes, where they haue alſo built a new temple for the *Engliſh* nation : within theſe twelue yeares they haue built a faire towne-houſe vpon the market place, not in greatneſſe, but in building much like to that of *Antwerp*. To conclude the towne, as wel in fortifications, as in buildings is now ſo changed, as hee that hath not ſeene it theſe thirty yeares, would not now know it. It is ſecond to *Middelbourg* in marchandiſe, but it exceedes it in herrings, where they are barreled vp, and marked, and from thence are tranſported throughout all Chriſtendome. This important towne (to ſpeake truelie) may rightly be termed the Key of the *Netherlands* for the ſea : for at all times

it

it cuts off the nauigation from *Antwerp* fo as nothing can come vnto them by fea : wherefore the
Duke of *Alua* fhould haue beene more carefull
to keepe it in time ; and not to haue efteemed it fo
little , as hee did when the newes of their reuolt
came vnto him: anfwering onely . *Pitcilingo*(fo
he called it) *es nada* . And in truth the Emperor
Charles the fift, knowing better the importance of
that place then the Duke of *Alua*, going laft out
of the *Netherlands* to returne into *Spaine* where
hee died, vpon his departure , hee did fecretly and
ferioufly recommend this towne vnto the King
his fonne . But as they fay. He that contemnes the
fathers admonitions, will be deceiued, as it prooued in this towne.

ARNEMVYDEN.

OLd *Arnemuyden*(which was wont to be fituated in an other place, not far from that where
it now ftands) was a goodly village with a good
caftle, well peopled with ritch Bourgers & Marchants, hauing a good commodious hauen, wheras many great fhippes might lie fafely , where at
that time there was greater traffick then at *Middelbourg* it felfe . This old *Arnemuyden* is by Inundations quite eaten vp by the fea , fo as there are
no reliks to be feene , neither can they conie&ture
that it ftood in any other place , but betwixt
the hauen of *Middelbourg* and new *Arnemuyden*,
vpon the plaine which is betwixt S. *Ioes Landt*, and
the

the right chanel of *Arnemuyden*, as it is at this day.

The greateſt breach which happened to old *Arnemuyden*, was in the yeare 1438 in the time of *Gyles* of *Arnemuyden* the Lord of that place, who cauſed all the Bourgers and the Inhabitants to go with their families vnto the *Dyke* out of the danger of the ſea, whereas now the town of *Arnemuyden* ſtands. The which as well for the cōmodity of *Roads* and *Deeps*, as for the ſituation vpon the ſea, hath and doth retaine vnto this day, the trade of many great ſhippes which arriue there daily laiden with diuers ſorts of marchandiſe, and from thence is tranſported into the other Prouinces of the Netherlands, except ſalt comming from *Spaine*, *France* and other places, the which remaines there to bee refined: for the which there are many ſalt-pannes' built along and vpon the toppe of the *Dyke*, where it is boyled and made white, and then they lade it and tranſport it to other places. And although that new *Arnemuyden* was not walled in vntill the yeare 1572. yet hath it beene held of all forraine nations for a towne of good eſteeme, by reaſon of the nauigation and trafficke; for which reſpect the Earles of *Holland* and *Zeeland*, did in old time eſtabliſh their towles and cuſtomes due vnto the county of *Zeeland*. This towne hath alwaies enioy'd the like priuiledges with the towne of *Middlbourg*, as Bourgeſes and ſubiects thereof, vntill the yeare 1572. that they followed the Prince of *Oranges*

part, of

partie : Soone after the *Spaniards* furprized it,
fpoiled it, flue fome, and the reft fled wandring vp
and downe, vntill that in the yeare 1 5 7 4. the
towne of *Middelbou g* being forced to 7eeld vnto
the Prince of *Orange*, *Arnemuyden* was alfo comprehended in the Accord, fo as the Ile of *Walchren*
beeing then freed, euery man returned to his
houfe, fo as by little and little the towne was fortefied as you fee it at this day. For the reedefy-
ing whereof the Prince gaue it goodly priuiledges and freedomes, beeing exempt from the fubiection of *Vaffelage*, being fubiect to *Middelbourg*
by vertue of their contract : and caufing it to bee
walled and ditcht, hee gaue them the rights and
prerogatiues that belong to a good towne, gouerned by their owne Magiftrats, Baylife, Bourguemafters, Aldermen and other Officers, which
they of *Middelbourg* were accuftomed to chofe:
but now they difpofe of all matters concerning
Iuftice and gouernment themfelues. The towne
of *Arnemuyden* had for many yeares a particular
Lord, carrying the title of Siegnior of *Arnemuyden*; the laft was called *Gyles* of *Arnemuyden*, who
in the yeare 1418. was made Knight, and married
the daughter of *Wolphart van Borffelle*, by whom
hee had two daughters, the one *Mary*, the other
Marguerite of *Arnemuyden* : *Mary* married with
Nicholas of *Borffele* Siegnior of *Brigdame*, *Coudekerke*, *Soeteland* and Saint *Laurence*; from whom
is iffued the houfe of *La Vere*. *Marguerite* married
William

William of *Vriefe* . Siegnior of *Oofteinde*, from
whence is defcended the houfe of *Trafigny*. And
as the fayd *Giles* was the laft Lord which carried
that name, his houfe fell to the diftaffe. Thofe of
this towne for the loue of him carry his armes in
their feales and armories, which they vfe to beare,
and they are at this day two Eagles *Or* in a field
Geules, armed and encompaffed with *Azure*, and in
the midft a fand-hill rifing out of the waues of
the fea.

DOMBOVRG.

ALthough this bee but an open place, which
is dayly more and more couered with fand,
notwithftanding all remedies, by reafon that the
winde driues the fand of the fea and downes,
which couers their gardins and paftures, yet beeing efteemed the moft ancient towne of the *Ifle* of
Walchren, whereof there are yet to be feene fome
old ruines of walles, it retaines ftill the ancient
priuiledges &municipall rights, as the beft town
of the fayd Ifland.

WEST CAPPELLE.

THis place, Bourg or village, (howfoeuer you
will call it) doth enioy the like priuiledges of
other townes: for that the ancient *Weft Cappelle*
which ftood in the fame place, was wont to bee a
good towne, and had the beft port in al the Ifland
of *Walchren*, which about 1 5 0. yeares fince was
carried away by the inundations of the fea, fo

as there remaines nothing ibut what wee fee of the old buildings, hauing notwithstanding bin inlarged with new houfes within thefe thirty yeares, the which makes it more commendable.

SOETELAND.

IS yet at this day a good place, fo termed as a fweete country, and fo it is the fweeteft foyle and the beft feat in all the Ifland, which makes the Marchants of *Middelbourg* and *Fliffinghe* to walke thether, whereas after they haue recreated themfelues, they returne at night to their houfes.

There are alfo in this Ifland many goodly villages, as *Ooft* and *Weft Suybourg* a quarter of a league one from the other, betwixt *Fliffinghe* and *Middelbourg* : At Weft *Suybourg* there is a good caftle the which with the village, doth now belong vnto the heires of *Phillippe de Marnix*, Siegnior of Saint *Aldegonde*, the light of learned men of our age, in which caftle the Emperour *Charles* the fift remained, vntill the winde prooued faire to imbarke, to make his laft returne into *Spaine*, but wee may not forget the important caftle of

RAMMEKEN.

OTherwife called *Zeebourg*, which about 60. years fince, ɏ Lady Mary *Queene* of *Hungary*, fifter to the Emperor *Charles* the 5. gouerneffe of ɏ *Netherlãds*, caufed to be built vpon the *Dyke* betwixt *Middelbourg*, & *Fliffing*, feruing as a bulwark

for

for all fhippes that are forced for want of a good winde,to come and anchor in the *Roade*. This caftle is alwaies well manned with a good garrifon, and with all things neceffary for a place of fo great importance, being as neceffary to be entertained and well kept, as any other in all the vnited Prouinces. By reafon whereof, the Queene of *England* defired to haue it with the townes of *Fluffinghe* and *Bryele* for caution of the money which fhee did lend vnto the vnited Eftates fome twenty yeares fince.

SCHOWEN.

IN Latin called *Schaldia*, a *Fluuio*, *Schaldi*, of the riuer of *Efcault*, in old time a great Ifland, but the tempefts and breaches of the fea haue wonderfully dyminifhed it. It hath yet at this day aboue eight leagues in circuit : and it was in thofe daies fo nere vnto the Ifland of *North-beuelandt*, as the Inhabitants did talke together from one banke vnto the other ; whereas fince there hath beene a great diftance. But within thefe twelue years that the fayd Ifland of *North-beuelandt* hath beene recouered, they are neerer. This Ifland is as fertill and plentifull of all things, as any other in *Zeeland*, and therefore it holds the fecond ranke at the Eftates of the fayd Prouince, in the which the foueraigne Iudges of the Eaft of *Zeeland*, do commonly refide,whom they call the Receiuer of *Beoofterghelt*, who hath all power of cryminall
caufes

caufes in that quarter;the cheefe towne whereof is.

ZIRICZEE.

THis towne is held for the firſt and moſt ancient
of the countie of *Zeeland*, and as ſome ſay, it is
found in the *Annales* of the *Netherlands* that it
was built in the yeare of our Lord 849. by one called *Zyringus*, whoſe name it carries : in ancient
time very famous for the trade of Marchandiſe,
wherevnto it was verie commodious by reaſon of
their goodly port, which the marchants did vſually
frequent ; But the ſands hauing in tract of time
ſtopt vp the hauen, it is now leſſe frequented: within theſe twelue or fourteene yeares the towneſmen
haue made a newe hauen which goes directly vnto
the ſea, the which is faire, large and commodious,
notwithſtanding ſince that *Middelbourg* grew ſo
famous, it cannot recouer the accuſtomed trafficke
touching nauigation , yet is it good , faire and
ſtrong, retayning their ancient trade for ſalt and
graine to die withall, with the fiſhing for herring.
In this towne the Receiuer of *Beooſterſchelt* doth
commonly remaine, who is (as I haue ſayd)chiefe
Iuſtice for the countie of *Zeeland*, to whom (as to
him of the *Beverſterſchelt* at *Middelbourg*,) all
commiſſions are directed, comming from the ſu-
periors, to put them in execution euery one in his
iuriſdiction in this towne was borne that famous
Amandus Zirizxeus, a relligious man of the order
of Saint *Francis*, who hath written many goodly
N Poems,

Poems, as may be feene in the Library of *Cornelius Gefnerus* . From thence alfo came *Leuinus Lemnius* Doctor of Phifick, & a man of great knowledge, as his workes do witnesse: whofe fonne called *William* of the fame profeffion was called to be Phifition to the King of *Sueden*. *Petrus Peckius* was alfo borne in this towne, a man of rare learning, who hath written many printed bookes.

BROWERSHAVEN.

IN this Ifland of *Schouen* two fmall leagues from *Ziricxee* , is that great Bourg of *Browerfhauen* more inhabited by fifhermen then any other : and yet there was borne one *Petrus*, carrying the furname of his towne, a learned man, who writ many bookes in diuinity. This towne did fome-times belong to *Maximilian* of Bourgogne, Lord of *Beueren* Admirall of the fea : thus hauing fallen vnto him with many other goodly Siegneuries by the Ladie *Anne* his Grand-mother iffued from the Noble houfe of *Borffele* : which familie hath fayled long fince for want of lawfull heires ; which *Maximiliam* died alfo without children in the yeare 1558. whofe fucceffion fell to the children of the Earle of *Boffu*, who had married one of the Sifters of the Lord of *Beueren* , and to the children of the Siegnior of *Cruminghen*, who had married the other Sifter, from whome is iffued the Siegnior of *Cruminghen*, who keepes commonly at the *Hage* in *Holland.*

In

In this Iſland of *Shouven*, there are many caſtles and villages, belonging to certaine Gentlemen and other priuate perſons, amongſt the which is the village of *Bomene* ſeated at one end of it, verie famous for the great loſſe of *Spaniards* which the great Commander of *Caſtille* had entring into the ſayd Iſland, the which in the end hee tooke by force, and ſlue all that were in the fort, except one man who eſcaped dangerouſly, but let vs paſſe to the other Iſlands.

ZVYT-BEVELAND.

THis Iſland is ſo called for that before it was rampared with Dykes, it trembled (for *Beuen* ſignifies to tremble, and *Beuelandt* a trembling country) as if it had no firme ſeat and foundation. This Iſland is the greateſt of all thoſe of *Zeeland*, and at one time it had twenty leagues circuit: but by reaſon of the tempeſts and inundations of the ſea, and the contynuall flowing and ebbing of the riuer of *Eſcault*, which runnes with a violent ſtreame betwixt *Romerſwael* and *Berghen vp Zoom*, it is halfe conſumed. In this Iſland of *Zuytheuelandt* there was in old time three townes of Marke, the chiefe whereof was *Romerſwal*, then *Borſſele*, which ſtood towards the South: but in the yeare of our Lord 1 4 3 2. the Dykes were broken by the high tides and great tempeſts and it drowned, with the countrie depending thereon, which they called the Siegneury of *Borſſel*.

N2   *ROMERS-*

ROMERSWAL.

HEld in that time the firſt ranke among the
townes of the ſayd Iſland, looking towardes
Berghen vp Zoom vpon the Eaſt, from the which it
is not aboue a league diſtant, but the ſame tempeſts
and inundations (wherewith *Borſſele* was ſwallced
vp) diuided this towne from *Zuytbeuelandt*, leauing it a part in a ſmall Iſland, beeing forced to defend it ſelfe continually with great toyle, coſt and
amazement, for feare of the ſea and the riuer of
Eſcaut, againſt the which they muſt fight continually, as a cittizen of that towne, a man of great
knowledge doth wittely ſhewe by theſe verſes
following, which hee planted at his doore in the
yeare of our Lord 1549 when as Prince *Phillippe*,
(afterwards the ſecond of that name, King of
Spaine) came thether to receiue the othes of the
countie of *Zeeland,*and to take poſſeſſion thereof,
as followeth.

Vidimus aſſueto priuatum lumine Solem,
 pallida turbato vidimus aſtra die:
Vidimus vndantes horrendos æquoris æſtus,
 nos miſeros Belgas, *cum obruit* Oceanus.
Vidimus aſt poſtquam te gloria noſtra Philipe,
 Cæſarea proles,ſemi-deumque decus:
Cuncta refutamus,tranſacti triſtia ſæcli,
 quod præſens noſtrum teſtificatur opus.
Sit licet exiguum, ſit pro ratione voluntas,
 ✠ *nil facit ad vaſtum parua catena fretum.*

Wee

We haue beheld faire *Sol* depriu'd of fight
pale ftarres at noone,and nooneday like the night:
We haue beheld the furious waues make way,
through all the ftrengths of wretched *Belgia.*
But when we but beheld that face of thine,
great *Phillip,*glorious bud of *Cæfars* line:
It clear'd our hearts frō woes,our eies frō fhowres:
witneffe this prefent monument of ours.
Which be it fmall,our loues muft be our pleas:
fmall chaines cannot ore-reach the broadeft feas.

GOES.

WHich is otherwife called *Tergoes*, is the onely
places which is left ftanding on the North-
fide,vpō an arme of the *Efcault,*called *Schenge.*It is
now a good towne, beeing fince thefe laft troubles much inlarged and fortefied with large rampars, and goodly bulwarkes, there is reafonable
good-trade, efpecially of graine for diars, where-
with the countrie abounds. There growes alfo the
beft wheat of all *Zeeland*, more then they need for
their owne vfes, tranfporting the furplufage into
the other Iflands. Their hauen is long and ftraight,
at the mouth whereof there are two forts, one of
either fide, fo as nothing can paffe without defco-
uery. Not farre from this towne is the village of
*Cloetinghen,*belonging to the fonne of the deceafed
Floris of *Brederode,*heire apparent to all that houfe:
a little farther off is the village of *Barlandt*, where
that learned man *Adrianus Barlandus*, who hath

care-

carefully written the chronicles of *Brabant* , and a sommarie of the Earles of *Holland* . Then *Cruyningen* , *Zeaetskerke* , *Hynckesandt* , *Capelle* , *Cattendyke* which are all villages, and many others . In this Island of *Zuytbeuelandt* there are yet some pleasant groues and busshes fit for hunting for there are many hares found in the Island, and great store of wild foule.

TOLEN.

IS one of the East Islands of *Zeelande*, belonging to the countrie , it is now wholie enuironed with good trenches and some forts betwixt, fearing the irruptions of the *Spaniards* , who haue twise or thrise attempted to get footing , for there is but one chanell to passe vpon *Brabant* side : It is verie neere the *Dyke* of Saint *Martin* , for there is but one little chanell which diuides them , and therfore some affirme (as it is likely)that in former times they were two Islands , although in effect it be but one, in the which are two good little townes, both well fortefied with bulwarkes , rampars and counterscarps, whereof the first is called by the name of the Island.

TOLEN.

THis towne shewes the effect by the name, beeing the towle or custome of marchandises due vnto the Prince , and now vnto the Estates of the countrie, who choose the Officers of Iustice , as Bayliffs, Sheriffs and others.

Saint

Saint Martins Dyke.

IS a pretty town, some times belonging to *Adolph* of Bourgogne, Siegnior of *Beuren*, the which came afterwards to the house of *Buren*, and now belongs to *Philip* of *Nassau*, Prince of *Orange*, Earle of *Buren* by his mother. In this territory is the village of Saint *Annelandt*, which is as much to say, as a good Bourg, belonging also to the sayd Prince : Ioyning vnto it is a little Island called *Philips Landt* : these are the foure principall Islands with their townes.

Noort Beuelandt.

THis Island was drowned (as wee haue sayd) in the yeare of our Lord 1 5 3 2. in which inundation there perished the townes of *Coortgeen* and of *Cats*, the villages of *Campen*, *wele*, *Emelisse*, *Haemste* and others, beeing also the patrimonie of the Prince of *Orange*, which Cont *Philippe* of *Hohenloo* his Brother in lawe within these tenne yeares, by an agreement made betwixt them, hath recouered from the sea, and fortefied it rounde about with good bankes, so as at this daie it is a good countrie both for tillage, and pasture, likelie to bee soone built againe with goodly villages, as it was wont to bee.

N4 *WOL*

WOLFERS-DYCK.

SO called by the name of the Lord *Wolphart*, as much to fay, as the *Dyck* of *Wolphart*; it is the leaſt of all theſe Iſlands aboue mentioned, in the which there are but three villages, *Wolfers Dyck*, *Sabbinghe* and *Hogerſdyck*, but there is good paſture for cattel: the Inhabitants being moſt giuen to fiſhng.

There are moreouer in *Zeeland* ſome other ſmall *Iſlands*, which are daily recouered from the ſea, riſeing firſt like bankes of ſand, ſo as ſeeing them thus riſe by little and little and to beare graſſe, they ſend their ſheepe ouer to feede there, whereas the ſhepards haue little lodges, and for their cattell they make great barnes or ſtables, where they lie drie in foule weather, and there the owners prouide them haye before winter.

It ſeemes alſo that theſe Iſlands of *Zeeland* haue beene recouered from the ſea, long before *Charles Martel* Duke of *Brabant*, father to King *Pepinne* of *France*: wherein the *Danes* laboured much, who in thoſe daies had continual war againſt the *French* and great *Brittanie*: for they did chooſe theſe ſand-hills, as a ſafe retreat for their Incurſions vpon the neighbour countries, which they made their *Rendezvous*, making it the magaſin of their ſpoiles. Firſt they ſeazed vpon the Iſle of *Walchren*, the which they did fortefie as well as they could againſt the violence of the ſea: before which enterpriſe they made many high mounts of earth as are

yet

yet to be feene, heere and there, which remaine vnprofitable , fome neere vnto townes, applied to the
vfe of Gardens: vnto which mountes (being any extraordinary tide) they did driue their cattel, and retyred therher them-felues , vntill the waters haue
falne , and then they returned to their lodgings.
Thefe *Danes* or *Noortmans* hauing thus recoucred
the country, began to Tille it , efpecially after the
defcent of their great Captaine Duke *Rollo* : who
was head of the *Norman* Nation in *France* : But in
the end the *Danes* being expelled out of great *Brittaine*, they were chafed alfo out of thefe Ilandes: the
which in fucceffion of time were peopled and made
ciuill: And fo after many Accidents, reuolutions &
quarrels in thefe watery parts, in the end they were
by force made fubiect to the Earles of *Holland*, being giuen vnto them long before , & made a County by the Emperour *Lewis* the gentle: as the Emperor *Charles* the bald his father had made *Holland* a
County and giuen it to *Thierry* the firft Lord of
thefe two Earldomes . But after that the Emperor
Henry the third of that name , had giuen vnto *Baldwin* Earle of *Flanders* , this Iland of *VValchren* and
other fmal neigbour Ilands , there fell great warres
betwixt the *Flemings* and the *Hollanders*: efpecially
that furious battaile in the yeare one thoufand two
hundred fifty three : wheras *Floris* brother to Cont
VVilliam King of *Romaines*, and the Prince of *Cleues*
defeated the Ladie *Maguerit* Conteffe of F *landers*
neere vnto *VValchren* before the King came , in
which

which defeat(as hiftories report) there were fifty
thoufand *Flemings* flaine,as many drowned , and
almoft as many prifoners, whom the victors intreated ignominioufly,ftripping thē naked :among the
prifoners were the two Commaunders , *Iohn* and
Guy of *Dompierre*, fonnes to the Conteffe *Marguerite*;with *Thybault* Earle of *Guife* , *Geffrie* Earle of
Bar,and aboue 2 3 o. Noblemen, Kn ghts and men
of accoumpt : King *William* being puft vppe with
this victory,hauing fuch prifoners,would not giue
eare to any conditions of peace,but fuch as he propounded to the Conteffe , which fhee would not
yeeld vnto. But the King beeing flaine two yeares
after in *Freezeland* , a peace was made betwixt the
Conteffe and *Floris* Brother to the deceafed King,
Vncle and Gardien to his fonne,who v as Earle of
Holland and *Zealand*,named F*lorens* the fift. By the
which peace it was faid that all prifoners fhould be
fet at libertie,paying great ranfomes:And that the
young Cont F*lorens* fhoulde marry *Beatrix* Neece
to the Conteffe *Marguerite*,Daughter to Cont *Guy*
her eldeft fonne. By which Accord and ma riage,
the F*lemings* did tranfport and giue in marriage to
the faid *Beatrix* all fuch rights and pretenfions as
they might haue in the Conties of *Zealand* and in
the Conty of *Aloſt*. But this was but a counterfet
peace,and of fmal continuance:for that *Guy* of *Dompierre*,being Earle of *Flāders*,could not indure that
the Earles of *Holland* fhould inioy this Iland of *Walchren*,but began to make warre to his great difho-
nour

nor and preiudice; the which could neuer haue any
end vntill that all the Seigneuries of *Henault*, *Holland*, *Zeland* and *Frisland* fel to the house of *Burgon-
ne*, at one instant in a manner with the Dutchy of
Brabant, vnder the good Duke *Philip*.

The Estates of the conty of *Zealand*, which wee
haue described, consists of the Nobilitie, and of the
townes of the Ilands of *Walchren*, *Schouuen*, *Zuit
Beuelandt*, *Tolen*, *Noort beuelandt* (newly recouered
from the Sea) *Duyuelandt*, *VVolferfdick*, and *Phillips-
landt*; wherof Prince Maurice is Gouernor & Admiral general : which Estates hold their general Assé-
blie in the town of *Middelbourg*, wheras commonly
the colledge of their Deputies do reside who Assé-
ble euery day to treat and determine of all occur-
rents touching the Estate, or otherwise in stead of
the Court of *Zeland*, in the said town- the which was
wont to be the Abbay of S. *Martin*: At which Colledge doth first appeare by his Deputy the sayd
Prince *Maurice*, in quality of Marquis of *La vere*, the
first Gentleman of *Zealand* speaking for the whole
Nobility of *Zealand*, then the Treasoror generall of
the country ; then the Deputies of the townes of
Middelbourg, *Zirczee*, *La-Vere*, *Flissinghe*, *Tergoes* &
Tolen, which are the six principall townes (the
rest hauing no voyce nor accesse vnto the sayd
Estates) with their Recorder and Secretary. Behold
wherin the Estates of *Zeland* consist: In that Court
there doth also remaine the Councel or College of
the Admiraltie of the saide Contie , consisting
for

for the moſt part of the Deputies of the ſayd
Eſtates, with an Aduocate fiſcall and a Secretarie
in which Counſell all Sea-cauſes are determined.

The County of *Zealand* hath drawne vnto it ſelfe as wee haue ſaid before the chamber of
Accoumptes, touching the demaines, and of all the
reuenewes proceeding as well from cuſtomes, Im-
poſts, rents, collections and contributions, as other
dependances of the receits, concerning the whole
Eſtate, which was wont to be intreated of and decided ioyntly with the Contie of *Holland* and *VVeſt-
freezland*, for which three there was but one chamber of Accoumptes at the *Hage*. This Chamber of
Zealand hath a Preſident, Maiſters, Auditors, Re-
giſters, Vſhers and other Officers. The ſaid Conty
of *Zealand*, hath now a particular coyne, eſtabliſhed
in the Court of *Middelbourg*, which they were not
accuſtomed to haue no more then *Weſt-freezeland*;
hauing but one Mynt thirty years ſince for al three
in *Dordrecht* the capitoll towne of *Holland*, where it
remained long and was much priuiledged during
the raigne of the Emperor *Charles* the fift. As for
their gouernment and religion, it is al one with the
vnited Prouinces their Confederats: Eccleſiaſtical
cauſes, as wel for their diſcipline as otherwiſe, are
referred to their Synodes, whereas ſome Deputies
of the Eſtates do aſſiſt.

All Appellations in ciuill cauſes, be the ſenten-
ces prouiſionall or definitiue of all the Townes,
Bailywiks and Iuriſdictions in the Conty of *Zealand*

land (Notwithstanding the Estates of this Prouince haue sought to sequester them-selues) resort to the Prouincial Councell at the *Hage* in *Holland*: Except they of *Middelbourg*, who by a special priuiledge haue choyce to appeale to the said Prouinciall Councell or to the great Councell, which is also at the *Hage*, like vnto that at *Macklyn* : whereof there is but a reuision before the Councellors deputed out of the vnited Prouinces. The sentences of which reuisors are held for holy and inuiolable decrees. But criminall sentences are executed without Appeale, by euery officer in his Iurisdiction. They haue also in *Zealand* their *Dickgraues*, as in *Holland*, which are Iudges, hauing their Iurisdictions apart, with certaine assistants or Sheriffes whome they call *Gefwooren*, that is to say Iurats, to heare & determine of all controuersies concerning the entertainment of dikes, Slufes, large ditches, waies, fludgates; which Dickgraues & Iurats are in the Iland of *Walchren*, in manner of a Colledge, the which consists of the Marquis of *La Vere*, or his Deputie of the townes and of the Deputies of the best proprietaries in the Iland of *Walchren*. The like is obserued in the other Ilands of the Conty of *Zealand*, euery one according to his priuiledges.

The Contie of Zutphen.

THis Conty hath taken his name of the Capitol Towne of the countrie, w hich is *Zutphen*, standing

ding vpon the right banke of the riuer of *Iſſel* , by the which the riuer of *Berckel* doth paſſe , which falles into *Iſſell*. This towne before the firſt troubles, and that the Duke of *Alua* did exerciſe his cruelties , was rich , well traded, faire and great, with a goodly Bridge to paſſe towardes the towne of *Arnhem* in *Geldres* , the which was broken by the *Spaniards*, part of the towne burnt , and the Inhabitants miſerably intreated ; which were the firſt fruites of the *Spaniards* gouernment: Since it hath been twiſe or thriſe taken and re-taken by the one and the other partie , hauing continued ſince the yeare one thouſand fiue hundred ninety one , vnder the vnited Eſtates. Although that this towne and the Iuriſdiction therof be numbred for the third member or quarter of the Dutchy of *Geldres* , it hath yet a long time beene a Conty of it ſelfe, hauing a particular Earle, the laſt whereof was the Earle *Gerlache*, who left no other heires but one Daughter , the w was marryed to *Otto* Earle of *Naſſau* and of *Geldres*, who brought him the ſaid Earldom of *Zutphen* for her Doury : by meanes whereof he augmented his Demaines: Since which time the ſaid Towne with the Iuriſdiction hath been incorporate to the Dutchy of *Geldres*, ſubiect to one Chancerie , Gouernment , Chamber of Accoumptes, and making one member at the generall Eſtates of both Countries, which as we haue ſaid before are held in the towne of *Arnhem* : whereas they of the ſaid Towne and
Conty

Contie haue their Affiftants and ordinary Deputies, who affift in the Affemblie of the general Eftates of the Vnited Prouinces, that is to fay of euery one of the faid quarters and of the Nobility of
Geldres, who change as the Eftates of the Prouince
fhall thinke it fit.

The Townes and Iurifdictions of the faid Contie are thefe which follow., after, the cheefe
Towne ; *Doesbourg*, a league and a halfe from
thence, *Dotecome*, *Bronckhorst*, *Lochom*, *Groll,*
Bredenoerd, *Keppel*, *Bourg*, *Sherenbourg*, which
are or haue beene heretofore walled Townes,
befides many good Villages. So as this Conty hath larger limmittes, and is richer then that
of *Namure* : Wherefore it merites to bee held,
as it hath alwaies beene, and as the Emperour
and King *Philip* haue carryed it in their Titles,
for one of the feauenteene Prouinces of the *Ne-*
therlandes: And at this prefent one of the eight vnited and confederate. There is in this Contie a generall Officer called Droffart, which depends vpon
the Chancery of *Arnhem* : Whofe Iurifdiction
extendes cheefly to the champian country, who
is bound to bring all Offenders to *Arnhem,* or to
the other townes that haue right to take knowledge thereof: The townes are gouerned by their
Gouernors, Councell and other ordinary Officers.

DOES-

DOESBOVRG.

IS an ancient Town which some call *Druisburgum*, other moderne writers will haue it the same towne which *Tacitus* names *Asceburgum*. It is sea the at the mouth of *Fossa Drusiana* or *Drusus* ditch, the which is a chanell which *Drusus* (to keepe his soldiers from idlenesse made them to digge at *Isseloort*, drawing it out of the *Rhyne*, and carrying it into the Riuer of *Issell* at *Doesbourg*, the which hee made to haue a shorter passage to make warre against the *Frisons*, then if he should haue beene forced to haue gone downe the riuer of *Rhyne*, and so entring into the *Brittish* sea, to haue compassed about all the country of the *Battauians*, and so to haue entred into *Frisland* by the riuer of *Flye*. It is a good towne and well peopled, the which during these wars hath not felt so many alterations as many other townes.

In the yeare one thousand fiue hundred ninetie eight the Admirall of *Arragon* Lieutenant of the Arch-duke *Albert* hauing taken the Towne of *Berck* vppon the *Rhyne*, and past his armie there, he resolued to besiege this towne; But *Prince Maurice* raizing his camp out of the Ile of *Geldre* (which they call *Gelderscheweert*) he went and put himselfe into the said towne, lodging part of his troopes in a little Iland right against it, in the middest of the Riuer of *Issel*, and the body of his armie lay intrencht without the towne towards the fields, whereas the

Admirall

Admiral thought to make his approches, to besiege it, but finding such lettes, hee durst not affront the Prince, who attended him long in battaile, but retyred, and went to winter vppon the Territory of the Empire: where he carryed himselfe as you haue heard in the history of the *Netherlands*.

DOETECVM.

THis towne stands in ihe Champian country, a League from *Doesbourg*, vppon the old *Issel*, it is a reasonable good towne, with a double wall, yet none of the strongest. The Admiral of *Arragon* hauing past the *Rhyne* to besiege *Doesbourg*, he went first before it, and tooke it by composition within three daies. But the Admirall beeing retyred, Prince *Maurice* went and beseeged it againe, the which was as easily yeelded to him as to the *Spaniard*, remaining at this day vnder the obedience of the vnited Estates, as it had beene aboue thirty yeares before, except those few daies the Admirals men held it.

BRONCKHORST.

IT is within a league of *Zutphen*, seated vppon the right side of the riuer of *Issel*, erected to a Contie, hauing a particular Earle. The familie of *Bronchoorst* is ancient, from the which are issued the houses of *Battenbourg*, *Anholt*, *Megen* and others. The towne hath beene much ruined during these warres: But the Castle which is of

O a reaso-

a reasonable strength)stands still , where there is a
continuall garrison for one party or other.

LOCHEM.

IS a good little towne, two leagues from *Zutphen*,
well fortified for the importance thereof, beeing
very necessary during the troubles : for holding the
States partie in the yeare one thousand fiue hundred eightie two , the Duke of *Parma* sent *Charles*
Earle of *Manffeldt* to besiege it in the King of
Spaines name : But the Prince of *Orange* knowing
that three of his Nephewes *Herman*, *Frederic* , and
Adolph vanden Berghe , sonnes of his Sister and of
Cont *Van Sheeren Berghen* were within it, hee sent
the Earle of *Hohenloe* with an armie to raise the
siege, as he did, and freed them ; forcing *Manffeldt*
to retire with losse: Since which time the said town
hath continued constant vnder the obedience of
the Estates, vntill that in the yeare 1 6 0 5.the Marquis *Spinola* Lieutenant to the Arch-duke *Albert* of
Austria , besieged it , and tooke it by composition,
but soone after it was recouered by Prince *Maurice*,
and continues as before.

GROLL.

IN old time was a good Borrough, but by these
last warres within these thirtie yeares , it hath
beene walled in with rampars and Bulwarks hauing
broad

broad and deepe ditches, fortified with casemats and counterscarps. Being held by the *Spaniards* Prince *Maurice* went and besieged it for the vnited Estates: Whereof *Peter* Earle of *Mansfeldt* Lieutenant for the King of *Spaine* by prouision, beeing aduertised, he sent Collonel *Mondragon* Captaine of the Castle of *Antwerp*, with a small Armie, to raise his siege, or at the least to cut of his victuals. The Estates beeing ill informed of the strength of this *Spanish* armie, which was made greater vnto them then it was, they commanded Prince *Maurice* to retyre as he did: But hearing what *Mondragons* forces were, who retyred towards the Rhyne to passe at *Berck*, hee pursued him beyond the town of *VVezell*, in which pursuite Cont *Philip* and *Ernest* of *Nassau* Brethren, Cousins to the Prince, and Cont *Ernest* of *Solms*, beeing too farre aduanced contrary to the Princes order, after they had defeated two Cornets of *Spaniards*, were them-selues in the end put to route, and the two Earles *Philip* of *Nassau* and *Ernest* of *Solms* slaine, and Cont *Ernest* of *Nassau* was taken prisoner: Where-vppon the Prince leauing his pursuit brought backe his Armye and *Mondragon* repassing the Rhyn, returned with his into *Brabant*. But two yeares after, in the yeare 1597. the Prince went agayne to beseege it, in the which Cont *Frederic Vanden Berghe* commanded with 1200. men who finding him-selfe very hardly prest, he yeelded it by composition: Since in the yeare 1605. the

O 2   Marquis

Marquis *Spinola* recouered it (although it were held very ſtrong) beeing yeelded vppon an honorable compoſition : It is two leagues from *Breefort*.

SHEERENBERGHE.

A Towne and Caſtle erected to an Earledome, wherofthe laſt Earle was called *William*,whom King *Phil p* the ſecond made Earle : he had to wife the Prince of *Oranges* ſiſter , by whome he had many ſonnes , the eldeſt called *Herman* is now Earle: Hee with two of his bretheren being beſceged in *Lochem* , were deliuered by the dilligence of the Prince their Vncle : But ſoone after abandoning him vngratefully , they followed the *Spaniards* partie : yet the Eſtates ſeazed vppon the towne in the which they had their garriſon:vntill that the Prince paſſing that way in the yeare 1 5 9 7. the Conteſſe their mother obtained of him that the town ſhould remaine neuter, and that ſhe and her daughters liuing in the caſtle ſhould bee freed from garriſon : The like ſhe obtained from the Arch-duke *Albert*: It is a little towne of ſmall importance,a League and a halfe from *Dotecom*.

BREDEFORT.

IS but a ſmall Towne with a Caſtle ſituated in a Moore, to the which there is but one paſſage to come vnto it vppon a Cauſey, ſo as it is of hard acceſſe : yet in the yeare 1 5 9 7. Prince *Maurice* ſurmounting

surmounting all difficulties, did befeege and batter it, and hauing caufed it to be fummond, the *Burgers* hauing a difpofition to yeeld, yea the women and children falling on their knees vppon the Rampar , and crying for mercy , the Captaine who commanded them being refolued for to hold it, the Prince caufed an affault to be giuen, and took it by force , commanding the foldiars to fpare the Inhabitants. The Captaine like a coward fled with his foldiers into the caftle , and hid him-felfe : The Prince caufed certaine peeces of Ordinance to bee brought to batter the Port, which the foldiers feeing, they yeelded vpon condition that they fhould be all taken to ranfome. This braue Captaine was found hiddē in a feller, yet he was no worfe intreated then the reft : only he indured many affrōts for his cowardly brauery. This town lies two leagues from *Anholt* : fince it hath bene well fortified by the vnited Eftates.

KEPPEL.

IS a little towne of fmall importance , as al other Land-townes be, it ftands vpon the old ftreame of *Iffel*, halfe a league from *Doesbourg*.

BVRG.

IS not much better then *Keppel* , feated vppon the fame torrent, a League from *Doesbourg*.

Heere you may fee tenne townes as well great as fmall, ftrong as weake , in the Contie of *Zutphen*,
O 3 befides

befides Boroughes, Villages and Caftles , whereof
there is good ftore , which make this Prouince to
haue a large Iurifdiction : It hath indured much in
thefe laft warr, but now they begin to take breath,
whereof they haue great need as well as diuers o-
thers, but wee will content our felues with this defcription.

The Prouince and Seigneurie of Vtrecht.

THis Eftate and Seignieurie in old time belonging vnto a Prince and particular Prelat, whom
they called the Bifhop of *Vtrecht*, was firft giuen by
the meere liberalitie of the Kings of *France*, vnto S.
Wildeboord the firft Bifhop , and afterwards by the
Emperours to his fucceffors , all vnder a coullor of
pietie, which Eftate did confift of two Dioceffes:
the one called the lower Diocefe , where are the
capitol Towne of *Vtrecht, Wick-ter-Duyrfted* (called
Batauodurum) *Amerffort*, *Rhenen*, and *Montfort*,
with aboue fixtie Boroughs and villages. The other
was called the high Dioces , which contained all
the country of *Oueriffel* , where there are fourteene or fifteene townes, wherof the three Imperiall and Hans townes are *Deuenter Campen* and
Swolle : the which together with the reft, now make
a Prouince apart : which wee will defcribe hereafter. The lower Dioces is good and fertill,
better manured then the vpper , a higher ground
and

and much dryer then *Holland* , which is neere neighbour vnto it, to defcribe which we wil begin with the cheefe towne.

VTRECHT.

WAs firft (as fome write it) called *Antonia* or *Antonina* , of one *Antony* a *Romaine* Senator, who (flying *Neros* tyranie) retyred into that quarter, and did begin this place. Others fay that *Marc Antony* was the founder,from whome it tooke the name : Some alfo maintaine , that it was fo called of *Antoninus Pius.* But be it what it may : it is moft fure (as many affirme,and as it may bee gathered by Medalles and other Antiquities) that this towne of *Vtrecht* was for a long time called Antonina, whereof there are yet fome markes to be feene vpon the Town-houfe. After that the *Wiltes* had taken and ruined it , they built a Fort which they call *Wiltenbourg* , the which was taken by *Dagobert* fonne to *Clotaire* King of *France*,who did fortifie it more then before , and called it *Traiectum*, for it was a trauers or paffage whereas an Impoft was paid(which in many places in *France* they call *Le droit de Travers* , the due or right of trauers or paffage)for all Marchandife , that was carryed and recarried on either fide : and it retaines at this day the name of *Traiectum.* It ftandes vppon the head of the Rhyne , the which paft directly there, before that they forced it (in making a Scluse
O 4   at

at *Wicter-duyrsted* some eight hundred yeares since) to cast it selfe into the riuer of *Leck* :passing through which towne, it did pierce through *Woerden*, *Oudwater* and *Leyden*, and did ingulph into the Sea at *Catwick*; yea since it had an other course:the waters and chanels which passe by the said townes, are at this day called the old *Rhyn*:It is an admirable thing, that this towne is so situated that they may go to what towne they please of fiftie, which lye round about them in a day, the which being shewed visible to *Philip* the 2. King of *Spaine*, being vppon the place, he tooke a wonderful delight. And it is most certaine that there were some Noblemen which layed great wagers for the tryal thereof, and found it true. Moreouer in one of the longest daies in Summer, if one parts early in a morning from *Vtrecht*, he may dine at any one of 2 6. townes, where he please, & return to his own house to supper:the Emperor *Charles* the 5. in the yeare 1 5 4 2. caused a castle to bee built neere vnto *S. Catherins* port, to keep the town in awe, when as by the cession of the Bishop of that place, he was put in temporal possession of the said town & the dependances:the which hee called *Vredenbourg*, that is to say a Castle of peace. The Cittie is great & mighty, wel fortified with ten good Bulwarks flanking one another, with their counterscarps and diches al of Masons work, and the rampars in like manner:some Bulwarks are also of stone, the rest only of earth:there are goodly buildings, furnished with caues & vauted sellers.

There

There are alſo goodly churches, among the which there are fiue,that haue chanoins:Thefirſt which is the cathedrall church , is called Saint *Martins* , the ſecond Saint *Sauiour* neere vnto it , but now pulled downe:the 3.Saint *Peter* ,the 4.Saint *Iohn*,and the 5. of our Ladies founded by the Emperor *Frederic Barberoſſa* , hauing bin enioyned therevnto by the Pope,to expiate the fault which he had committed in ruining the towne and all the churches and monaſteries of *Milan* : But aboue all , the cathedrall church is ſtately,hauing a faire high goodly tower, tranſparent:in the which the ſayd Emperor *Charles* the 5. did celebrate the order of the golden fleece, in the yeare 1546 the old temple was pulled down by the biſhop *Adelbold*,for that he held it to bee too little , and did reedefie it in the eſtate we now ſee it. This new temple was conſecrated in the yeare 1023. in the preſence of the Emperor *Henry* the 2. by 12.biſhops. There are alſo in the ſame towne two commanders , one of the knights of *Malta*,and the other of the order of the *Teutons* , vnder the great Maiſter of *Pruſſia*,both hauing churches and very ſtately lodgings , either of them hauing his commander.Hee of *Malta* is called the Bayliff of S. *Catherins* , and the other carries the name of commander or great Prior of the Prouince , by reaſon that he hath vnder him many ſmall commanderies, and great poſſeſſions in many places of the *Netherlands.* They hold an honorable ranke and doe good to many which are entertained by the bounty of

theſe

thefe men, as chanoins, abbayes and monafteries
which are in the fayd towne, who(although there
be no other publicke exercife then of the reformed
religion) hold their prebends and entertainments,
the cloyfters within precinct of the towne ftanding as they did,except the houfes ofbegging Friars
which are applied to other vfes : Of which abbaies
and cloifters there is that of Saint *Paul* of the order
of Saint *Benet*, and two of gentlewomen. There
were alfo three of gentlewomen without the town,
but thefe laft warres haue beene the caufe of their
ruine, fearing to leaue lodgings for their enemies,
beeing to neere the towne, but the Nunnes enioye
their entertainement ; and when any Monke or
Nunne dies,the Eftates of the Prouince put others
in their places, to eafe the poorer fort of the gen-
trie. The cittizens of this cittie are courteous,
ciuill, induftrious and ritche amongft whome
there are,and haue alwaies beene men that are vertuous and of great valour;and aboue all Pope *A-
drian* the fixth of that name, firft of all a Doctor
of both lawes, whereon hee hath written goodly workes, and withall hee was a great *Mathematician*. Hee obtained in the vniuerfitie of *Louaine*,
(where hee ftudied long) without feeking it,
diuers degrees of honour, and not without profit; and fo fparing his reuenues, hee founded and
built a colledge which at this day doth honour
his memorie : whofe fame was fo pleafing to
all men, as hee was chofen to bee Scholemafter

to

to the Emperour *Charles* the fifth in his Infancie:
by whose Maieftie hee was fent Ambaffador into
Spaine, to the King *Don Fernando* of *Arragon*,
who for his merittes made him bifhoppe of *Tor-
tofo*. Beeing afterwardes recommended to the
Pope by the Emperour *Maximilian* the firft hee
was made Cardinall. The King *Don Fernando*
and the Archduke *Philippe* his Sonne in law beeing dead, cardinall *Adrian* was chofen for a time
to be Gouernor and Viceroy of *Spaine* in the name
of Prince *Charles* who was foone after Emperour.

In the end on the fixth day of Ianuary in the
yeare of our Lord 1522. hee was chofen Pope,
the newes, whereof being carried him into *Spaine*,
hee made no fhew of ioye; beeing anoynted hee
would not change his name as others did; hee liued but twentie monethes and fome daies after, in
continuall trouble of minde and griefe: Amongft
all his Epitaphes this agrees beft with him. *Hadrianus fextus hic fitus eft, qui nihil fibi infeli-
cius in vita duxit, quam quod imperaret*. Heere
lies *Adrian* the fixth who thought nothing had
happened vnto him more vnfortunate in all his
life, then that hee had commanded. Hee caufed a
goodly houfe to bee built in *Vtrecht* the place of
his birth, which they call at this day the lodging
of Pope *Adrian*.

In this cittie refides a Prouinciall councell to the
which all the appeales of the towne, country and
Siegneury

Siegniory of *Vtrecht* do refort: In which councell
there is a prefident and nine councellors, a receiuer of the Prouince, Regifters, and other Officers.
This Siegneury was greater in the time of King
Dagobert, who ioyned the temporalty to the fpiri-
tualty, giuing it to Saint *Willebrord*, who was an
English man borne, and the firft bifhop, to whome
fucceeded *Boniface*, in whofe times this cittie was
in great reputation, hauing the title and dignitie
of Archbifhop, but *Boniface* hauing beene marti-
red by the *Frifons*, this preheminence and authority, was with the confent of the chapter (then
much afflicted by the *Danes*, and *Normaws*) confer-
fed to the bifhops of *Cologne* who haue euer fince
retayned this dignity: notwithftanding *Pepin* and
Charlemayne Kings of *France* reftored this cittie,
who not onely eftablifhed the Epifcopall dignitie,
but to the end the bifhoppe might defend himfelfe
from his aduerfary, hee did fo augment his iurifdiction, as his Siegneury did extend it felfe in a manner ouer all the country of the *Battauians* : And although the *Frifons, Danes* and *Nortmans* did fpoyle
and burne it often, yet they did foone recouer their
former eftate and gather new forces : To confirme
that which wee haue fayd, it fhall not bee from the
purpofe to infert here fome Latin verfes though ill
pollifhed fauoring of the harfhneffe of the ftile in
thofe daies, the which were written in two great
tables of wood, hung vpon two pillers before the
Quier of the fayd cathedrall church, written in
great

great Letters, halfe worne out by continuance of time, thofe of the right fide were.

Circumquaq ic fluens Hollandia *gurgite* Rheni,
   cingitur Oc ano fluminibufque maris.
In qua cum muris vrbs Antonina *nouellis,*
   tempore Neronis ædificata fuit.
Hanc deuaftauit fera S auica *gens,et ibidem*
   caftrum Wiltorum *conditur inde nouum,*
Turribus excelfis , quod adhuc plebs Abroditorum,
   funditur euertens dirruit vfque Solum.
Hinc Traiectenfe caftrum cum mænibus altis,
   conditur a Francis Chrifticolis *fed idem*
Vulgus Danorum confregit humo tenùs,omnes
   cum clero ciues,infimul enfe necans.
Denique Baldricus *Præful noua mænia ftruxit,*
   quæ modo fubfiftunt auxiliante Deo.
Sic Hollande fi *terræ veraciter omni,*
   Traiectum *conftat vrbs capitalis adhuc.*

The famous *Rhine* through *Hollands* bofome glides
   and(with the fea)enguirts it on all fides.
Here, *Vtrecht* ftands, firft built(as authors fay)
   in *Neroes* time,and called *Antonia.*
Thefe walles the *Slauons* raz'd, vpon repaire,
   of which,the name of *Wiltenburch* it bare.
Then came the *Abrodites,* a nation wood,
   and leuell'd it euen with the place it ftood.
In place whereof the chriftian *Frankeners* came
   and built a fort cal'd *Vtrecht :* but the fame
Was by the *Danes* made a rude heape of ftones,
                                          and

and they that held it flanghtered, all at ones.
But bifhop *Baldrick* fince repaired it,   (ftand yet,
  and rail'd thofe walls which (God bee thankt)
And thus remaines it *Vtrecht* ftill, of all,
  the land of *Holland,*firft, and principall.

On the fecond piller on the left hand hung thefe
verfes.

Tempore Francorum Dagoberti *regis, in ifto,*
  prefenti fundo conditus ecce decens.
Primitus Ecclefia Sancti Thomæ *prope caftrum*
  Traiectum,quam gens Frifica *fregit atrox.*
Sed prior Antiftes, Dominus.&c.

This church which men S.*Thomas-his* do call,
  vpon this plot was founded firft of all.
When *Dagobert* rul'd *France,*nere to the towne
  of *Vtrecht*: the fierce *Frifons* raz'd it downe.
But the firft prelat, Lord.&c.

The reft of thefe verfes were fo worne as it was
not poffible to read them.

WYCK-TER-DVYRSTED.

IT appeeres by the ancient Hiftories, that this
 towne of *Wyck-ter-Duyrfted*, hath in ancient time
beene a great and fpatious towne, in the which they
write were 32. parifh churches. It was before this
towne that the *Rhine* was dambde vp, and forced
(fome 8 o. yeares fince) to leaue his right courfe
and to caft it felfe into the Lecke, as we haue fhewed before. But they fet not downe the caufe why
                                                    they

they cut it off in this place, and made it take the
courfe it now holds. The which happened, for that
when as the winde was at the Norweft, and blew
hard, the riuer of *Rhine* being driuen backe, and not
able to paffe out by his gulfe at *Catwyck* into the
Britifh fea, was forced to difperce it felfe ouer all
the conntries of *Holland*, *Vtrecht* and the *Betuve*,
which is of the Dutchy of *Geldres*. The which happened often, whereby they fuftained great loffes,
wherfore the Eftates of thefe 3. Prouinces affemb-
ling together, they confulted how they might pre-
uēt it, & in the end refolued to turne the *Rhine* from
his right courfe, which was to the Norweft, and to
giue it an other, which fhold fall, crokedly into the
fea, as it doth at this prefent: for the effecting wherof they dambd it vp, drawing it by little & little into the Lecke which is nere vnto it making high
bancks of either fide, fo as in fucceffion of time it is
become a good nauigable riuer, falling into the
Meufe beneath *Dordrecht*, and fo enters into the
Ocean fea before *Bryele*. This towne of *Wyck*
is verie ancient; Whereon *Cornelius Tacitus* a
Knight and *Romaine* Hiftoriographer makes honorable mention, calling it *Batauodurum*. It was
ruined by the *Danes* and *Normans*, but afterwards
built againe: yet nothing fo bigge as at the firft,
notwithftanding it hath alwaies beene, as it
is at this prefent, for the commoditie of the fituation, a good and a ritch towne, hauing a verie
ftrong caftle, whereas the Princes, Bifhoppes of
Vtrecht

Vtrecht did for a long time keepe their court, when as they would lie in the lower diocese, as they did at the castle of *Vollenhof Gheelmuyden* in *Oucryssel*, a league from *Campen*, when as they kept in the higher Diocese. This town had in former times a priuat Lord, who was also Siegnior of *Abcoude*; But the bishops of *Vtrecht* would neuer be quiet vntill they had gotten it, this house declyning as wee haue shewed in the chapter of the Nobility of *Holland*.

AMERSFORT.

THis towne was in olde time built at twise, for there is a little towne al walled about in the very midest of an other greater, the which at this present is verie strong with rampars and bulwarks flanking one an other, and large ditches. It is three leagues from *Vtrecht* standing vpon a little riuer which they cal *Do.* It hath beene often taken and retaken by the *Geldrois*, the last was in the yeare 1543. when as *Martin van Rossen* Marshall of the Duke of *Geldres* army tooke it by force but he sodenly yeelded it againe according to the accord made in the towne of *Venlo*, betwixt the Emperor and the sayd Duke. To speake the truth it is a faire and a good towne, well peopled for a land towne; the inhabitants are courteous and of good conuersation, among the which there are many learned men and louers of musicke, who in certaine daies of the weeke meet togither in honest company to make musicke: for the which they haue certaine gardins and faire chambers of the sworne companies, as

plea-

pleafant in fommer as can bee feene in any place wherfoeuer, and in winter they make choife of fome of their houfes: Maifter *Iohn Fouck* Prouoft of our Ladies church in *Vtrecht*, was borne in this towne, he was honored with other degrees and Ecclefiaftical dignities, a learned and vertuous man, and therfore he was called by the King into *Spaine*, and there made Prefident of the councell of the *Netherlands*, for the affaires of *Flanders*. In this towne was alfo borne that great perfonage, *Iohn* of *Oldenbarneuelt* Knight, Siegnior of *Tempel* and *Groeneuelt*, firft councellor and aduocate for the county of *Holland* and *Weft-Frifland*, a man of great Iudgement and experience, vpon whom the affaires of Eftate do chiefely depend, not only for the faid coūty, but alfo of the generall Eftates of the vnited Prouinces, which remaine not atthe *Hage* in *Hollād*.

RHENEN.

SO called for that it is fituated vpon the banke of *Rhine* fiue good leagues from *Vtrecht*, & as much from *Arnhem* in *Geldres*, whereas they doe moft commonly dine, going or comming from one of thefe two townes vnto the other, which is a great paffage towards *Deuenter*, *Zutphen*, *Doefbourg* and other places, as well in *Geldres*, as *Cleues*, or to *Cologne* or any place where they pleafe in *Germany*. This towne hath towardes *Vtrecht* a large country, the foile whereof is fit to make turfes to burne, but not fo good and durable, neither make they fo good a cole as thofe of *Holland* : And a league frō thence,

P   there

there hath beene within thefe 6 . yeares, a village
built more for the making of thefe turfes, then for
any other reafon. There remaines yet fome forme
of a caftle in this towne, the which is little and of
fmall importance, if this great paffage were not,
which makes it to be frequented. It confifts moft of
Innes and Tauerns. It hath alfo fuffred much during the warres againft the *Geldrois*.

MONTFORT.

THis towne hath a particular Lord at this day,
who writs himfelt Vicont of *Montfort*, it ftands
vpon the riuer of *Yffel*, a league in equal diftance frõ
the townes of *Woorden*, *Oudewater* & *Ifelfteyn*. The
place is little but ftrong, founded by *Godfry* of *Rhenẽ*
bifhop of *Vtrecht*, to ferue as a bar & fronter againft
Holland, who did alfo build againft the *Geldrois* the
caftle of *Horft*, againft the *Traiectins* the towne of
Woerden, and againft the *Frifons*, *Vollenhouen* in the
contry of *Oueryffel*: the which appeeres fufficiently
by his Epitaph.

Godefride *tui Rhenanam prouidus arcem*
    donafti iuris æreque mox proprio,
Quatuor en patriæ, largus munimina noftræ,
    Horft, Woerd, *et* Monfort *conftruis et* Volenhoe:
Wife *Godfry* firft with *Rhenen* did enlarge
    our ftate, and then at his owne coft and charge.
He *Montfort*, *Venlo*, *Horft*, and *Woerdt*, did reare,
    the foure chiefe forts that keepe our foes in feare.
Lambertus Hortenfius, a learned man who hath com-
                                                    pofed

poſed many good bookes, was borne in this twon.

Of the Eſtate of Vtrecht in generall.

THe Biſhoprike and Eſtate of *Vtrecht* was in former times very great and powerfull, the which
Charles the *Bald* King of *France* did with the temporalty make an Earledome, wherevpon there grew
great and long warres, betwixt the biſhops of *V-
trecht* & the Earles of *Holland*, for that the biſhops
ſought to recouer by fauour of the Emperors, all
their ancient demeins, granted vnto them by *Dagobert*, and *Charles* the *Bald*: And the Earles of *Holland*
ſeeking to maintaine, yea to augment that which
had bin newly giuen them, were ſupported by the
Kings of *France*. I ſay that this Eſtate was in old
time ſo great and their territories ſo large, (as *Æ-
neas Siluius* otherwiſe called Pope *Pius* the 2. doth
write) as the biſhop or prince therof, might at need,
put 40000. armed men of his owne naturall ſubiects to field. And although they had continuall
warres againſt their neighbors (wherof they themſelues were euer the firſt motiues) as the *Hollanders*,
Friſons and *Geldrois*, yet they made head againſt thē
all as well as they could, as appeered by *Godfrie* of
Rhenen. But in the latter age *Charles* of *Egmond* duke
of *Geldres*, a proud Prince, warlike and fierce, made
ſuch ſharpe warres againſt the Biſhops of *Vtrecht*,
as he reduced them to great extremitie, & eſpecially *Henry* of *Bauaria*, brother to the Cont *Palatin* of
Rhine from whom hee tooke a great part of his

Siegneury

Siegneury , as well of the higher as the lower dio-
cele. Moreouer the cittizens of *Vtrecht* were grown
lo proud by reafon of their freedomes and preuiledges , and fo infolent by reafon of their welth,as
they grew into factions among themfelues,caufing
many diforders in their towne , and attempting a-
gainft their bifhops ; they d.d often reuolt againft
them,& it they were not chofen according to their
humors,they would not accept them, but did them
a thoufand indignitie s,yea killing their Officers,&
taking fome prifoners before their faces, not without danger to the bifhoppes owne perfon,who was
forced to efcape their fury) to fly to his caftles of
Wyck or *Horft*.The laft reuolt and affront which they
did vnto their Prince and bifhop , was vnto the a-
boue name *Henry* of *Bauaria* who had enioyed this
dignitie foure yeares,beeing incenfed againft him,
hauing beene one day abroad in the country , and
returning home at night,they fhut the gates againft
him, and would not fuffer him to enter into the
towne: and (which was worfe)foone after they receiued *Martin van Roffen*,Marfhall of the campe
to the Duke of *Geldres* , into the towne with a garrifon of *Geldrois* , who from thence did wonderfully annoy the *Hollanders* , and at one time made
an incurfion as farre as the *Hage* , the which
they fpoyled, and retired fafely with their bootie to *Vtrecht*. Bifhop *Henry* feeing himfelfe thus
braued by the *Geldrois* , and by his owne fubiects,
refolued to caft himfelfe into the armes of the
                                              Emperor

Emperor *Charles* the fifth and to tranſport vnto him all that he held of the temporaltie : to the end hee might ſuccor him, to preſerue that which belonged vnto the ſpiritualtie in this towne and ſtate. And for that the Emperour was then in *Spaine*, hee did impart it to the Lady *Marguerite* his Aunte, who was Douager of *Sauoy* and Regent of the *Netherlands* : ſo as in the end it was concluded, that on the 15 of Nouember 1527. he ſhould come in perſon to *Schoonhouen*, whether the Emperor ſhould ſend ſome men of account on his behalfe : amongſt which were the Earles of *Buren* & *Hochſtraten*, the chancellor of *Brabant* and the Preſident of the Prouincial councel of *Holland* : where being arriued at the day appointed, after many conſultations, they concluded that the Biſhop ſhould yeeld vp, reſigne & tranſport, all the rights, intereſt and pretenſions, which hee had to the temporall iuriſdiction in the dioceſe of *Vtrecht*, and the country of *Oueryſſel*, to the benifit & profit of the ſayd Emperor, of which rights he did put his Imperial Maieſty in poſſeſſion, as Duke of *Brabant* & Earle of *Holland*, (not in quality of Emperor) as well for himſelfe, as for his ſucceſſors deſcended of his bloud: whervpon the Earls of *Buren* and *Hochſtraten*, the chancellor and other deputies, did promiſe vnto the biſhop in the Emperors name their maiſter, and did bind themſelues to make war againſt his enemies, and to ſettle him in his Epiſcopal ſeat, and make him duly to enioy his ſpirituall dignity . The Duke of *Geldres* beeing ad-

uertiſed

uertifed of this treatie and accorde,hee made sharper warres then before , and so incenfed the cittizens of *Vtrecht* againft their Bishoppe *Henry*, as they fought by all meanes to depriue him of his Epifcopall dignitie , choofing in his place (by the Dukes instigation and counceli) the Earle of *Bilg*,a chanonine of *Cologne*. Thē did there grow a furious warre betwixt the Emperor and Bishop *Henry* , againft the Duke of *Geldres* and the comunalty of *Vtrecht* , holding the Dukes partie, and their new Bishops : So as after much bloud spilt , and many spoiles done in the country ; there were some citizens of *Vtrecht* well affected to Bishop *Henry* , who brought the Emperors men into the towne the 1. of July 15 28.who entred early in a morning by surprize,where there was some little oppofition,& the Earle of *Mæurs*(lieutenant to the Duke)was taken prifoner,with many of the chiefe of the towne,and some chanoins.Three daies after the bishop entred, and caufed some of the mutines to bee executed by the fword,yea he made two chanoins to bee put into a fack and caft into the riuer , and he would haue taken a sharper reuenge without the interceffion of the Earle of *Hochftraten* : eight daies after he affēbled the three Eftates in the publick place, by the which he was acknowledged to bee their bishop & Prince,all follemnly fwearing fidelity & obedience vnto him.Afterwards the bishop hauing conferred againe with the said Eftates, hee propounded vnto shem,how that being in the town of *Schonhouen*,he

had

had let them vnderstand his resolution to submit
the temporalty of his Siegneury to the Emperour,
shewing them how necessary it was, for their quiet
and publike preseruation, to the end that this Estate
being vnder the gard and protection of so mighty
a Monarke; it should bee defended and preserued
from all enemies which did enuiron it; intreating
them to like well of that which he had resolued, and
to yeeld vnto it. The matter being diuersly debated
after many allegations on either side, in the end (for
that they could not auoide it, the Emperors men
being already in possession of the town) seeing they
had comitted an error, and that their opppposition
would auaile them nothing, but incense the Emperor & their Prelat, they yeelded vnto it. That is, that
the citty of *Vtrecht*, with the iurisdiction and limmits of al the townes, villages, borroughes, forts,
territory, champian country, mountaines, woods,
forests, riuers, pooles, lakes, mills, rents and reuenues to conclude all that was of the temporall demeins, of the sayd Estate and countrie of *Vtrecht*,
together with all the right, title and interest, which
hee had to the high diocese, that is to say, to the
country of *Oueryssel*, and ouer the town of *Groning*,
the iurisdiction of the *Groningers* and the *Omelands*,
with all their rights, should be vnited and incorporated to the demeins of the Dukes of *Brabant* and
Earles of *Holland*. The which hauing beene a-
greed vpon and concluded, the *Traiectins*
were absolued of their othe of fealtie which
P 4 they

they had taken vnto the fayd bifhoppe,who freely
difcharged them, vpon condition that they fhould
take the like othe ,and doe homage to the Emperour, and to his lawfull heires iffued of his bloud,
Dukes of *Brabant* and Earles of *Holland*: The Bifhop referuing nothing for himfelfe and his fucceffors,but the fpirituall iurifdiction and reuenues,
and that fumptuos Palace in the towne,ioyning to
the cathedrall church,built by *Charles Martel* Duke
of *Brabant* , father to *Pepin* King of *France* , who
gaue it to *Gregorie* the third Bifhop of *Vtrecht*. All
things being thus concluded betwixt the Bifhoppe
Henry of *Bauaria* , and the Emperor; *Charles* Duke
of *Geldres* finding his forces to weake to incounter fo great a Monarke , hee purchafed a peace
with his Maiefty,the which was concluded the firft
of October following: And the 21. of Nouember
the Earle of *Hochftraten* , as gouernor of *Holland*
for the Emperor, was fent by the Ladie *Marguerite*
Regent into the fayd towne of *Vtrecht*,who tooke a
follemne poffeiffion in his Maiefties name(as Duke
of *Brabant* and Earle of *Holland*)and receiued their
othes and homages: the like hee did at *Amerffoort*,
Wyck-ter-Duyrfted, *Renen* , and *Montfort*, (as for the
foueraigntie this laft towne hauing a particular
Lord and Vicont of that place)returning back to *V-*
trecht the chiefe towne of the country,he difpofed
of the Eftate & gouernment. And as al things were
well fetled vnder the Emperors authority , bifhop
Henry had a defire (for fome reafons)to retire into
Germany

Germanie to his other Bifhoppricke of *Wormes* chofing for Bifhop & fubftituting in his place *William*
of *Enckwoort* borne at *Boifleduc* Cardinall and Bifhop of *Tortofe*,as Pope *Adrian* the fixt had beene
before hee was Pope,who refigned the faid Bifhop-
prike vnto him before hee came to the Popedome.
This *Enckwoort* was a Courtier at *Rome*, and came
not to his Bifhoprike of *Vtrecht*(making *Iames Vte-
nengen* his Vicar)vntill he died in the yeare 1533.
In the meane time Pope *Clement* the feauenth hauing feene the Contracts and Inftruments of the
ceffion and tranfport made by the Bifhop *Henry* of
Bauaria to the Emperour of the temporaltie of *V-
trecht*,and the appourtenances , hauing had therein
the aduice and confent of the Colledge of Cardi-
nals,they did approue and ratifie all,decreeing that
this ceffion and tranfport fhould be of force , and
take full effect. But for that this Eftate and Seig-
nieury is a fee of the Empire, and doth hold of the
Imperiall Chamber , the Emperour was forced to
demand the Inueftiture of the faid Chamber in his
owne priuate name . as well for him-felfe as for his
fucceffors lawfully defcended from him.The which
he did eafily obtaine. And by this meanes the Citties, Townes,Territorie and Iurifdiction of the Eftate and Seigneiury of *Vtrecht*(which had bene gouerned by their proper Princes and Bifhops,aboue
nine hundred yeare) came vnder the obedience of
the Emperor *Charles* the fift , and after him to his
fonne *Philip* the fecond King of *Spaine* , Duke of
Brabant

Brabant, Earle of *Holland* &c. Of which Eftate of *Vtrecht* (being two Dioceffes) the Emperor made two Eftates, reducing them into two Prouinces, which make the number of feauenteene in the *Netherlands;* that is, into ỹ prouince of *Vtrecht,* & that of *Oueryffel* : That of *Vtrecht* making the fourth in ranke of the confederate *Belgick* Prouinces, vnder the generall Eftates, and that of *Oueryffel* the fift, hauing their voyces and fuffrages in that order in their Ceffions.

The Eftates of which Prouince of *Vtrecht* confift at this day, as in former times, of three members; the Clergie of fiue Colledges that haue Chanoins, the Nobility, and the townes: Of which Colledges the Deputies are indifferently chofen, to affift daily in their Affemblies, with them of the Nobility and townes; who haue their Secretaries and other Officers.

This Seigneury of *Vtreeht* hath (as we haue faid) a Prouincial Councel, from which at this prefent there is no appellation, as had bin heretofore to the Imperial Chamber at *Spier,* at fuch time as it was meerly a member of the Empire : but fince that the Emperor *Charles* the 5. did vnite it to his demaines, excluding the faid Imperiall Chamber, hee made it fubiect to the great Councel at *Macklyn:* vntil that the Eftates of the faid country and of *Oueryffel,* hauing within thefe thirty yeares recouered their libertie, it hath bene difcontinued. Notwithftanding in cafe of remiffion they may haue their recourfe

vnto

vnto the Eſtates of the Prouince; where as the reuiſion is made by the ſame Acts: In which Prouincial
Councel there is a preſident, ſix Councellors, an
Attourney general, and a Regiſter. The Chamber
of accoumpt, is kept by the colledge of the Eſtates,
wheras the Treſorers as well generall as particular
are bound to come and yeeld vp their Accoumpt.
The ſaid Seigneury hath alſo a particular Mynt, as
it hath alwaies had; the which is alſo ſubiect to the
general of the Mynte for the vnited Eſtates. The
gouernment and Religion is generally maintained
as in other Prouinces their confederats. There are
foure Marſhals for the whole Seigneury, euery one
of which hauing charge in the quarters that are aſ-
ſigned them, where they are to command their Archers to apprehend all vagabonds and other offenders which they ſhall meet in the country. The de-
ceaſed Prince of *Orange* of famous memory, was
Gouernor of this Prouince, as of *Holland* and *Lea-
land*, placed there by King *Philip*, before his laſt returne towards *Spaine*; after the violent death of the
ſaid Prince, the vnited Eſtates did ſubrogat Prince
Maurice of *Naſſau* his ſonne, Marquis of *La Vere*,
and *Fliſſingue*, making him moreouer their Captain
General and Admirall of all the vnited Prouinces,
as he is at this preſent.

FRISLAND.

NO man can denie but this *Friſon* Nation is very
ancient, as it appeares by the ancient greeke
and latin writers, as *Strabo*, *Ptolomey*, *Plinie*,
Tacitus,

Tacitus and others : for it retaines at this day the
same seat and the same name, which they gaue them
and had before them: Seeing that in a manner al o-
ther Nations of *Germany* haue either quit their old
abodes, or elſe haue receiued new names: the which
needes no farre fetcht proofes, seeing their neereſt
neighbours do verifie it. For the names of *Holland,*
Vtrecht, Oueriſſel, Weſtphalia and others, were neuer knowne by any of the aboue named Authors:
neither was the name of *Geldre* euer in vſe (the Inhabitants whereof, and of *Cleues, Iuilliers, Monts,* &
Berghe were then called *Sicambres*) but eight hundred ſeauenty eight yeares after the Natiuitie of
our Sauiour I E S V S C H R I S T.   That which they
now call the country of *Saxony,* was not the abode
of the ancient *Saxons,* wherof *Ptolomey* makes mention. So as it is hard for moderne writers to iudge
(by reaſon of the alteratiõ of names) if thoſe which
be at this preſent neighbours vnto *Friſland,* bee the
ſame Nations which in ancient time were wont to
be, or whether they bee now more remote. But as
for the *Friſons* there is no diſpute nor doubt, wher-
ofto giue more firme and ſolide reaſons both of
the name and of the Antiquity, the Reader ſhal vn-
derſtand that the ſucceſſion of their Princes, the families, the foundation of townes , caſtles and villages, may in their regard, bee drawne, if not farther,
yet with more certainty then any other Nation of
Germany. The *Danes* although they bee very ancient , and equal touching their beginning with the

Friſons

Frisons, cannot make a true extraction, nor giue a reason of the time, but since their King *Frotho* the third; during whose raigne our Sauiour IESVS CHRIST was borne. The *Franconians* likewise although they bee very old (whatsoeuer they pretend that their freedome was purchased in the seruice of the *Romaine* Emperours) yet are they in doubt of their first beginning, issue and denomination : so as they cannot decipher their true and continued Chronologie, but since *Charlemaignes* time. But the *Frisons* hauing to this day alwaies kept one name and one dwelling, may directly and by a plain computation of times, report their gestes from the beginning vnto the ending: so hauing taken beginning 313. yeares before CHRIST, and since that time foure times made proofe of the change and Estate of their Common weale: they may by a cleer computation of yeares, shew how long they were vnder princes, then vnder dukes, after vnder Kings, vnto *Charlemaigne*, and since vnder *Podestates*, vntill their *Anarchia*; how long also vnder the *Factions* vnto the resignation which *George* Duke of *Saxony* made vnto the Emperour *Charles* the fift, and how long vnder the house of *Austria* vntil their Emancepation and liberty, which they inioy at this present, prouing from the beginning of their Princes the foundation and building of the towne of *Staueren*, which then was the cheefe of al the Realme of *Frisland*. By reason of which Antiquity this town hath had a prerogatiue from the Kinges of *Denmarke*, that

that in paſſing the ſtraight of the *Sonde*; their ſhips
haue priuiledge to go firſt before all others, either
going or comming out which muſt attend their
turnes, but not thoſe of *Staueren*, which muſt bee
preſently diſpatcht by the Impoſt gatherers.

To deſcribe the queſtions which are betwixt the
ancient and moderne Authors, to find out the truth
from what place *Friſo* and his two bretheren *Bruno*
and *Saxo* are firſt deſcended, were in my opinion a
tedious and endleſſe labour, ſeeing they can determine nothing that is certaine, no more then of the
Anceſtors of theſe three princes; which ſome maintained to be deſcended from *Ragau*, ſonne to *Sem*,
the ſonne of *Noe*: But it appeares plainely that they
were of the reliques of the *Macedonian* Armie, hauing ſerued *Alexander* the great in his conqueſt of
Aſia and the *Indies*, who placed them in garriſon in
the *Emodian* Mountaines. But the *Indiens* after the
death of *Alexandar*, beeing perſwaded by *Sandroco-
tus* to rebell; *Friſo* with his two bretheren and all
their friendes imbarked in three hundred ſhips in
the yeare of the creation, 3 642. & before the Natiuity of *Chriſt*, three hundred twenty one, & ſo put
to ſea, ſailing from one country to another, ſeeking
ſome new dwelling, but they wandred vp and down
eight yeares and could not bee receiued: In the end
of ſo many ſhips (whether that the Seas had ſwal-
lowed them vp, or ſpoyled with age, or otherwiſe
loſt) there were but fitty foure which arriued at a
ſafe Port, wherof eighteen landed in *Pruſſia*, twelue

in

in *Ruſſia*, and twenty foure (in the which were *Friſo*
and his bretheren) entered by the *Flye* about Au-
tome into theſe quarters of *Friſland* without any
let or oppoſition of the *Suedens* , who at that time
(for feare of tempeſts and Inondations) where retyred into the higheſt part of the country.

Hauing taken land they preſently built a Temple
to *Iupiter*, which in their language the called *Stauo*,
and there they built a towne, which of the name of
their God they called *Stauora* , which is now the
towne of *Staueren* ſtanding vpon the *Friſons* ſea, the
which they fortified: wherby they defended themſelues not only againſt the *Suedens*, but alſo againſt
the *Danes, Brittons* and others , getting their liuing
as well of pyracie at ſea, as by tilling of the ground,
vntill the people beeing multiplied , and queſtions
growing daily among them by reaſon of the ſtrait-
nes of their country , which was not ſufficient to
feed al their cattel: Prince *Friſo* fearing that this cõ-
tention of the Commons (he being the elder of his
brethren) might breed ſome diſlike betwixt them
three, propounded a meanes to maintain loue & a-
mity betwixt them ; who hauing imparted it vnto
the people ; this was found the moſt expedient:
That *Bruno* and *Saxo* with their families (leauing
this part of *Friſland*) ſhould ſeeke forth ſome new
habitations neere vnto it , as well for themſelues
as for their ſucceſſors : So as beeing neighbours
one vnto an other, they might not onely enter-
tain themſelues in the Diſcipline and Inſtitution of
their

their Anceſtors, but alſo ſuccor one another with
their common forces, againſt all incurſions of their
enemies. So three hundred years before CHRIST,
Saxo and *Bruno* parted from *Staueren*, and paſſing by
the *Flye*, they ſayled towardes the Eaſt, vntill they
came to *Haldrccht*, or *Saxony*, neere vnto the *Germaine* Sea, whereas entring into the gulph of *Albis*,
they landed by little and litttle, and hauing chaſed
away the Inhabitants by force, they wonne a great
country. *Bruno* (for that hee would not diſcontent
his brother) went towards the Weſt, by the *Viſurge*
or *Wezer*, where hee founded a Cittie of his owne
name called *Brunſwick*. (VVhat this word of *Wisk*
ſignifies wee haue ſhewed before) the which although it hath beene often deſtroyed, built againe
and augmented, yet when as the poſterity of *Bruno*
came once to faile, it hath alwaies retained the title of a free towne: So as in the time of *Charlemaign*
it was wholy deſtroyed but in the yeare eight hundred ſixtie one it was re-edified againe by *Bruno*
Duke of *Saxony*, ſonne to *Ludolph*; wherof I thought
good to make mention, for that *Albert Crantz* doth
maintaine, that the towne of *Brunſwick* was firſt
founded by this *Bruno* ſonne to *Ludolph*. Touching
the geſts of *Bruno* and *Saxo*, and of their ſucceſſors
Saxons and *Brunſwickains*, wee will leaue them to
ſuch as haue written the hiſtories of *Saxony* and
Brunſwick, and will onely ſpeake of our *Friſo*: who
beeing the firſt Prince of the *Friſons*, after the departure of his Bretheren, retained al *Friſlana* for his
inheritance

inheritance, the which did extend it felfe along the North-fea coaft, from the riuers of *Flye* and *Ems* (or *Ameris*) on the Weft fide on the riuer of *Zidore* to the Eaft, which is the length and breadth from the North and the *Brittifh* fea, vnto the *Battauians* or *Hollanders*, and to the *Sicambrians*: which are the *Geldrois* on the South fide. Al which country *Bruno* diuided into feauen parts, according to the number of his fonnes, which he called *Zeelandts*, for that they are all vppon the fea, moft part Ilands or Peninfules ioined to the continent: his fons were *Adel* his eldeft, and the fecond Prince of *Frifland*, *Witto, Hetto, Hayo, Scholto, Gailo* & *Asgo*: to whom he gaue by his Teftament certain precepts of that which they fhould do or not do to entertaine amity and correfpondency with their neighbour Princes: he him-felf left vnto his fons their portions in writing, and alfo a certain treaty of allyance which he made with the Princes of *Germany*: who by a cõmon Accord and confent made him and his fucceffors Gardiens of the North fea, to defend the whole country from the Inondation of the fea, as alfo of the publike waies againft robbers and theeues, to that end that Marchants might paffe and trafficke freely vnto the R*hyne*: and in this refpect he was allowed to take cuftomes & impofts of marchãdife at diuers paffages: he had alfo an Immunity of Armes granted him, which was a priuiledge, whereby neither he nor his were bound to go to the war when as the other Princes and Prouinces went to defend

Q   the

the liberty of *Germany*. The Frifons had many other good priuiledges, of their liberty & freedome, the which were giuen them by *Cefar Auguftus*, *Charlemaigne* and other Emperors, and ratified by *Charles* the fift, which they haue alwaies maintained.

Thefe feuen parts of *Frifland* called *Zeelädts*, were diuided & compaft in by certaine riuers, wherof betwixt *Eldere* and *Flye* were fiue that is, *Lanwer*, *Eems*, *Wezer*, *Elbe*, and *Iadua*. Betwixt the *Flye* and *Eems* there were three of thefe *Zeelandts*, very wel peopled vpõ the South fide, for that the North part was not habitable by reafon of ÿ lakes, moors, & bogs, which were inacceffible, & for want of banks to defend them from the Inondation of the fea. wherfore the places moft frequéted were that of *Staueren*, the feauen forefts, *Steenwick*, *Twent*, *Drent*, a part of the Territory of *Groning*, *Benthem* and *Oldenburch*, all which lay togither vpon the maine land: All which vntil *Charlemaignes* time was called High *Frifland*, as it may appeare by the writing of fome Saints which haue preacht the Word of God there. But 120. years before C H R I S T, *Frifo* the yong (whom they alfo cal *Friftus*) fon to *Grunnius* who was founder of *Groning*, fon to *Gaylo* the fon of *Hago* the 4. fonne of *Frifo* the firft Prince of the *Frifons*, made a new Collony of *Frifons* not far from the reft; hauing had to wife the daughter of *Vbbo* third Prince of *Frifons* who was named *Frou*, which fignifies Lady, by which name *Oppinus* faith, the Emperor *Seuerus* wife was called. This *Frifo* obtained from his

father

father and father in law, a troupe of men, with the which hee paſt the *Flye* on the VVeſt part, into an emptie Iland, where hee ſtayed, and there made his aboad, calling it new *Friſland*, whereof the Inhabitants were called *Friſiabenes:* And on a certain place (where as ſince the towne of *Alcmar* was built) he ſeated a towne which by his wiues name hee cal'ed *Frougaſt:* But as in the *Friſon* tongue as wel as in the *Germaine*, they do vſually pronounce a *V.* conſonant for an *F.* In ſucceſſion of times this word is changed into *Vrougaſt* or *Vroulegaſt*, with which word *Geyſt* there are many places end in *Friſland.* This towne of *Vrougaſt* became afterwards, great, and of good trafficke: The which the *Remaines* making warre againſt the *Battauians* and *Friſons*, for the affinitie which this name had with their towne of *Verona* in *Italie*, they alſo called it *Verone.* Of this *VVeſt-Friſland* is that to be vnderſtood which *Tacitus* writes was done by the *Friſons* for their neighbourhood with the *Battauians.* In this Eſtate was *Friſland* maintained ſince the comming of *Friſo* their firſt prince the ſpace of one hundred ninety three yeares, wherof *Staueren* was the chiefe town, whereas the Princes kept their Court, gouerning the other quarters called *Zeelandts* by their Lieutenants. This Towne of *Staueren* grew ſo proud by their wealth and Nauigation, as they ſeemed all gold, gilding the poſts of their houſes, and their vanitie was ſo great, as a rich widdow hauing commaunded the Maiſter of her ſhippe to bring

Q 2   her

her the beft Marchandife hee fhould finde in the
Eaft Countries : For that hee brought nothing
backe but Wheat , which hee held to bee beft;
This vaine woman commaunded the Maifter, that
if hee had laden it on the larboord fide , hee fhould
caft it into the Sea on the ftarboord fide, which hauing done, God fent a tempeft which did fo moue
the fandes of the fea, as in the fame place where the
Wheat had beene caft forth, there did rife a barre
or banke of fand , which hath euer fince fpoyled the Hauen of the faid Towne, which hath depriued them quite both of their Nauigation and
wealth , fo as fince the Inhabitants (hauing
beene often fpoyled) are now growne more
modeft.

All that Prince *Frifo* had left in writing, was not
done in the *Frifon* tongue, but in *Greeke* letters; hauing raigned fixtie yeare hee died, two hundred
twenty feauen yeares before *Chrift*. *Adel* his eldeft
fonne fucceeded him , who raigned ninetie foure
yeares, and dyed one hundred thirty one yeares
before *Chrift*. After him came *Vbbo* his fonne who
gouerned eighty yeares , and died fifty one yeares
before *Chrift*. *Frifo* or *Frifius* fon to *Grunnius*, who
built the towne of *Groning* (as wee haue faid) marryed the Ladie *Frou* ; To whome fucceeded his
fonne *Afniga Afcou* 4. Prince of *Frifland*, who raigned 82. yeares, and died 31. yeares after the birth
of *Chrift* : *Diogarus Segon* was 5. *Dibaldus Segon* 6.
& *Tabbo* 7. al which together liued 443. yeares: thē
                                                    had

had they as many Dukes, whereof *Afcon* was the first, who had foure fonnes, whereof *Adelbold* the eldeft fucceeded him, and was fecond Duke of *Frifland*; dying withont children hee left his bro-ther *Tito Bocaial* his fucceffor, who dying alfo without children, had *Vbbo* fonne to his brother *Richold*, Nephew to *Afcon* for his heire, who was 4. Duke of *Frifland*: To whome fucceeded his fonne *Haron* fift Duke, who dyed in the yeare of *Chrift* three hundred thirty fiue. After him came his fon *Odibald* fixt Duke, then *Vdolph Haron* feauenth and laft Duke. For after him vnto *Charlemaigne Frif-land* had nine Kings. Thefe feauen dukes altogether raigned two hundred fixty two yeares. Then came *Richold Vtto* who was firft King of Eaft *Frifland*. (wee call it fo in regard of *Weft-Freezeland*, into the which *Frifo* the young fonne of *Grunnius* ledde the firft Collonies.) To him fucceeded *Odibaldus*, fecond King of *Frifland*: Then *Richold* third King. And after him *Beroald* fonne to *Valck* fourth King of *Frifland*, in the time of *Clotaire* King of *France*, and by him flaine in battaile. *Adgil* was fift King of *Frifland*: *Radbod* the firft of that name, 6. King of *Frifland*: After whom came *Adgil* the 2. the 7. King who had three fons, *Gombauld* the 8. King of *Frifons Iohn* called the Prieft, & *Radbod*: *Gobauld* was a good Chriftian, & went to ferue *Charlemaigne*, where he was flain with *Rolland* and other peeres of *France*, at the battaile of *Ronfeual*. *Iohn* called the Prieft (fo called for his holynes of life) followed *Charlemaigne*

in

in his voyage to *Ierusalem*: from whence (as *Suffridus Petri a Frison* writer sayeth) hee paſt on with a Collonie to the Eaſt *Indies* , where hee erected a Kingdome, the which was called by his name , the Kingdome of *Preſtre Iean* : whoſe ſucceſſors which came afterwards into *Affricke* , into the Kingdome of the *Abiſſens,* are at this day called *Preſtres Ieans.* *Radbod* the third ſon of *Adgil* , the ſecond of that name , was King of *Friſland* , a great perſecuter of Chriſtians, he was twiſe vanquiſhed by the *French.* It was he which retyred from the font, being ready to be baptized , vppon a fooliſh anſwer which the Biſhop of *Soiſſons* made him, going to baptize him. He did great ſpoyles vnto Chriſtians , as farre as *Vtrecht* , the which hee ruined, aud deſtroyed the Temple of S. *Thomas* , which King *Dagobert* had built. He raigned fifty yeares ; and with him ended the Kings of *Friſland* ; the Realme beeing after that anexed to the Crowne of *France.*

Wee haue before made mention of *Friſo* the yong, who led the firſt Collony into Weſt *Friſland:* let vs now ſpeake of the ſecond , who was brought into that quarter which is now called *Waterlandt,* which hapned in this manner: wee haue before ſaid that *Aſcon* firſt duke of *Friſland,* had four ſons, *Adelbod, Tito, Richold* & *Raabod :* that the two firſt were dukes ſucceſſiuely, and that *Vbbe* the ſon of *Richold,* was the 4. Duke of *Friſland* ; there then remained *Radbod* the 4. ſon of *Aſcon* : hauing taken a wife out of *Weſt-Friſland,* of the race of *Friſo* the yong ; hee had

had by her one fon, called *Thierry*, who in the 300.
yeare of C H R I S T s natiuity , which was the 2 of
the raign of *Haron* the 5. duke of the old Fr*efons* his
coufin, led a Collony into that quarter of *Weft-frif-*
l nd, with the help of the faid *Haron*, and other four
of his coufins , the which at that time by reafon of
the multitude of Ilands, Moores, Lakes , and other
ftil waters, was not yet inhabited : yet with that aid
and the intereft he had by his wife, he made this fecond part(which at this prefent is *Waterlandt*)habi-
table and fertil, in the which are *Edam, Monikendam,*
Purmerends, Woormer, Ryp, *Graft* and other good villages, fo as of thefe two parts ioined togither, with
that which he added afterwards on the weft part, he
made an Eftate , and built a Pallace at *Medenblike,*
which he made the cheefe town of the whole country. VVho pretending to make it a Kingdome, *Ha-*
ron his Coufin, Duke of Eaft F*rifland* hindred him,
for the which they were long in controuerfie, til in
the end *Haron* forced him to content him-felfe with
the title of a Duke.

This *Thierry* Duke of *Weft-Frifland* had one
fonne which fucceeded him , named *VVilliam* the
firft, who had *Dibauldi* , *Dibauid* had *VVilliam* the
fecond, who had *Elim*, hee dyed without heires
male , and in him fayled the lyne of this *Thierry*:
Hauing before his death adopted *Beroald* (beeing but feauen yeares old) the fon of *Richold* the fecond of that name, the third King of *Frifland* : fo as
al thefe Dukes of *Weft-Frifland* fucceffiuely raigned

two

two hundred thirty three yeares, fiue and twentie
yeares after the death of *Elim*, in the yeare of *Chriſt*
fiue hundred thirty three. *Beroald* after the death
of *Richold* his father did inherit the Realme of Eaſt
Friſland. Thus were the two *Friſlands* vnited together ; the which *Beroald* inioyed ſixtie yeares:
whereof he was afterwards depriued, and of his life
alſo , by *Clotaire* the ſecond of that name King of
France, father to *Dagobert*: Notwithſtanding *Adgill*
the ſecond ſucceeded him, and after him *Gombauld*,
then *Radbod* the ſecond , whome *Charlemaigne* vanquiſhed , and freed the *Friſons* from the yoake of
Kinges: reſtoring them to their liberty, to whome
hee gaue goodly priuiledges , the which they haue
long maintained with the priſe of their bloods.

Since the *Friſons* were long vnder an Ariſto-
craticall Gouernment , ſometimes vnder Poteſ-
tates whom they did choſe them-ſelues , and not
able to agree vppon the election by reaſon of dangerous factions , the Earles of *Holland* hauing in
ſucceſſion of time and long warres , ſeazed vpon
that part which they now call *Weſt-Friſland* and
Waterlandt , the which the *Hollanders* will haue,
(but the Inhabitants of the country cannot indure
it) called *Northolland*. On the other ſide, the dukes
of *Brunſwicke*, the Hans townes of *Breme* and *Ham-*
bourg , the Earle of *Oldenbourg* , *Schowenbourg* and
Embden haue vſurped much of Eaſt *Friſlād*, euen vnto the Territory of *Groning* : the which although it
be an Eſtate & territory apart, is cōprehended notwithſtanding

withftanding vnder the territory of that which
hereafter we will fimply call *Frifland*, inclofed betwixt the *Flye* and *Ems*, to diftinguifh it from *Eaft-
Frifland* held by the Earles of *Embden*, and *Weft-
Frifland*, anexed to the county of *Holland.*

That then which we will fimply call *Frifland*, and
the Inhabitants *Frifons*, as *Tolomey* and *Tacitus*
tearme them, faying that they are *Germaines*, and
people from beyond the *Rhine*, whom *Pliny* calls
Cauches, the great and the leffe, are *Aborigines*, or
originally comefrom that place : who aboue all the
people of *Germanie* retaine their ancient appellation, keeping in their ancient and firft feat, hauing
the fame language they haue alwaies had. True
it is that in the chiefe townes they vfe the Dutch-
tongue, but in the champian country they keepe
their *Frifon* language, which the gentlemen take
pleafure to entertaine in regard of the antiquitie.
Although I bee well acquainted with the high and
low Dutch tongue, yet I muft confeffe that in this
ancient *Frifon* language I vnderftand nothing.

Wee haue fayd before that the *Frifons* did for a
time entertaine themfelues vnder factions, wee
muft therefore relate fuccinctly the beginning
thereof : which was that in the yeare of our re-
demprion. 1390. there did rife two factions in the
country of *Frifland*, the one *Vetcoopers*, which fignifies in their vulgar tongue, marchants of greafe,
that is to fay, marchants of fat oxen, which they
hold for an honeft kinde of marchandife, and of

Schyer-

Schyeringers , which are butchers and fellers of tripes , which is a bafe kinde of trade , which factions they fay came from Eaft and Weft *Frifland.* The firft fpring and beginning thereof was; that all thefe marchants of cattell and the butchers beeing togither at a publick banket according to their cuftome , there was a gueft to choofe a Prouoft , a Deane or a King amongft them , whofe charge fhould bee to looke that no diforder fhould bee committed , which might trouble the companie. There was amongft them of either of thefe two companies,one that exceeded the reft , and both e-quall in wealth , in refpect and loue towards all the guefts . Whom both the one and the other partie contended to chofe,their Deane, Prouoft or King: the one and the other maintayning that this dignity & authority at the table, was moft befitting him that had the honefteft trade. Wherevpon a queftion grew among them,which of thofe two marchandife was the honefteft: the one preferring the marchants of cattell , the other the butchers . Vpon which difpute their braines being het with wine, in the end they fell from words to blowes one againft another,party againft party,euery one with his Al-lies and Kinfmen , meaning to maintaine the one quarrell or the other : fo as in the end there was a great fight , in the which many were either hurt or flaine . In reuenge whereof , either party holding it felfe wronged, they began to make factions,and to bandie one againft an other : fo as this canker eat-ing

ing more and more; ftrangers (who had no intereft, nor were any way wronged) ingaged themfelues, vpon hope of bootie of the one or the other partie : euerie one wrefting what hee could from his Aduerfarie , without either lawe or iuftice (fo confufed were things then and full of diforder) but fuch as they made by the fworde , where as the ftrongeft carried it . The fruits of thefe factions were fuch, as they not onely rained amongft priuate perfons, but amongft whole fam lies, villages, bourrougs and townes, yea among whole Prouinces, fo as the whole country was ful of thefrs and murthers , and no man was free from their infolencies. In like maner about that time *Hollãd* was afflicted with the factions of *Hoecks* and *Cabillaux* that is to fay, the *Hamefons* and the *Merlus*, wherof we haue made mentiõ heretofore : which was, that the one party (as the *Merlus* or *Coddes* bee fifhes which prey) did threaten to deuower the other: and they of the *Hamefons* did threaten to take the others by the throat: which to fpeake truth were quarrels fcarce fit for children . And at that time were the factions of *Gelphes* & *Gibelins* in *Italy*: Of the diuerfity of colloured caps in *Flanders*, & of thofe of the ftarre in *France*, al which were factions raifed from the diuill . This mifchiefe proceeded fo farre in *Frifland*, as from the leffe it came to the greater, and from Marchants and Bourgers to the Nobility and Clergie: The gentlemen ruining the houfes & caftle one of an other; and the Abbots and Monkes doing al the mifchief they could one vnto an other:

So

So as to appeafe thefe factions, and to reconcile the Noblemen, the Emperor *Maximilian* the firft, fent *Otto van Langen* to perfwade them to choofe a Poteftat amongft them, which fhould gouerne the country according to their preuiledges, vnder the authority of the Empire. But their fplene was fo great, as euery one feeking to choofe one of their faction, the fayd commiffioner preuailed nothing, but returned as hee came. So as the Emperour to force them to an accord, tooke occafion to giue the gouernment hereditary of all *Frifland* and *Groning* to the houfe of *Saxony*, to hold it in fee of the Empire.

For the attayning whereof, the Dukes of *Saxony* hauing fpent a great part of their means with fmall profit, finding this people fo impatient of a ftrangers yoake, in the end Duke *George* refigned all his intereft vnto the Emperour *Charles* the fifth who enioyed it quietly, as his fonne *Philip* King of *Spaine* alfo did, till within thefe thirty yeares that they freed themfelues by their adiunction vnto the generall vnion of the confederate Prouinces of the *Netherlands*. Thus much we haue thought good to fpeake of the beginning and Eftate of *Frifland* in generall; Now wee will defcribe the townes in particular.

LEEWARDEN.

IS at this day (as in old time *Staueren* was wont

to

to bee) the chiefe towne of *Frifland*, fituated almoft in the center of the countrie, called in ancient time during the Paganifine, *Aula Dei*, and in
the vulgar tongue 𝕲𝖔𝖉𝖗𝖘·𝖍𝖔𝖋𝖋: that it to fay, the
court of God, in the which was a colledge or fchole
for the *Druides*, Philofophers and wife men of
that time, which were come out of *France* to plant
their colleges there. In witneffe whereof, there
are yet in this towne two Temples, the one named
the ancient court, the other the new, whereof the
gentlemen of the country were in former times
called *Hovelingen*, that is to fay courtiers, for
that they were conftituted publike defenders of
this houfe of *God* taught by the *Druides*. And in
truth this towne hath more gentlemen in it, then a-
ny other in *Frifland*. Of this fchoole of the *Druides*,
Synard the wife, a diuine and councellor to *Radbod*
the laft King of the *Frifons* was Rector, whom hee
councelled to perfecute the Chriftians; hee cenfu-
red and caufed *Tullies* bookes of the nature of the
Gods to bee burnt, condemning them as full of errors and contrarie to the doctrine which they
taught, of the falfe Gods of the gentills. This
towne in proceffe of time hauing taken the name
of *Leewarden*, and the country beeing conuerted to
the chriftian Religion, this fchoole of the *Druides*
was changed into a cloifter of Nunnes, by *Vboalt*
in the yeare 1 2 3 3. the which *Dodo* the fourth Abbot of *Fleurencamp*, would haue alfo called, *Aulam
Dei*, for that he would not haue the memory of that
name

name loft . But in the vulgar tongue it hatth beene called *Nyen-cloofter*, that is to fay a New cloifter. They of *Leewarden* haue alwaies continued (as it appeeres by all ancient and moderne writers) and entertained their fchoole in good learning : which hath euer beene the chiefe of all *Frifland*. Vntil that within thefe 20. yeares, the Eftates of the Prouince haue erected an vniuerfity in the town of *Franiker*, two leagues from thence; for the entertainement of which fchoole, as at this prefent of the vniuerfitie, and of the learned profeffors which are there, in all faculties, the magiftrates of *Leuwarden* haue neuer fpared any charge.

In this towne is the court of Parliament for all *Frifland*, which doth determine of all caufes both criminall and ciuill : whether all caufes come and are to bee decided according to the fincerity of the *Romaine* lawes , the which are obferued there with the like purity as they were made by the Emperor *Iuftinian*, and as they are taught in vniuerfities, hauing not aboue twenty municipall lawes or cuftomes, derogating from the written law . All proceedings and other publike acts are made in the Dutch tongue, their ftile of writing, and the forme of their letters and caracters, as wel printed as written, are as pure and neate as in any other courts of *Brabant*, *Flanders*, *Holland*, *Vtrecht*, and other places of the *Netherlands* : So as the naturall *Frifons* as alfo the *Brabanfons*, *Hollanders*, *Flemings* and other Dutche , may eafilie execute all Offices of Magiftrates,

ftrates, Secretaries and Notaries, as well in one countrie as in an other, depending vpon writing, bee it of Iuftice, Pollicy, Account, Treafure or otherwife.

This town of *Leuwarden* is feated in the quarter of *Oftergoe*, being great and fpacious, and conteyning in circuit neere halfe a French league; the ftreetes are faire, large and ftraight, in the whish it is not lawfull to leaue any filthineffe, euery houfe hauing a boate, into the which they caft it; the which beeing full, they tranfport it by barkes into the fieldes: the towne beeing fo diuided by nauigable chanells (whereon there are manie bridges) to ferue as well for the trafficke of marchandife, as for other commodities, fo as moft houfes maie bring their prouiffons vppe to their doores, or not farre from them : The which doe alfo ferue greatly for the clenfing of the ftreetes, the raine wafhing awaie all the filth (if any remaines in the ftreetes) into the chanelles. The ayre is cleere, but fome-what brackifh by reafon of the exhalations of the fea which is nere : which is the caufe that it doth not lightly ingender any putrifaction, neither is it often infected, with any contagious difeafe.

It ftandes in a verie pleafant countrie, full of goodlie Medowes, euen vnto the towneditches, beeing a pleafant fight on Sundaies and Feftiuall dayes, to beholde the Bourgers walking and fupping vppon the greene graffe

by

by troupes. It hath alfo many pleafant villages round about the towne, which feeme as walkes for the Inhabitants. The fituation is (as we haue faid) in the mideft of *Frifland*, fo as on a fommers day they may goe either in wagon, or horfe-backe or on foote on which fide they pleafe, either to *Oftergoe Weftergoe*, or the *Seauen Forefts*, out of the country, where they haue good meanes to goe and tranfport their marchandife by fhipping either great or fmall.

In regard of which commodities and the goodneffe of the feat, *Albertus* Duke of *Saxony* and *George* his fon, hauing obtained the hereditary gouernment of *Frifland* from *Maximilian* the Emperor, did there fettle the Parliament for the whole Prouince, which the Emperour *Charles* the fifth and his fonne King *Philippe*, haue fince allowed and confirmed; moreouer *Frifeland* hath good hauens on euery fide, by the which they may commodioufly and fpeedely bring all forts of marchandife and commodities vnto the town, which makes it cheape lyuing there.

This towne hath vnder his Griteny, that is to fay, Baylewicke or Iurifdiction, which they call *Leewarderadeel* feauenteene good villages depending thereon: for in all the quarter of *Oftergoe*, whereof this towne is the chiefe, there are ten Gritenies, euery one of which hath his villages depending thereon, fome more, fome leffe, conteyning alltogither one hundred thirty and two villages

lages in the fayd ten Gritenies : befides the towne of *Dockum* which is the fecond towne of that quarter of *Oftergoe,*wherof we wi'l prefently fpeak.

In this towne doth commonly refide the colledge of deputies for the Eftates of the whole Prouince,confifting of the nobility and townes,which gouerne the whole Eftate , as well for matters of policy and warre,as for religion,who with the voices of the Gritenies , difpofe of all Eftates and Offices, both of fuftice, treafure and demains,as alfo of captaines places,and others concerning the war and the Ecclefiafticall Eftate.

There is alfo the minte for money for the whole country, both for gold and filuer,according to the order which the deputies for the Eftates fhall fet downe : the which notwithftanding is fubiect to the generalls of the mints of all the vnited Prouinces, when need requires.

The people there are as courteous , humble and affable , yea more then in any other towne of the whole Prouince,or in *Holland* & *Zeeland,* although the *Frifons* haue beene held to bee fome-what rude and inciuill ; the which appeeres contrary by the frequentation of learned men of the court of Parliament,& by the exercife of learning:for that there is not a Bourger,if he haue any means,but he fends his children to fchoole : The which is feene at this day by many learned men,whom I wil not now flatter, for that they are yet lyuing , as alfo by thofe which for their knowledge haue beene of great

R   authority.

authority: Amongſt which was *George Ratalder*, councellor to the King in the great councell at *Macklin*, doctor in the lawes, and a good Poet, who in the yeare 1 5 6 6. was ſent by the Dutcheſſe of *Parma*, Gouerneſſe of the *Netherlands*, in Ambaſſage to the King of *Denmarke*, for the affaires of the ſaid countries. And ſince in regard of his vertues and ſufficiency, he was choſen Preſident of the Prouinciall councell at *Vtrecht*.

A league from this towne is the village of *Zuychem*, famous at this day by the memory of *Viglus Aita Zuychemus*, in his life time Preſident of the councell of Eſtate for the King of *Spaine* at *Bruſſels*, whoſe wife being de d, he was made a Biſhop and Prouoſt of Saint *Bauon* at *Gant* : where hee built a goodly houſe, where one of his heires liues whom I haue viſited within theſe ten yeares : Hee alſo erected a free ſchoole for a certaine number of poore children and a ſchoolemaſter, and beſides it an Hoſpitall for old men and women of that village, the which are well lodged and entertained according to the capacity of the foundation.

DOCKVM.

IS the ſecond towne in all that quarter of *Oſtergoe*, hauing a chanell which goes vnto the ſea, and another which leads vnto *Groning*, which is fiue leagues diſtant from thence, and eight from *Franiker*, whereas commonly the councell or colledge
of

of the Admiralty for the whole Prouince of *Frise-land* doth remaine. This towne hath suffred much during the first troubles, as well in the Duke of *Aluas* time as afterwards, being sometimes forced to obay the one party and then the other; so as yet to this day there appeere some ruines of this intestine warre. I haue not beene in any towne in *Holland*, whereas they liue better cheape in their Innes then here, wherby we may Iudge how the Burgers do, which make their prouisions at the best hand. I haue found there learned men and very courteous, and it is famous for that it is the place where-*Gemma* Frisius was borne, whom in my youth I knew at *Louuain* a great Phisition and Mathematicien, whereof his workes giue sufficient testymony. He died at *Louuain* in the yeare 1 5 5 5. leauing one son called *Cornelius Gemma Frisius*, of the same profession that his father was. In this town is carefully kept and with great reuerence, the booke of the holie *Euangelists*, written by Saint *Boniface* himselfe, who was before called *Winfrid*, hee who after Saint *Willebroard* (otherwise called *Clement*) did greatly augment the faith of I e s v s C h r i s t in *Frisland*, where afterwards he was made a martir, with 52. of his companiõs, in *Westfrisland*: where they say there are yet some of that race which massacred thé, who from their birth carry a white marke, or rather a tuft of white haire on their heads. They may go easily from this towne by boat vnto all the townes of *Frisland*, and by sea to all parts of the world.

R 2   *F R A.*

FRANIKER.

THis is one of the moſt ancient and renownedſt townes in *Friſland*, in the which not farre from the port of *Harlingen*, there is a little caſtle, in the which *Henry* ſonne to Duke *Albert* of *Saxony* was for a time as it were beſieged by the other townes of *Friſland*, which hee tooke ſo diſdainefully, as hee reſigned all his intereſt in the ſayd countrie to his Brother *George*, who ſince ſold it to the Emperour *Charles* the fifth. Although that the caſtles of *Leuwarden* and *Harlingen*, were during the warres ruined, yet this beeing of ſmall importance ſtands ſtill; for that it hath no meanes to a-noy the towne, hauing no paſſage without it wher-by they might giue entry vnto the enemy, but doth onely ſerue for a gentlemans lodging. The towne is ſeated in the quarter of *Weſtergoe*, which is the ſe-cond part of *Friſland*, in the which beſides *Franiker* there are eight townes more, which are, *Harlin-gen*, *Bolſwaert*, *Sneck*, *Ylſit*, *Worcum*, *Hindelopen*, *Sta-ueren* and *Sloten*, vnder which quarter there are eight *Griſtenies* or *Baylewycks*, the which one with an other haue 1 2 5. villages depending on them. It is a good towne, being three quarters of an houres circuit, in which many gentlemen of the champi-an country make their reſidence, and ſome lyuing in the country during the Sommer, retire thether in the Winter.

The

The Eftates of *Frifland* defiring to prouide for
the inftruction of their youth, haue within thefe
twenty yeares erected an vniuerfity in the fayd
towne, with great priuileges, the which maks it the
more famous, in the which they entertaine many
profeffors in al faculties, with good penfions, which
drawes many fchollers thether from all parts, euen
out of *Poland* and *France*: whereas the Eftates of
the country haue a fworne printer. They of the
Magiftracie haue of late yeares built a faire towne
houfe. It is two leagues from *Leuwarden*, and one
from *Harlingen*, whether they may goe in Sommer
both by water, and by wagon, but in Winter onely
by boate.

BOLSWAERDT.

IS a free *Hans* towne, fituated in the third diuifion
of the quarter of *Weftergoe*, in a good countrie, a league equally diftant from *Sneck*, *Ylft* and
Worcom, a league and a halfe from *Hindelopen*, and
two leagues from *Staueren*, *Sloten*, *Franiker* and
Harlingen: three from *Leuwarden*, and fiue from
Dockom, and fo enuironed in a manner by all the
townes in the countrie. It is a good towne, with
a chanell which goes to all thefe other townes and
villages: whereby the ftreetes are alwaies cleane
from filthe, by reafon that the rayne doth clenfe
them: it is equall with *Sneck* in bigneffe. The Inhabitants for the moft part liue of their handiworkes,

R 3 marchandife,

marchandife, and nauigations, traffiking for the
moſt part with the *Hamburgers*. It hath a paſſage
vnto the ſea by the Sluſe of the village of *Mackum*,
a leagúe from thence, whereas the ſhippes of the
ſayd towne lie as ſafely as in a good hauen. The
Gouernors of the Eſtate of this towne are called
Bourguemaſters, Aldermen and Councell. The
Bourguemaſters and Aldermen haue the admini-
ſtration of Iuſtice, beeing ſixe in number. Two
which are of the councell haue care of the works,
reparations and entertainement of the fortifications and gates of the towne, and meddle not with
the Iuſtice, but their charge is alſo to looke vnto
all crimes that are commited, and to deliuer the
offenders to the Officer, to bee puniſhed according
to the exigence of the fact: which Regents and
Adminiſtrators receiue their authorite and commiſſion yearely from the Gouernor and councel of
the Prouince. There was in old time three Monaſteries in the town. The pore haue good entertainmēt,
the *Orphins* founded by *Rheine*, Bourguemaſter
of the towne, the which was indowed with more lyuing by *Hyde* the daughter of *Hero*, being a widow.
   Then the ritch Hoſpitall, whereas many poore
people are fed all at one table, with their lodging.
Then the poore Hoſpitall, whereas many poore
old people haue euerie one a chamber a part and
are entertained there with bread, beere, butter and
firing, from whence the poore people of the
towne haue once a weeke releefe. This towne is
                                             ſince

since the yeare of our Lord 1 5 7 2. much increafed , and well fortefied as well in portes, rampars, bulwarkes , as otherwife . The Burgers haue endured much,as well in their trafficke at fea,as in lodgging of fouldiars . This towne hold a market euery Saterday, whether the inhabitants of all the nereft townes and villages , *Grieteines* or *Barlewyckr* come and bring their marchandife and victualls, with greatftore of wild-foule & venifon:they want no fifh alfo,both from the frefh water and fea. The Bayliff of *Wouferadeel* comes thither euery marketday to hold his feat of iuftice,and to do right to all men of his iurifdiction,where the *Grietemin* or *Bailife* doth prefide,withhis Afleffors & Iurats,hauing vnder them 29. villages, and two monafteries, that is the Abbay of *Fleurecampe* of men and one of women called *Oogecloefter* , now ruined in thefe laft wars,& their reuenue applied to the comon caufe. Nere vnto this town is a village named *womels*,famous for the birth of that learned man *Cyprianus womelius* a doctor of the law and a great Poet,councellor in the Imperiall chamber at *Spyer* . Thefe of this towne of *Bolfwart* did many years fince ioyne thefelues to the *Hans* towns of *Germany*,with whom they are confederate , and are regiftred among the members thereof,inioying the like priuileges,freedomes and exemptions of impofts and cuftomes, as the other townes of *Denmarke*, *Sueden*, *Norwaie*, *Liuonia*,*Pruffia*, *Eaft* country,and other Principalities and common-weales.

R 4   Hauing

Hauing alfo their chamber or lodging of Efter-
lings in *Antwerp*, and at the Stylliard in *London*, the
which is now out of vfe, which priuiledges the inhabitants of the faid towne inioye, bringing onely
a certificate of their Bourgefie vnder the feale of
the towne of *Bolfwaert* : The which was wont to
yeeld them great profit in nauigation and traffick:
It was practifed generallie throughout all the
Hans townes, the better to entertaine their com-
merce, and mutuall correfpondencie, and to traine
vppe their youth in the trade of marchandife, from
one Prouince to an other, no married men beeing
admitted in thofe places of *London* and *Antwerp*,
onelie young men doing their owne bufineffe or
their Maifters, fo as they bee members of this companie. As for the foundation of this towne of *Bolf-*
waert wee finde that it was built by the Ladie *Bolf-*
wine daughter to *Radbod* King of *Frifland*, in the
yeare 7 1 3. which Ladie was married to the Siegnior of *Teekenbourg*, iffued from the Noble houfe
of *Dockenburg*, the which of a caftle was made a
towne, and is now called *Dockum*. This Ladie being
a widowe, retired her felfe from *Teekenburg*, into
this quarter of *Frifland* whereas King *Radbod* her
father gaue her a houfe of pleafure, and there fhee
built a fmall towne, which fhee called by her owne
name *Bolfwaert*, for that it was feated in a halfe
Ifland : the which the *Danes* and *Normans* did often ruine, yet in the end it became a good towne
of trafficke.

Being

Beeing in that towne it was told mee that at that time of the foundation, the sea came vp vnto it, but since the land hath wonne much of the sea, so as it staies at the village of *Mackum*.

STAVEREN.

IT is the most ancient, and was in former times, the cheefe towne of all *Frisland*, wherof we haue sufficiently discoursed, of the same society and company, but more ancient then that of *Bolswaert*, whose priuiledges (especially their precedence at the *Sond* in *Denmarke* before all other shippes) wee haue made mention of before, being needlesse now to make any further repetitiõ: it stands vpon the sea on the South side, on the entry of the gulph of *Zuyderzee*, at the point which lookes towards *Holland*, almost opposite to the passage of *Enchuysen*, halfe a league from *Hinderlopen* vppon the same shoare. It seemes that this is the place whereas time the people kept, whome *Plinie* cals *Sturi*, of which name all *Frisland* was sometimes called *Regnum Stauriæ:* Which Kingdome did extend to *Nymegen*, where was wont to be ingrauen on the East Port, *hic limes Imperii*, Heere is the bounds of the Empire, and on the West gate, *Hic finis Regni Stauriæ*, Heere is the end of the *Stauriens* Kingdome : so as there is no doubt but heretofore it hath been a rich and mighty Towne, but the tempests and Inondations of the sea haue often annoyed it, and driuen it farther into

the

the country, beeing told mee when I went to view it , that the old towne was a League nerer to the Sea , and now in the bottome of the Sea : Besides certaine barres of Sand haue ſtopt the Hauen , and taken away their nauigation, as wee haue formerly obſerued. There was wont to bee a ſtrong Caſtle at the end of the towne, looking towardes the Sea and the Hauen: But during theſe laſt troubles , the Captaine which was put in gard there with a garriſon, beeing beſeeged by the Eſtates growing wilful and reſolute to keepe it, his ſoldiers hauing ſmal hope of any ſuccors, yeelded vp the place, and deliuered their Captaine to the Eſtates ; who cauſed it to bee preſently raized , as wee may ſee by a great part of the ruines. The towne is long and narrow, inlarged and fortified with rampars and bulwarks, but of ſmall importance and ill intertained , as beeing held at this preſent time not greatly neceſſarie : The houſes in the great ſtreete are reſonable faire and well built , the Inhabitants liue by their handy-workes and by the Sea , but not of ſuch nauigation and trafficke as they were wont to haue.

HARLINGEN.

IT is now a good and ſpatious towne , and of good trafficke , ſince that *Gaſper Robles* Lord of *Billy*, Gouernor of the country of *Friſland* and *Groning* , for the King of *Spaine* cauſed the bankes
behinde

behinde the Caſtle, to bee repayred and inlarged, with great labour and coſt, which doth now defend it from the tempeſts and waues of the ſea which beate againſt it, which worke the Inhabitants (notwithſtanding the hard gouernment of the ſayd *Robles*) cannot ſufficiently commend.

The Eſtates of *Friſland* hauing ſince theſe laſt troubles reſumed their liberty, haue cauſed the ſaid Caſtle to bee ruined ſo farre as it did ouerlooke the Towne, retaining the fortification which lookes towards the Sea and the Bankes, hauing in the ſame place where the ditch was drawne a goodly new Hauen into the Towne, which paſſeth vnder a great draw-bridge, to go vnto the Port and not farre from it, whereas a great number of Shippes may lye ſafely. The reſt of the Towne that is inlarged, is fortified with good rampars and Bulwarks. There are two chanells which comming from the ſea to the olde hauen, paſſe through the towne, whereof the one goes to *Franiker* a league from thence, from whence at all houres of the day Boates doe go with paſſengers, at an eaſie rate. This towne being thus ſituated vppon the Sea, hath the beſt hauen and neereſt vnto the ſea of any other in all *Friſland*, where they are rich Marchants, who beſides their ordinary trade in the country, aduenter much in long voyages, for the which they make goodly ſhippes.

SNECKE.

SNECK.

IS a good little country Towne, feated in a plaine three leagues from *Leuwarden*, and one from *Ilſt*: the which hath Deputies alſo at the Eſtates of Friſ. *land* : Heretofore it had goodly Cloyſters, both within and without the town, the which at this day are all ruined and applyed to other vſes, and their reuenues imployed to the common cauſe, or to ſome workes of Hoſpitality, Piety or Schooles. It is honoured for that it is the place where *Doctor Hopperus* was borne, who hath written many goodly workes with great credit, and hath ioyned practiſe & wiſdom to his knowledge: for which reſpect he was firſt of the Priue Counſell for the King of *Spaine* at *Bruſſels*, and from thence was called into *Spaine*, to ſupply the place of *Tiſeuach* Preſident of the Counſell of Eſtate for the *Netherlands*.

SLOTEN.

A Little towne neere vnto the gulph of the *Zuy-derzee* lying on the South part vppon the ſea, a league and a halfe from *Staueren*; it hath no other trade then Nauigation, and that which depends on the ſea.

ILST.

STandes vppon the VVeſt, halfe a league from
Snecke,

Sneeke , and vppon the *Nortweſt* a League from *Bolſwaert*,on the South ſide as farre from *Sloten:* It is an open towne,yet hath it municipal lawes , it is inuironed with a large ditch , which may defend it from the incurſions of the enemies,or of any other inſolent perſons. It conſiſts of two long rankes of faire houſes,from the Eaſt vnto the Weſt: through the which doth paſſe a chanell, the which on either banke is planted with high trees,which do beautifie the towne. There is but one Pariſh Church,which was wont to be a Couent of Carmelites; being ruined in theſe laſt troubles,but the Temple ſtands ſtil.

It appeares by the Antiquities of *Friſland*, that in the yeare one thouſand two hundred ſixty three, this town was one of the moſt ancient of the country , famous for their Nauigation and trafficke. Now it is the Store-houſe for ſhip-timber,for ſuch veſſels as paſſe from one place vnto an other within the country , more then to any other towne in *Friſland. Albert* Duke of *Saxony*, according to the Donation made vnto him by the Emperour *Maximillian* the firſt of the Hereditary gouernment of *Friſland* , tooke poſſeſſion of that towne , as the whole Iuriſdiction of *VVeſtergoe*,and moreouer beeing neere vnto that of the ſeauen Foreſts, after that hee had raized the ſiege and freed his ſon at *Franiker* , hee became in a manner Maiſter of all *Friſland*.

WOR-

WORCVM.

TO ſpeake truly , is but a good Bourough,
yet hath it the priuiledges of a Towne ioyning vppon the ſea , entering into it by a great
Scluſe which pierceth the banke , a League fom
Bolſwaert , from whence I haue gone thether
both by water and by land. It hath alſo a Chanell from one end vnto an other which goes
vnto the ſayd Scluſe. According to the ſituation it is a place which hath good meanes to liue
in , and good cheape. It is gouerned by Bour-
guemaiſters and Aldermen , but for all matters
of Iuſtice it reſorts to the Prouinciall Councell at
Leuwaerden.

HINDELOPEN.

SO called by reaſon of the retreate of the wilde
beaſtes (at ſuch time as *Friſland* was halfe
Foreſt) which they doe call *Hinden* in their countrie language , and *Loopen* which is to runne,which
is as much to ſay , as the courſe and recourſe of
Stagges and Hindes : it was firſt a place for hunting,then by a little and a little made a Village,and
the Sea eating vp to it, which gaue it a good roade
it became a Bourough, well knowne at this daie,
for their Nauigation, which is the peoples cheeſe
practiſe.

Hauing

Hauing defcribed the two principal quarters of
Frifland, that is *Oftergoe* and *Weftergoe* , with their
townes : we muft now fpeake of

THE SEAVEN FORESTS.

THis quarter fo called by reafon of the feauen
Forefts which were wont to bee there , but
now turned for the moft part into pafture and
land for tillage , which make the third quarter of
Frifland , confifting of eight Gretenies or Baylywicks , all which together haue feauenty fiue villages, among the which there are good Borroughs,
the which ioyntly haue their Deputies (bee they
Gryetmen or others) at the ordinary Affemblie of
the Eftates of the faid Prouince , in the towne of
Leuwaerden. Thefe names fhould bee troublefome
to the Reader, by reafon of the ftrangeneffe therof.
to fet downe in writing the appellations of all the
Gretenies of the three quarters of *Frifland* , beeing
in number 28. the which I cannot terme more properly, then Bailywicks , & their Grietmen Bailiffs.
    There are fome Ilandes depending vppon *Fri-
fland* , among the wich *Amelandt* & *Schellinck* are
the chiefe , the firft belonging to a particular Lord,
who during the troubles hath held it free and neu-
ral paying fome contribution vnto the Admiralty,
of *Dunkerke*, fo as the fhips of the faid Iland might
faile freely to al places, as alfo the *Dunkerkers* might
go and refrefh them-felues in the fayd Iland.
                                                        There

there are three good Villages in the said Iland, besides *Amelandt* (whereas the Seignior hath his lodging) recouered from the sea- The Estates of the said country haue also within these thirty yeares a good portion of ground which they call the *Bildt*, which is now wel defended with Dikes, and is made the fertilest quarter in al *Frisland*, where they haue appointed a Bayliffe or Receiuer, for it is of great proffit and reuenue.

There are in diuers parts of *Frisland* turfes, some hard and firme, others more light, which make not so good coale as the first: and wheras they haue no turfes, the Peasants vse the dung of their cattel, with which they cutte reedes very small, and mingle it together, and then they dry it for the Winter: they say that bacon dryed with this fire, is more firme then any other. This Country yeeldes many good and strong Horses, which are transported through all Europe: as also great Oxen and very fatte. Their Kine are very fertill, the which do often bring forth two calues at once; & the ewes two or three lambs, and sometimes foure together, where the Sheepe are very bigge of bodie, but not so sweete and sauory as those of *Berry*, *Arthois*, *Cempenie* in *Brabant*, which haue a dry feed, and are lesse.

OVERYSSELL.

THis Conty of *Oueryssell* in former times vnder the Principallitie of the Bishops of *Vtrecht*,
was

was then called the high diocefe , But fence that
the Emperor *Charles* the fifth obtained from the
bifhop the temporality of both diocefes the higher
and the lower; hee made two Prouinces , one of *V-
trecht* and the other of *Oueryfel*, the which are numbred among the 17. Prouinces, and now vnder the
vnion of the Generall eftates of the confederate
Prouinces: who by armes haue fhak't of the Spanifh yoake , and haue purchafed their liberty,
which they enioy at this day. This country is fo
called for that it lies beyond the riue of *Yffel*: this
Duch word *Ouer*, fignifying beyond, and in Latin
Trans, fo as it was called *Tranfiffalana*. On the north
fide it hath *Frifeland*, and a part of the country of
Groning; on the South the Conty of *Zutphen*: to
Eaft the country of *Weft-phalia*, and vpon the Weft
the *Zuyderzee*. It is watred by many riuers, the *Yffel*,
Vidre, *Regge*, *Dan-noire* and *Wahal*, befids the chanels
which are kept in by the Sluce : A good and fertill foyle, and fat paftures, where they doe yearely feed many fatte cattell. There is abundance of
good butter and cheefe and all other forts of
victuall.

The whole Prouince is diuided into three great
Baylywicks; that is of *Salandt*, of the old *Saliens*: of
Tuent, fo called of the ancient *Tubantins*: and of
Vollenhouen, which is in the mideft of the other two,
whereof the one bends to the North and the other
to the South. The quarter of *Salandt* compre-
hends vnder it many good townes among the
S   which

which are thefe three Imperiall *Hans* townes. *De-uenter,Campen* and *Swolle:*the leiſer are *Haſſelt,Couo-erden*, *Genemuiden*, *Ommen*, *Hardenbourg*, *Wilſon* and *Graff-horſt* . That of *Tuent* hath the townes, of *Oldenzeel,Otmarſon*, *Enſchede,Ghoor*, *Diyepenham, Delden*, *Riſſen*, and *Almeloo* : The quarter of *Vollenhouen* hath a towne of that name with a **Caſtle** which was wont to be the Biſhop of *Vtrechts Pallace* when they came into the high diocefe : then the towne of *Steenwieke*, to which the *Cuyndert* did belong,which was wont to be famous for the ſtrength of the Caſtle, the which was ruined in thefe laſt **warres.**

Among the fortefied townes, befides the three Imperiall *Hans* townes of *Deuenter*, *Campen* and *Swolle*, are thofe of *Haſſelt* vpon *Vidre* (to diſtinguiſh it from *Haſſelt* a good towne in the country of *Liege)Oldenzeel,Steenwick,Otmarſom* and *Enſcheede.* There are alfo a great number of caſtles and aboue 120.*Borroughs* and villages.

The fouerainty of this Prouince,before the troubles in the Netherlands, did belong vnto *Phillip* the fecond King of *Spaine*, who fucceded the Emperor *Charles* the fift his father , who had the intereſt (confirmed by the Pope) from *Henry* of *Bauaria* Biſhoppe of V*trecht*, vpon certaine conditions, the cheefe whereof was, that hee ſhould maintaine their priuiledges ; for want whereof and to free them from the oppreffion of the *Spaniards,* they haue(as all the other vnited Prouinces) treed
them-

them-felues and recouered their liberty: whereof the people (as well as the *Frifons*) are wonderfully defirous, and impatient to beare the yoake.

The fayd Prouince hath neuer acknowledged but two members in their gouernment, that is, the Nobility, of the which are chofen the particular gouernors, and high officers, and they three Imperiall townes, *Deuenter*, *Campen* and *Swoll*, and no others. By the voices & fuffrages of which two members, all difficulties in the Eftate are decided: And whatfoeuer hath bin decreed by them according to the conftitutions of the country, fhall remaine firme and ftable: And as the nobility in precedence yeeld not to any; no more do the towns, but in their order and degree: whereof *Deuenter* is the firft, then *Campen*, and laft *Swoll*: euery one of which townes iudge by decree as well in ciuill as criminal caufes; and either of them hath priuiledge to coine money. Let this fuffice for a breefe defcription of the Eftate of the country of *Oueryffell*: Let vs now come to a particular defcription of the townes

DEVENTER.

THE firft of the three Imperiall *Hans* townes is feated vppon the right banke of the riuer of *Yffell* three leagues from *Zutphen*, and foure from *Swoll*. It was a goodly great town, and of great traffick before the laft troubles: But the two fieges which they haue beene forced to endure with

S 2   in

in thefe thirty yeares by the vnited Eftates, hath much decayed it. The firft time in the yeare 1 5 7 8. when it was yeelded to the Earle of *Reneberg*, Lieutenant for the faid Eftates and the country, fince the earle of *Lecefter* gouernor for the Queene of *England* Protectreffe of the vnited Prouinces, gaue the Gouermnent thereof to Sir *William Stanley* an *Eng ifh* Collonel, who fold it to the *Spaniard*: So as it remained fubiect to the *Spanifh* infolencies, from the yeare 1 5 8 7, vnto the yeare 1 5 9 1. when as Prince *Maurice* went to befeege it with the faid Eftates, in the which Cont *Harman Vanden Bergh*, Coufin german to the Prince commanded, whome hee forced to yeelde by compofition, after a great battery; the ruines whereof will not be eafily repaired in many yeare., efpecially towards the kaye.

But whereas the cannon could not anoy them, it is well built, with faire high houfes, the ftreets broad and cleane with a faire market place, in the mideft whereof is the houfe of the fworne companies, whereas a gard is kept day and night, before the great Collegiall Church is the townehoufe which they call *Raed huys* that is to fay, the councell houfe, whereas the Bourguemafters and Senators doe affemble dayly to doe iuftice to euery man. The Magiftrats there fhew them-felues modeftly graue, and the Burgers ciuill, among whome there are rich Marchants, by the trafficke which they haue of all forts of Marchandife, as

well

of marchandife, as well by Land into *Weftphalia* and other places of Germany, as by the riuer of *Yf-fel*, which on one fide mounts vp the *Rhin* vnto *Colo-gne*, and defcends downe before *Campen* to the *Zuy-derzee*, vnto *Amfterdam*, *Horne*, *Enchuyfen* and other Towns of *Holland* and *Frifeland*, Since it was laft yeelded, it is wunderfully fortified with ram-pars and good Bullwarkes, befides that it hath al-waies had a double wal of Bricke round about it. In ould time when as matters fuceeded not well in the diocefe of *Vtrecht*, the Bifhops retired themfelues to *Deuenter*, as we reade of Bifhop *Baldric*, who to fly the fury of the *Normans* and *Danes* which ruined the towne of *Vtrecht*, retired with all his clergy to this towne: then the *Danes* being chafed away, he returned and repared the Cathedrall Church, which they had made a ftable for their horfes. In this towne doth vfually refide the *Droffart (or* great *Bay-liffe)* for the quarter of *Salandt*, whereof this is the chiefe towne, and in the which there is great ftore of gentlemen.

CAMPEN.

THis is the fecond of three Hans townes in the Prouince of *Oueryfell*, although it be not like to all the reft, on the other fide of the riuer of *Yffel*, but on *Gelders* fide, it is a faire great towne, of more length then breadth, the which after that it had beene yeelded vnto the Earle of

Renelerg

Reneberg in the name of the Eftates, it was much better fortified then before. It hath a-goodly bridge vpon the riuer, at the end whereof they did then build a good fort to defend it ; by which bridge they may goe both on horfe-backe, Wagon and foote, to all the townes of *Oueryfel*, *Frifeland* and *Groning*, or elfe if they will by the chanells which rune through the country. Hauing paft this bridge, going towards *Vollenhouen* & *Geelmuyden*, you enter into a goodly great and fpatious pafture, full of diches, which they cal *Maefter brouk*, which yeelds as good butter and cheefe as any part in *Holland*: befids, that in a fhort time it fats a great number of goodly Oxen. This pafture hath at the leaft foure leagues in circuit, from the bridge of *Campen* vnto *Geelmuyden* along the riuer of *Vidre*, paffing before the towne of *Haffelt*, then paffing on to *Swolle*, it returnes from thence to *Campen*, which circuit is a halfe dayes iorny. It is good cheape lyuing in this towne, there is aboundance of frefh water fifh and good cheape, as Salmon, Sturgion, Carpes, Barbels and Pikes. I did once buy three Carpes there, either being a foote and a halfe long for fixe Patars a peece, the which tide to the barke, and fwimming in the *Zuyderzee*, I brought a liue to *Amfterdam*, All forts of victuall are good cheape there, efpecially foules and Ducke and Mallard. This towne is full of Gentlemen and learned men: the houfes are faire and high built, and ftreets very cleane. It is much inlarged and beautified
within

within thefe twelue or thirteene yeares . The Magiftrates are affable and the people ciuill and courteous, whereas thofe that are fled thether for relligion are kindly entertayned, yea they are drawne thether to fet vp their trades, being very fit for it, for that the Marchants and workemen may goe in one night with a good wind to *Amſterdam*, and going from thence at night, af-⸱er the difpach of their bufines, they may bee the next day againe at their owne houfes, which is a great commodity. This towne hath priuiledge to coyne mony, and they carefully entertaine a free fchole.

SWOLLE.

IS a land towne, of a round forme, fituated vp-on a little Brooke running into the riuer of *Vidre*, and from thence by the blacke water into the *Zuyderzee* : It is held to bee ſtrong, hauing euer had double walles and double diches : fince thefe troubles it hath beene fortified with new rampars and Bulwarks. In former times it was wont in time of daunger to bee the retreat of the Gouernor and of the Councell of that country, who made his refidence at *Vollenhouen*. It is good cheape liuing there, but the ſtreets are not fo cleane kept as at *Campen*, by reafon of the Cattell which they keepe within the towne and the great multitude of Wagons which come thether

S 4   from

from all parts;for it is of greater trafficke then *Campen*. It hath not bene any way anoyed by fiege during thefe troubles,like to *Deuenter* and *Campen*,be-
ing fallen into the Eftates power,by the preuention
of the well affected *Burgers*,who chafed away them
of the *Spanifh* faction , whereby they are become
rich. It hath two chanels which paffe through it,
vpon the greateft of them ftands the Market place,
which is faire and fpatious, and ioyning vnto it the
great Temple of Saint *Michel*; then a little lower,
is our Ladies Church.In honor of this Town thefe
foure latin verfes were made.

S-wolla *diu celebris meruit virtutibus arma,
Quæ populum fortem nobilitare folent:
Inde falutifera vetere pietate,fid que,
In* Tripolim *recipi fædere digna fuit.*

Swolls vertue whilom got thefe armes , that grace,
the vndanted troop that won them and their race:
And for hir faith and Martial brood ,'t was fhee
was only held fit guard for *Tripoli*.

For that it is the third imperial *Hans* Town of this
Prouince of *Oueryffell* , hauing priuiledge to coine
both gold and filuer , as the two others , wee haue
defcribed thefe three chiefe Townes : let vs now
come vnto the leffer , but ftrong and wel fortified.

STEEN-

STEENWYCK.

IS situated vpon a brooke called *Blockerzyel*, comming out of the country not far from the towne, and falls nere vnto *Vollenhouen* into the *Zuyderzee*; In lesse then twenty years it felt two sieges, the one by *Charles* Earle of *Manffeldt* for the Prince of *Parma*, who was forced to retire, the towne beeing victualed by Count *william*, *Lewis* of *Naffau*, *Philippe* Earle of *Hohenloo* and Generall *Norris*. Being afterwards surprised by the *Spaniards*, Prince *Maurice* went to besiege it in the yeare of our Lord 1592. the which hee did so importune both by batterie and myne, as (notwithstanding the great losse of his men, he himselfe being also shot in the cheeke,) hee forced them to yeeld by composition. It is not ten yeares since the *Spaniards* made another enterprise, but it succeeded not. It was much defaced by these two sieges, but it now begins to recouer it selfe.

HASSEL.

THis town is called *Haffel* vpon the *Vidre*, to distinguish it from *Haffel* nere vnto *Tongre* in the country of *Liege*: it is two leagues from *Volenhouen*, in ancient time a good and ritch towne by reason of the commoditie of the riuer of *Vidre* which runnes into the *Zuyderzee*, at *Gheelmuyden*,

being

beeing mingled with the two little riuers of *Regge* and *Veecht*. It is at this day reasonably well fortefied, but it hath no such trafficke as it it was accustomed, yet it is a prettie towne and well gouerned.

OLDENZEEL.

IS the towne which they call in Latin. *Veteres Salij*, from whence some will maintaine (but without any great ground) that the lawe Salike comes. It hath also felt the fruits of their last warres, hauing beene besieged in the yeare of our Lord 1605. and yeelded to the Marquis *Spinola*, for the Arch-dukes *Albertus* and *Isabella* of *Austria*, Dukes of *Brabant* Earles of *Flanders* &c. It is a reasonable great towne and of good trade, where they make great store of fine lynen cloth, which they sell in the *Netherlands*, and is sent into *Spaine*.

OTMARSVM.

IS called in Latin *Veteres Marsii*, which are the old *Marsians* whom *Pliny* and *Titus Liuius* doe often mention, being seated in the country of the *Tubansins*, which at this present is *Tuent*, a quarter in the Prouice of *Oueryssel*. It is a little towne and of small importance, yet hath it thrise tasted the fruites of warre, as well by siege as otherwise: Beeing vnable

to

to endure a long fiege by reafon of the weakneffe
thereof, lying in an open country, whereas either
partie(being Maifter of the field) might eafily cut
off their victualls. In the yeare 1 5 9 2. Prince
Maurice tooke it in leffe then foure and twenty
houres, where as the Siegnior of *Famas*, Generall
of the artillery for the Eftates was flaine, a gentleman much lamented by the Prince, and of all men
of warre of his partie : within thefe three yeares
the Marquis *Spinola* recouered it with as much
eafe . To conclude this towne and *Oldenzeel*
are fo weake , as they muft yeelde to the firft
enemie that comes with any force for to befiege them.

ENSCHEDE.

THis towne is of reafonable good traffick, fituated in the open country, in the quarter of *Tuent*, a league from *Oldenzeel*, and two from *Otmar-
fum* : it felt in the yeare 1 597. the waight of Prince
Maurices forces, to whom it was forced to yeeld by
compofition, at the fame time when as *Grolle, Bre-
fort, Lingen* and others were taken.

VOLLENHOVEN.

VVAs not 30. years fince a good town, lying vpon the gulphe of the *Zuyderzee*. two leagues
from *steenwyck*. It was wont to haue a faire, great
and

and pleafant caftle , which was the court of the
Princes , Bifhoppes of *Vtrecht* , when as they came
into the high diocefes, and therefore it was a town
renowned , where there was good commoditie of
victualls , brought thether both by water and by
land : And moreouer after that the temporall E-
ftate of *Vtrecht* came vnto the Emperor, the Gouernor of the Prouince and the councell made their
refidence there . But the laft troubles haue greatly
impayred it, and the caftle is ruined.

GHEELMVYDEN.

HAth runne the fame fortune that *Vollenhouen*,
from whence it is a league diftant , and as
much from *Haffel*, that ftands vpon the Gulphe of
Vidre, towards the *Zuyderzee*, hauing towards the
land the pleafant paftures of *Maefterbrouck*, in like
manner a league from *Campen*. The caftle wherein
the King of *Spaine* was wont to keepe a garrifon,
hath beene alfo ruined.

MEPPEL.

THis towne is feated vpon a little brooke, which
neere vnto *Gheelmuyden* falls into the *Vidre*. It
was neuer of any great importance, and now it is
in a manner all ruined.

HAR-

HARDENBERG.

WAs in ancient time a good towne vpon the same riuer of *Beecht*, where there was wont to bee a good caftle, whereas the Bifhops of *Vtrecht* tooke great delight, for that it ftood in an open country. It is mid-way betwixt *Coeworden* and *Ommen*, both the towne and caftle are to this day almoft ruined by thefe laft warres.

COEWARDEN.

BEfore the laft fiege which Prince *Maurice* of *Naffau* laied before it, the which hee tooke by compofition, it was but a little bafe towne, commanded by a great and ftrong caftle. The *Droffart* hearing of the Princes approach, caufed the fayd towne to be burnt and ruined, to the end the enemy fhould haue no commodity to lodge there: yet hee did fo preffe this towne both by battry and myne, as the *Droffart* was forced to yeeld it; fome two moneths after the taking of *Steenwyck* by the fayd Prince, lying in the fame countrie of *Oueryffel*, In the yeare 1593. Cont *Herman vanden Berghe* and *Verdugo* went to befiege it, but when as they faw, they could not preuaile any thing, neither by battery nor myne, hauing changed their firft refolution, and thinking to famifh it in time, they ftopt vp all the paffages with forts, fo as nothing could
enter

enter into it : yet the Princes men that were in garrison within the caftle, maintained themfelues with great conftancy and refolution a whole winter; vntill the Spring, when as the Prince came with a good army to victuall it in defpight of all thefe forts : which Cont *Herman* and *Verdugo* feeing, abandoning all their forts or burning them, they retired : wherefore the Prince hauing victualed it at eafe, and fupplied it with frefh men, the fame Sommer, being in the yeare 1 5 9 7. hee went to befiege the towne of *Groning*, the which hee tooke, as wee wil fhew hereafter. Since the Eftates haue giuen order for the repayring of the towne, for that it is a good paffage to goe by land into *Frifland*, the countries of *Groning*, *Weftphalia*, *Breme* and other places.

RYSSEN.

IS feated vpon the riuer *Regge*, the which runnes into *Vidre* at *Heffel*, and paffing from thence before *Gheelmuyden*, it falls into the *Zuyderzee*. It is fo little and at this day fo deformed, as it merits not the name of a good towne.

DIEPENHEM.

VPon the fame riuer of *Regge*, it is a league or little more from *Ryffen*, and two leagues from *Enfchede*. At this prefent it is but a Bourrough, although

although with all the small townes, it hath the priuiledges of a towne.

GHOER.

IS a Borrough standing vpon a brooke which runnes into *Regge* at *Diepenhem*, from whence it is a league distant. It hath during these warres had a great fort, which was alwaies taken, when as either party was maister of the field.

DELDEN.

THis was wont to bee a good towne, and of trafficke but now is much decaied by reason of the last warres ; hauing beene subiect to the passing and lodging of souldiars of either party, for (as I haue sayd) hee that was maister of the field, was alwaies maister of those petty places.

AMELOO.

IS built vpon a brooke comming from *Oldenzeel*, the which two leagues from thence falls into the *Vidre*, it is at this present but a Bourg.

WILSEN.

IS at this daie but a village, seated vppon the waie as you goe from *Campen* to *Swolle*,

yet

yet hath it the priuiledges of a towne, and is numbred among the leſſer townes.

GRAFFHORST.

IS ſituated vpon the gulfe of the riuer of *Teſſl*, entring into *Zuyderzee*, halfe way betwixt *Campen* and *Gheelmuyden*. It is but a ſmall village, not ſo good as *wilſen*, yet hath it the title and rights of a towne.

All this is comprehended in the country of *O-ueryſſel*, which is the ſeauenth in ranke of the eight vnited Prouinces of the *Netherlands*, which haue recouered their liberty by armes, and acknowledge at this day no Soueraigne Prince but the generall Eſtates of the ſayd vnion: which eight Prouinces are, the Dutchie of *Geldres*, the Earledomes of *Holland*, *Zeeland* and *Zutphen*, the Siegneuries of *V-trecht*, *Friſland*, *Oueryſſel* and *Groning. Weſt-Friſland* (whereof they might make a Prouince by it ſelfe) is comprehended vnder the county of *Holland*, who giue it the name of *Noort-holland*; which the *Weſt-Friſös* wil not willingly heare of: for they haue their particular Eſtates, Admiralty, Officers and Mynte. Prince *Maurice* of *Naſſau* hath this Prouince of *O-ueryſſel*, vnder his gouernment, with *Geldre*, *Holland*, *Zeeland*, *Zutphen* and *Vtrecht*.

The aſſembly of the Eſtates of the ſaid Prouince, both generall and particular is diuerſly made, according to the ancient cuſtomes & preheminences

of

of euery quarter, not tied in that regard to any
townes, but according their order and ranke; the
deputies changing often, I haue feene them held in
a country houfe. Wherefore wee cannot fpecefie
any certaine place of their affembly, by reafon of
their often change. Yet there remaines a certaine
forme of a colledge of Eftate in the towne of *Deuenter*: But it cannot refolue of any affaires of importance, which muft bee referred to the affemblie
of the Eftates for the whole Prouince, wherefoeuer
it fhalbe held. Yet when as the affaires fhall tend to
the good or preiudice of the generality of the vnion, they muft referre them to the affemblie of the
generall Eftates of all the vnited Prouinces, the
which is commonly kept at the *Hage* in *Holland*.

Groningue with the Omme-lands.

THe Eftate of the towne of *Groningue*, and the
Ommelands (which are country iurifdictions
confifting of many good Borroughs Villages, Abbaies and Monafteries) are fituated betwixt the riuers of *Ems* and *Lanwers*, and make a Siegneury or
Prouince, which is numbred among the 17. of the
Netherlands, and the eight in ranke of the vnited
Prouinces: which are reprefented and gouerned
by the common confent of the Eftates of the fayd
Prouince. Before that we treat of this Eftate in general, we wil firft fpeake of the town of *Groningue*,
which giues the name vnto the whole Prouince:

T   which

which name fome hold was giuen it by *Grunnius*,
iffued from the bloud of the Kings of *Frifland*,who
was the founder, and not that *Troian* of whom *Se-
baftian Munfter* fpeakes. This towne is feated in a
pleafant foyle, enuironed with goodly paftures,
fome thinking that it hath taken the name from the
greenes thereof; this worde of *Groen* fignifying
greene, *Ingen* being as an adiectiue which makes
vppe the word, wherof there are many both in this
and other Prouinces of the *Netherlands*, as *Hu-
finghe*,*Finelinghe* & others in the country of *Groe-
ningue*; *Harlingke* in *Frifland*, *Vlaerdinghe* in *Holland*, *Flifinghe* in *Zeeland*, *Poperinghe* in *Flanders*
and others els where.

This towne with the dependances, was heretofore giuen to the Bifhops of *Vtrecht* in the yeare
1057. by the Emperor *Henry* the third and others
going before him, and by their fucceffors, (fince
that the *Normans* deftroied the towne of *Vtrecht*):
whereof they gaue letters of Eftate to the fayd
Bifhops,of the which they haue alwaies made vfe,
vntill the end of the laft age. The which notwithftanding was often taken from them,as well by the
Groningers themfelues, as by the Princes which
haue feazed vpon that Siegneury : amongft others
Albert and *George* Dukes of *Saxony*, who had the
gift from the Emperors *Frederic* and *Maximilian*,
and *Edfard* Earle of *Embden*, whom they accepted
for their Lord, all which did not acknowledge the
Bifhops of *Vtrecht*. This towne is inricht with two
fmall

small riuers , *Huneso* and *Aha* , comming out of the countrie of *Drenthe* , through the *Ommelands* the which compassing about the towne , meete in the suburbes which is called *Schaytendyep* , from whence passing by the towne of *Dam* , with other small brookes which ioyne there , they fall by the Sluses of *Delfzyele* into the *Dullart* , which is of the riuer of *Ems* : by the which all ships both great and small take their course , to ioyne with the greater, which anchor vpon the *Dullart* , and so to goe from thence to sea whether they please . There were wont to be twelue churches in this towne, whereof three were parish churches : the first was Saint *Martins* , the second Saint *Walburge* (which Temple hath the forme of a *Mosquee* , which they say was built by *Pagans* , the Parish beeing now annexed to that of Saint *Martin*) , and the third is that of our Lady , ioyning to one of the Market places. Other fiue are Monasteries, and the foure which remaine Hospitalls: among the cloisters that of *Franciscains* , being in the midest of the town, is conuerted to a colledge for schollers, for the study of humanity, wherof at my being there, doctor *Vbbo Ems* was Rector , the other cloisters & monasteries are applied to better vses, then to feed idle bellies. The foure hospitalls are entertained , whereof the first, which is great like a parish , is called of the Holie Ghost, the second Saint *Gheertruyde* : the third Saint *Iames* , and the fourth Saint *Anthony.*

There are in this town two goodly market places,

the one for the greatnesse, was called *Dat-brede marckt*, very great and spacious, the like whereof is not be seene in any other towne, beginning from Saint *Martins* church-yard, going toward the weſt, at the end whereof is the towne-houſe: nere vnto it is the other market-place not much leſſe, which goes to our Ladies church, which they call *Ter A-ha*, or fiſh market; At which two market places (which is a goodly thing to ſee) there meet 17. of the greateſt ſtreets of the towne: whereof ſix go to ſeueral gates, (being eight in al) that is to *Poel* port, *Ooſter* port, *Heren* port, *Ter Aa* port *Botteringe* port, & *Ebbing* port, which gates are called by the name, of the ſaid ſtreetes: The *Spaniards* in the Duke of *Aluas* time did builde a Cittadell at *Heren* port, which the Burgers did ruine, when as *Gaſpar* of *Rob-les*, Lord of *Billy*, a *Spaniard*, Gouernor of the town, was deteined priſoner by his owne ſoldiars and the towne reduced vnder the vnion of the Eſtates, but afterwards it was trecherouſly yeelded vnto the King of *Spaine* by *George* of *Laluin*, Earle of *Rhene-berg*, with the murther of the Burgue-maſter and ſome Burgers: vntill the yeare 1594. that Prince *Maurice* of *Naſſau* did force it by a ſiege and furious battery to ſubmit it ſelfe vnder the obedience of the ſayd generall Eſtates, as it continues vnto this day with the *Ommelandes*. This towne hath betweene *Poel* port and *Steeneille* port, a goodly ſuburbes with a chanell, where the ſhippes arriue which come from *Dam*, *Delfziell* and other places

of

of the country, with turfes and al forts of prouifion, neceffary for the towne which fuburbes are fo fortefied as the Inhabitants thinke themfelues as fafe there as within the towne : it is called *Schuytendiep.* Within thefe ten yeares the generall Eftates (for fome ieloufie which they had of the fayd towne)as weil for feare of intelligences of fome Burgers with the *Spaniards*, as alfo to rake away all occafion for E*nno* Earle of Eaft-*frifland* to attempt againft the fayd towne, caufed a cittadell to bee built, in the which they entertained an ordinary garrifon the which kept the mutins in awe.

There is yet an other fuburbe rampared like vnto a fort, at the Port *Ter Aa*; an other at the Port of *Botteringe*, and an other beyond the Cittadell, all which fuburbes haue much endured during the fiege, and in the laft warres; as many goodly houfes of pleafure, as well of gentlemen, cittizens, as ritch farmers, moft part ruined doe yet fmart for it. Finally the fituation of this towne is fuch, that as they may carrie and tranfport whatfoeuer they pleafe by water : fo may they alfo doe by land at all feafons of the yeare, by the *Drenth* and other neighbour places to the fronters of *Germany*, which brings great proffit to the towne.

As for the *Ommelandes*, that is to fay, the champian country thereabouts, which confifts of many good Bourges and villages, although they bee not fubiect to the towne, yet by a mutual accord, there is fuch vnity among them, as in many things, they

T 3 **haue**

haue yeelded vnto the towne; as the right of the
market, the ftaple of marchandife fold by great or
by retaile, to fell no ftrange beere nor ale through-
out all the country, but only fuch as they doe brew
within the towne: the which is fet downe at large
in the letters of the ftatute, in the yeare of our
Lord 1 4 5 5. renewed and augmented in the yeare
1 4 8 2. And the chiefe point wherein the *Omme-*
lands haue yeelded vnto the towne, the which they
haue enioyed for thefe many yeares, is touching
matters of Iuftice, by the which the wife men of
the country are gouerned, Inferior Iudges kept in
awe, the iurifdiction maintained, the pride of the
ritch and mighty reftrained, and the Edicts belonging to the common-weale, concerning their authoritie publifhed. For the which the Magiftrate or
Senate of the towne chufe fiue honorable perfons
fit for thofe charges to bee renewed euery yeare, if
for their fufficiencie and merittes they bee not continued two or three yeares, thefe are called *Hoft-*
mannem, they are feldome chofen if they haue
beene Bourgue-maifters, Senators or of the
councell.

Thefe fiue *Hoft-mannem* tooke knowledge of all
things were it by themfelues alone, or ioyntly with
the Senate. Their Court was called, their iudiciall chamber, their authoritie was great ouer all the
champian country: which by little and little did extend beyond the riuer of *Lanvvers*: and then into
Oftergoe and *Weftergoe*, two chiefe Cantons of *Frif-*
land,

*land,*wheerby there grewe great quarrells betwixt the *Groningers* and *Frisons*: yea among the *Frisons* themselues, diuided into thofe two curfed factions of the *Schyeringers* and *wetcoopers*. To pacefie the which the Emperor *Frederick* the 3. fent *Otto van Langhen* a Chanoine of *Ments* and his councellor into *Frifland*: but hee returned without any effect, by reafon of the wilfulneffe of the *schieringers*. The Emperor *Frederick* dying foone after, *Maximilian* the firft his fon, fucceeded in the Empire, who fent the fame *Otto van Langhen* again into *Frifland,*with an ample commiffion, giuing them authority (as they had before time)to choofe a Poteftate,(which is as much to fay as a Prouinciall Gouernor) and to fettle the *Frifons* in their ancient liberties: whereby the *Groeningers* had beene excluded from the confederation which they had with them of *Oftergoe* and *weftergoe*. But although the *Frifons* were well inclined to this Election of a Potef-tate, (wherein they proceeded fo farre, as there was one chofen of the chiefe of their Nobilitie and well qualified) yet one of the factions held him for fufpect, either partie defyring to haue one of his league, where-vpon their hatred did fo increafe, as *Otto* preuayled no more then at the firft, which made the Emperour *Maximilian* to giue the gouernment Hereditarie of *Frifland* and *Groningue* to Duke *Albertus* of *Saxonie* ;as wee fhewed in the defcription of *Frif-land.*

T 4   **Duke**

Duke *Albertus* hauing afterwards broken this
confederation betwixt them of *Groening* and *Frisland*; ouer whom hee held himselfe halfe Maifter,
feeking to difpofe of all things at his pleafure,
as well within the towne of *Groening* as in the
Ommelands, where hee pretended an abfolute fuperioritie: which they beeing vnwilling to yeeld
vnto, hee went to befiege the towne of *Groening*,
the which after a long fiege, hauing endured many Indignities from Duke *Albertus*, and fearing
in the end a badde iffue of this warre, they did call
in and receiue for their Protector Hereditarie,
Edfard Earle of *Embden*, or rather of *Eaft-Frifland*
(Lieutenant at that fiege to the Duke, but dif-
contented with Collonel *Vyt*) vppon certaine conditions, amongft others, to build a fort or block-
houfe the which was done.

The Duke feeing himfelfe deceiued by the Earle,
and difapointed of fo goodly a prey, ment for the
recouery thereof to imploy all his meanes, holding
the *Frifons* to bee halfe vanquifhed. The *Groeningers* feeing the Emperour to imbrace the Dukes
quarrell, and that there was a profcription fent out
by the Empire againft Cont *Edfard*, who could
hardly free himfelfe, & much leffe protect them: rather then to fal vnder the proud gouernment of the
Saxons, they called in *Charles* Duke of *Geldre*, a
Prince that was ftirring & high minded to vndertake their protection, & vpon the fame conditions
that they had receiued Cont *Edfard* onely the fort
which

which he had built fhould be razed, the which the *Geldrois* (to augment his *Signeuries*) would not neglect, fending the Seignior of *Oyen* to take poffeffion: and thus the towne and ftate of *Groning* fell into the hands of the *Geldrois* which was the caufe of gre t warres betwixt the two Dukes of *Saxony* and *Geldres*.

The *Geldrois* being put in poffeffion of the towne in the yeare, 1 5 1 8. and of the *Ommelandes*, 1 5 2 1. (as fuch an active fpirit cannot containe him-felfe within his bounds) hee began foone after to attempt as well vpon the rights of the towne as the preuiledges of the *Ommelandes*, The *Groningers* hauing difcouered his practifes with Captaine *Meinard van Ham*, for the King of *Denmarke*, vpon the towne of *Dam*, which is of their iurifdiction, the which hee pretended to fortefie to keepe *Groening* in fubiection, and then to doe all things at his pleafure. They feeing them-felues thus circumuented, and knowing the dukes intention, grew cold in their affection which they did firft beare him, turning it to the houfe of *Bourgongne*, where-vpon hauing refolued with the confent of the *Ommelanas* they did write vnto *George Schencke*, Baron of *Tautenburg*, knight of the order of the Golden-fleece, gouernor of *Frifeland* for the Emperor *Charles* the fift according to the refignation which the Duke of *Saxony* had made vnto him, to which effect the fayd Seignor *Schencke* (hauing receiued commiffion from

the

the Lady *Mary* Queene of *Hungary*, fifter to the
Emperor) marched with all the forces hee could
thether, where he entred in Iune in the yeare. 1536.
and there receiued their oth of fidelity, in the Emperors name, as Duke of *Brabant*, Earle of *Flanders*,
Holland, *Zeeland*, &c. Lord of *Frifeland* and *Oueriffel*,
but vpon certaine conditions, that the members and
ftate of the Seigneury of *Groning* fhould hold their
priuiledges, right and ftatutes, as they had receaued
them from their anceftors : that the towne fhould
hold their ancient Preture and the foraine: that they
fhould build a pallace in the towne for the Emperor fit for a Prince, but without any fortification:
the forts in the country fhould be razed, & noe new
built, if neceffity did not require it for the defence
of the country and of the towne, out of whofe reuenues there fhould be yearely payed vnto the Emperor & to his fucceffors 12000. crownes, vpõ which
conditiõ *Phillip* K. of *Spaine* was receiuedin Ianuary.
1550. Among all the priuiledges of the faid towne,
they haue one very notable, which came from their
anceftors, with an inviolable contynuation, which
is ; That noe King, Prince, Eftate nor common-
weale, can call any *Bourger* or Cittizen of that
towne into iuftice, nor caufe him to bee cited or
adiorned before any court, but onely before the
Senat or his ordinary iudge : more-ouer that noe
man might appeale from any fentence that were
giuen, either in ciuill or cryminall caufes, neither
from the court of *Hoffmans* or iudiciall chamber,

in

in that which concernes their iurifdiction, from the which no man of what quality fo euer may decline: moreouer the towne is Lady and miftriffe of her owne lawes and ftatutes, the which by a foueraigne power they may make and vndoe, create and abrogate without the authority of any perfon. The Eftates of the *Ommelands* haue alfo the like authority in their regard. The towne hath had a priuiledge to coyne filuer and copper for thefe foure hunderd years, and gold fince the yeare.1474.

The Magiftracy of the towne confifts as it hath done time out of mind, of foure Bourgue-maifters and twelue Senators (but of late daies, for before they were wont to haue 16.) which are the head of the common weale, all hauing equal voices, but not equall in dignity and authority. This Senat takes knowledge of all that concernes the towne: they haue power to choofe the *Hoftmans* or Pretors of ẙ country & to fend ambaffages wher need fhould require: to conclude, their duty is to prouide both in general & particular for the good of the common weale. Their charge is for two yeares and they are created with fuch order as euery yeare eight are depofed, and other eight fubrogated in their places, among the which I comprehend the Bourguemaifter.

After the Senat and *Hoftmans*, there is within the towne a colledge of 24. men, chofen out of the beft families, which they cal the fworne councellors for that from yeare to yeare they binde them-felues by oth to the Common-weale of *Groning*, without
whome

whome the Senat cannot refolue of any matters of importance.concerning the whole common-weale as to vndertake a warre, or to giue it ouer; to contract alliances, make lawes or to breake them, build new forts or other publike workes: change their mony; bring the towne in debt or chtage it with rents otherwife: To treat of which things, the fenat caufeth them to be called, which haue beene depofed, whom they call the old fenat: and fome-times they call fome of the beft cittizens of the towne, as the Deans or maifter of the cheefe trades, men of great credit among the people. This colledg of foure and twenty fworne men, hath as it were a triumuirat, which fpeakes for them all, and bind themfelues by oth vnto the Senat, to procure the townes good, and to make a faithful report of all, the which may properly bee called *Tribunes* of the people.

There are many other offices in the towne, feruing for the entertainment and preferuation thereof: as Prouofts of the wacth, Maifters of quarters: Heads, Captaine or *Deans* of the fworne companies, whom the Senat doth choofe for life: Maifters of workes, ouerfeers of the waights and mefures for bread and beere. To conclude it feemes there wants nothing for a well gouerned common-weale.

The manner of chofing the Magiftrat in that towne is as followeth. One halfe of the councell which are fixeteene and of the twenty foure fworne men are yeerely depofed, whofe places are filled by fiue perfonages well qualified among the twenty
                                                                     foure

foure Iurats whome the Gouernor of the Prouince doth name, which fiue do choofe out of all the towne eight new councellors, to fill vp the places of them that are depofed, which eight newly chofen, with eight old remaining, chofe foure Bourguemaifters, more-ouer the Gouernor names (befides the twenty foure fworne men) fiue other men who choofe twelue among the commons of the towne, to fill vp the place of twelue that were depofed, fo the twelue new Iurats with the twelue of the old remayning, make vp the number of twenty foure, all which together choofe the three Tribunes.

There is alfo in that towne an ordinarie free fchole or rather a colledge, which is very famous by reafon of Doctor *Vbbo Emmius*, an excellent Hiftoriographer, who was Rector and gouerned it : of whofe writing we haue for the moft part made vfe, in the defcription of *Freefeland*.

The *Ommelands* are diuided into three quarters; the *Fenelingo, Himfing*, and the weft quarter, euery one hauing their preuiledges written in diuers Seign'uries, as places of iudgement, which they call *Redgerrechten, Gretenies* or *Baylewiks*, whereof the bourguemafters, and councel of the towne haue fome, and the Nobles or proprietaries of the faid towne and *Ommelands* haue the reft : in the which the *Redgers*, *Gryetmans* or Bayliffes take knowledge both of ciuill and criminall caufes, and determine of them according vnto equity and iuftice, from which fentences in euery iurifdiction & Seigneury,
touching

touching the right therdof duties, Inheritances,
morgages by writing or otherwife, they may appeale before the aſſembly, which they cal *Varwen*,
compoſed of a Lieutenant, foure Capitoux, with
their Aſſeſſors, Redgers, Nobles, Proprietaries,
Grietmans or Bayliffs. In other cauſes not concerning the matters aboue ſpecified, in caſe of appeale,
they go vnto the Lieutenants and Captaines of the
towne of *Groning*, as the chiefe, and of the *Ommelands*, who in ſuch caſes iudge alſo by decree, (as we
haue ſaid) without any appeale, euocation or re-
miſſion: Being alwaies to bee vnderſtood, that the
ſaid lieutenant: who is choſen by the Eſtates of the
towne & country, and the 4. Capitoux by the Bur-
guemaſters and councell, may not meddle with the
ſuperintendency, nor the politik gouernment of the
Ommelands, but according to the commiſſion, oth
and inſtruċtions which they haue from the Eſtates
choſen by the towne and county: In the name and
behalf of the foueraignty of the whole Eſtate, and
Siegneury, they may adminiſter Iuſtice, according
to ẙ right & ancient cuſtomes of the Prouince. By
the which Lieutenant & Capitoux, in vertue of a
certaine grant made by the Emperor *Cha· les* the 5.
in 1538. vnto thē of *Wedde* & *Weſtuveldinger-landt*,
euen in caſes of appeall all matters within the ſaid
quarters of *Wedde* and *veſtuvoldinger-landt*, are decided, without any further euocation, prouocation
or reuiſion. Of this towne doth meerly depend the
towne which they call.

THE

THE DAM.

THis towne is two leagues from *Groning*, in ancient time a good towne of trafficke, as beeing
the Slufe to goe to the fea, the which is now at *Delfzyel* (for that which they call *Zyel* or *Dam* is all
one, fignifying a Slufe) but fince the yeare 1 5 3 6.
being taken by affault for the Imperialifts, when as
the *Geldrois* did hold it, the walles were demante-
led: and then it was accorded that it fhould not be
lawfull for the *Groningers* to wall it in any more,
nor to make any fort. The which notwithftanding
could not bee obferued, for fince the laft warres, it
hath bin fortefied, and taken and retaken againe.
Now it lies open, yet holding the forme of a town,
through the which paffeth the chanell which goes
to *Delfzeyl*, and from thence by the fame Slufes to
the *Dullart*, or into the riuer of *Ems.*

DELFZYEL.

IS at this prefent a great and mighty fort in forme
of a towne, much greater then before : for many
yeares fince there was one, but it hath beene often
ruined and repaired againe : It was concluded betwixt the Emperour and the *Groeningers*, that
this fort fhould bee razed, and that they fhould
not build any one there, or in any other place without the confent of both parties, yet in thefe laft
warres they haue fuffred both that and others to
be

be built, whereof fome are ruined as vnprofitable, fome are yet ftanding, which in time may bee alfo razed. But that of *Delfzyel*, for the greatnes; number of inhabitants, ftrength and commodity, ftanding vpon the *Dullart*, is likely to ftand ftill, and in time to become a good towne of traffick, yet vnder the fubiection of the *Groningers*.

This is all we can fay in breefe of the towne, Eftate and commonweale of *Groning* and their *Ommelands*; yet we may not forget that out of this towne are come great and learned men: among others *Rodolphus Agricola*, of whome that great *Erafmus* of *Rotterdam*, giues an honorable teftimony, forthat he was expert in the Greeke, eloquent in the Latine, an excellent Orator; a good Poet, a fubtill Philofopher, a perfect Mufition, being able to make Mufical inftruments himfelfe as he did the Organs of the great Church and others, of whome alfo that moft learned *Hermolaus Barbarus* doth make mention in an Epitaph which he compounded vpon his vntimely death, which was in the forty yeare of his age, in the citty of *Heidelberg*, in the yeare 1 5 8 5. where the Prefident *Viglius Aita* of *Zichem* paffing that way, as one honoring the memory of his countriman, he caufed a faire ftone to bee fet vpon his tombe, and the Epitaph of the faid *Hermolaus* grauen thereon, as followed.

Inuida

Inuida clauferunt hoc marmore,Fata Rudolphum,
　Agricolam, *Frifij,fpemque,decufque foli,*
Scilicet hoc viuo meruit Germania *laudis,*
　Quicquid habet Latium, Grecia quicquid habet.

The glory of the *Frifons* fhew is gone,
　through enuious fate,and lieth within this ftone:
*Rudolph Agricola,*whofe life did fee,
　All *Europes* praife deferu'd by *Germany.*

In this towne,and in *Agricolas* time was alfo borne,
the learned *Weffel Bafillius* an excellent Philofopher
who died in the yeare, 1489. who we may fay,were
the two ftarres of *Groning.*

Townes and places out of the eight Prouinces,
yet comprehended vnder
their vnion.

H Auing defcribed as particularly as wee could,
the eftate of the faid eight vnited Prouinces,the
fituations, the commodities, the trafficke and the
ornamants of euery one of the townes , & the forts
comprehended within them,and which are of their
iurifdiction,although that the generall eftates,haue
not all at their commandement; as there are fome
in *Gelders* and beyond the *Rhine* , held by the
Archduke *Albertus* and *Ifabella* of *Auftria* , yet
the vnited Eftates haue the greateft part and the
cheefeft places vnder their obedience: wee muft
V　　　　　　　　　　　　　　　　　now

now alſo deſcribed the townes and forts, which
they hold in thoſe Prouinces, which are vnder the
ſaied Archdukes, eſpecially in the Duchy of *Bra-*
bant and Conty of *Flanders*, gotten by armes, the
which they keepe. Firſt.

In the Duchy of Brabant.

BERGEN VP ZOOM.

WE place this towne firſt of all thoſe which the
vnited Eſtates hold in *Brabant*, for that it is
made a Marquiſate, although that *Breda* be one of
the firſt *Barronies* of the Duchy : This towne hath
a good hauen, at the mouth wherof there is a mighty fort which defends it : it is right againſt *Tertolen*
one of the Ilands of *Zeeland*. Before the towne of
Antwerp was in credit, and that *Bruges* began to decay, it had the cheeſe trade for Marchandiſe. There
were wont to be goodly buildings the which being
abandoned in theſe laſt warre by their proprietaries, and remayning as it were deſert, they haue
ſerued to noe other vſe but to lodge ſoldiars, and
are much decayed. It hath beene alwaies a good
garriſon for ſoldiars, who went to ſeeke there fortunes farre and neare, to the gates of *Antwerp*, and
as farre as *Luxembourge*, bringing home often times
very good booty, with whome the *Bourgers*,
Inne-keepers and Tauerners did ſo well agree as
they reaped great beniſit by the ſoldiars. This
towne

towne hath conftantly mayntayned the party of
the generall Eftates of the vnited Prouinces, fence
the time that it was yeelded in the yeare 1577. by
the *Germaines*, who deliuered vp their Collonel
Fronfbergh with the towne vnto the generall E-
ftates. In the yeare 1588. the Duke o' *Parma*
came to befeege it with a mighty army, thinking
to take the great fort by practife with an *Englifh-
man*, but hee was difapointed of his purpofe, and
was forced to retier with difhonor and loffe: And
in the yeare, 1605. the Marquis *Spinola*, Lieutenant to the Arch-dukes, made two furious attempts, the which in a manner fucceded, but they
were repulft by the valours of the *Bourgeis* and
foldiars with great loffe. Although it bee vnder
the obedience of the vnited Eftates, yet doe
they retaine ftill their ancient rights and preuiledges.

BREDA.

IS a faire great towne, with a pleafant Caftle ioyning vnto it; which was wont to bee the Pallace
whereas the Earles of *Naffau* held their Court, as
the deceafed *William* of *Naffau* Prince of *Orange*, did
for a time for it is but twelue leagues: from *Bruf-
fells*. It was wont to haue a goodly Heronrie in
the great Church-yard, but now they are difi-
perfed, yet there are fome of them remayne
ftill beehinde the Caftell. Collonel *Fousker* with

his *Germaines*, hauing escaped out of *Antwerp* in the
yeare 1 5 7 7. hee retired into this towne, whereas
Philip Earle of *Hohenloo* went and beseeged him,
in the Prince of *Oranges* name (the towne being
his patrymony) and for the Vnited Estates : the
which the soldiars deliuered vnto the Estates, with
their Collonel, as they had done *Fronsbergh* at *Ber-*
ghen vp Zoom, vnder whose obedience it did continue, vntill that the Baron of *Fresin* being prisoner
in the Castle hauing corrupted some soldiars, found
meanes in the yeare 1580. to deliuer it to the Duke
of *Parma*: from whome it was recouered in the yeare
1 5 9 0. by a hardy and dangerous enterprise which
Captaine *Charles* of *Heraugiere* a gentleman of
Cambray, seruing vnder Prince *Maurice*, made with
7 2. resolute soldiars, who being hidden in a boate-
full of turfes, in a thousand dangers of their liues,
hauing entred at noone day into the castle, without
descouery the night following they surprized it,
cutting the *Corps de gard* in peeces, & giuing entry
vnto the Prince and the Earle of *Hohenlo*, with their
troupes, which lay not farre of: which the Captaines
of the garrison seeing, fled, and the towne was also
yeelded by composition, since which time, the
towne hath continued vnder the obedience of the
Prince and the said Estates, who made *Herauguie e*
gouernot as a recompence of his valour, and gaue
good reward vnto the soldiars with promise of aduancement, as most of them haue had vpon the first
changes.

STEEN-

STEENBERGHEN.

IS a little towne betwixt *Berghen vp Zoom*, and *Breda*, along the sea-coast, the which the *Spaniard* did hold, vntill the yeare 1 5 9 0. when as *Charles* Earle of *Manffeldt*, by commandement from the Duke of *Parma*, went to besiege the fort of *Seuenberghe*, the which he battred, and did what he could to take it, but finding he should profit nothing, hee retired. The Prince hearing that the fort was thus freed, hee went to besiege this towne of *Steenberghen*, the which hee forced to yeeld by composition, and since it hath continued vnder the obedience of the vnited Estates.

WILLEMSTADT.

THat is to say *Williams* towne, built within these 30. yeares, by *William* of *Naffau*, Prince of *Orange* who gaue it that name. It is in the Island of *Rogheville*, which is in the duchy of *Brabant*, a good and a strong towne, at this time almost all built. It serues as a *Rendezuous* to the Estates armie, when they haue any incursion or enterprise to make; at it was at the enterprise of *Breda* whom it doth much import, as wel as the towne of *Dordrett* to haue it well kept: whereof the Estates do entertaine a sufficient garrison there, with a Gouernor, Sargent Maior and other Officers.

V 3 *CLVYN-*

CLVTNDERT.

IS a good bourg in the Duchy of *Brabant* whereas the Estates haue built a mighty fort, where for the importance thereof they entertaine an ordinary garrison, with a Captaine, superintendant, and other officers.

LILLO.

IS a mighty fort vpon the riuer of *Escault*, within three leagues of *Antwerp*, not far from the gulph of the said riuer, built within thirty yeares. It is a place of great importance, to stoppe the nauigation to *Antwerp* : which the Collonels and *Bourgers* of the said towne, (during the time they were vnder the vnion) did carefully (and to their great charge) preserue. And when as the Duke of *Parma* did resolue to beseege it, they did re enforce the garrison, and sent the Seignor of *Teligny*, Sonne to *Mounsieur de la Noue* to command their, and Collonel *Godin* to prouide for all things before the comming of Collonell *Mondragon* Captaine of the Castle of *Antwerp* : who hauing beseeged it, and seeing noe meanes to cut of their succors by water, after that he had spent some cannon shotte, hee raysed his campe and retyred. It hath continued euer sence

vnto

vnto this day vnder the obedience of the vnited
Estates, who in my opinion will not suffer it to bee
ruined by the peace, but rather to conuert it to a
good towne, the which in time, in steed of a place
for warre, may haue good trade of marchandise, and
proue rich, being seated vpon so goodly a riuer
and so neere the gulph thereof towards the sea,
right opposit to another fort which the Estates
now hold on *Flanders* side called *Lyefsken hook*.

TER-HEYDEN.

IS a fort at the mouth of the riuer, the which comming from *Breda* falls there into the sea. It was
first built by the *Spaniards*, but the towne of *Breda*
being surprised, and won (as we haue saued) Prince
Maurice (to the end that towne should not be brid-
led on that side) went to beseege it vntill it was yeelded vnto him by composition, the which he caused
to be presently raised.

For all which townes and places, together with
their *Baylewickes* and iurisdictions, there is a forme
of councel of Brabant at the *Hage* in *Holland*, before
the which there is appeall from subalternall and inferior iudges.

Townes and Forts which the Eſtates hold in Flanders.

SLVCE.

THis towne is a good port of the ſea, the which during the proſperity and trafficke of the towne of *Bruges*, ſome 100. yeares ſince, when as the nations floriſhed there was their Magaſin or Stoor-houſe, as their great and goodly Caues doe witneſſe, ſeruing for the wines that came from *Spaine*, the *Canaries* and *France*. For *Fliſſing* (which is but three leagues diſtant) was then but a village, and *Middelbourg* no great matter; the whole trafficke at that time was either at *Bruges* or at *Berghen vp Zoom*, and ſince at *Antwerp*. Since the pacification of *Gant*, vntill the yeare 1 5 8 7. this towne was vnder the obedience of the Eſtates, entertained, with a good gariſon, whereof the Siegnior of *Groenevelt* was Gouernor. But the ſame yeare the Duke of *Parma* went to beſiege it with all his forces, the which notwithſtanding his continuall battery, mines and furious aſſaults, was for a long time valiantly defended. In the end ſeeing no hope of any ſuccors, which they had expected from the Earle of *Leceſter* (Lieutenant for the Queene of *England* in the vnited Prouinces) and from the Eſtates, they were forced to yeeld it vpon an honorable compoſition, for want of munytion and other neceſſaries. Since which time, this towne did much anoy the

Eſtates

Eftates, efpecially the *Zelanders*, by the meanes of
ten Gallies which *Don Ieromino Spinola*, brother to
the *Marquis Spinola* brought out of *Spaine*, with the
which he did often affront the fhips of *Holland* and
Zeeland, vntill in the end he was flaine in a fea fight,
with great loffe of his men & fpoyle of his Gallies,
the which being repaired, fought ftill to cut off the
victualls and fuccors which the Eftates fent to *Oftend*, during the time of three years & three months,
that the Archduke *Albert* and the *Marquis Spinola* held it befieged, the which in the end hee tooke
by an honorable compofition : after that by an o-
ther fiege Prince *Maurice* had forced them of the
garrifon of *Slufe* to yeeld by compofition, beeing
preft by famine : which towne hee tooke without
battery or any other force, with all the Gallies and
other fhips, fetting the flaues at liberty, with many
other forts of importance, as you fhall heare, wheras the Archduke on the other fide got nothing but
a heape of ftones and earth, there remayning no
forme of a towne at *Oftend*, but onely the rampars.
Thus was *Slufe* reduced vnder the Eftates command, much againft *Spinolas* minde, who attempted twife to releeue it, but in vaine. It was yeelded
vnto them a month before *Oftend*, which from that
time was vnprofitable vnto them and of great
charge, feeing they had *Slufe*, fo as their gaine was
much greater then their loffe. For they did winne
at one inftant the Iflle of *Cadfandt*, and all the other
forts oppofite to the hauen of that towne, then
ARDEN-

ARDENBOVRG.

VVAs wont to bee a prettie country towne, a-
bout the which and in the Iſland of *Cadſant*
they did breed good horſes , whereof there was
twiſe a yeare a faire at this towne. But theſe ciuill
warres by the breach of dykes and inondations,
haue ſpoyled much of the country . Prince *Maurice* beſeeging *Sluſe*,did alſo beſiege this towne,the
which was yeelded vnto him , and is now ſtronger
then euer.

YSENDYCK.

¶S a mighty fort on *Flanders* ſide,right againſt *Fliſ-
ingue*,ſtanding toward the *Sas* of *Gant* & *Bocholdt*,
whereas the Archduke,for the importance of the
place, did continually entertaine a great garriſon
both of foote and horſe , to ſtop the incurſions of
them of *Fliſſingue* & *Berghen vp Zoom* in that quarter of the Waſt of *Flanders* . And although hee did
much rely in his fort,imagining it could not be eaſi-
ly taken: yet notwithſtanding that there were 800.
men in the fort, Prince *Maurice* beſieged it,battred
it,and forced it to come to compoſition in leſſe then
eight daies,before he gaue any aſſault. Since the E-
ſtates haue inlarged it,& it is now like vnto a town;
likely in time to be of good trafficke,for that the hauen is able to containe many ſhippes of 4. or 500.
tuns a peece,being well ſituated vpon the ſea,wher-
fore in my opinion the Eſtates will not ſuffer it to

bee

bee razed; nor leaue it in any fort, beeing fo commodious for them.

As for the other leffer forts about *Slufe* and in
the Ifland of *Cadfand*, wee will paffe them ouer, hauing fpoken of the principall.

LYEFKENS-HOECH.

THis fort was built at one inftant with that of
Lilloo, beeing oppofite vnto it vpon the riuer of
Efcault, fo as all fhips that come from the fea to goe
to *Antwerp*, muft paffe betwixt thefe two forts: But
it could not refift the enemies attempts like vnto
Lilloo: for in the yeare 1 5 8 4. the Vicont of *Gint*
Marquis of *Roubay* befieged it, and tooke it by affault, by a ftratageme which he made with a heape
of ftrawe and haie, which he caufed to bee burnt on
the dicke-fide where hee gaue the affault, fo as the
fmoake being driuen with the winde, did fo trouble
their fights that defended the breach, as they were
forced with great furie, the Vicont killing Collonel
Petain, (who commanded there) with his owne
hand, in cold bloud, and caufing many Burgers of
Antwerp to bee nanged: the which was afterwards
reuenged vpon the *Spaniards* and other prifoners
which they held in the vnited Prouinces. It was
fince recouered by the Eftates, vnder whofe obedience it hath continued vnto this day. Yet it is not
like to continue as *Lilloo*, but may well be razed vpon the conclufion of a peace, beeing of no fuch importance as the other.

TER.

TERNEVSE.

Is a good village of that quarter of *Flanders*, which hath a Baylife, Alderman and other officers, whereas the vnited Eſtates did long ſince build a fort, and entertained a good garriſon : it is ſituated in the mideſt of a drowned Land, and therefore not eaſie to approch nor to campe before it; for which conſideration the *Spaniard* (who will not willingly wet his feet) would not attempt it:remaining vnto this day vnder the Eſtates , being commanded by a captaine, ſuperintendent for them.

AXELLE.

IS a little towne in the land of *Waes* (which is one of the beſt quarters of *Flanders*)which *Seruaes van Steelandt* great Bayliffe of the ſaid country of *Waes* deliuered vnto the *Spaniard*, when as the Duke of *Aniou* was retired, after that great folly committed at *Antwerp* Six or ſeauen years after Sir *Phillip Sidney* Gouernor of *Fleſſingue* , and *Collonel Ihon Peron* ſurpriſed it, and deliuered it vnto the Eſtates in the yeare, 1587.the which they much fortefied ſince, by drowning of the great part of the country , which makes it inacceſſible , whereof the ſaid *Peron* hath recouered a good part , during the time that the Eſtates, left him gouernor of the place.

There are other forts in that quarter of *Axelle* and of *Terneuſe*, vpon *Flanders* ſide, as that of *Blockerſdyck*, Saint *Marguerits* and Saint *Anthonis-hoeck*
the

the which we omit, beeing of no great importance nor likely to continue.

Forts beyond the riuer of Rhine.

BOERENTANGHE.

IT is a goodly fort, none of the greateſt, but at this preſent like a little towne vpon the fronters of the countie of *Lingen*, which is the high-way to goe out of *Friſeland* and *Groning* into the country of *Weſtphalia*, and by *Cloppenbourg* to *Delmenhorſt* and *Breme*, and ſo to *Hamburg*, *Lubecke* and other towns of the Eaſt country, along the Baltique ſea. Is is entertained with a good ordinary garriſon, conſiſting of many halfe companies (at the leaſt when I was there) wherby (in my opinion) the Eſtates did wiſely cutting off many Monopolies and occaſions of mutynies, for that there is ſeldome any accord where there is diuerſitie. The countrie about is all mooriſh or full of turfes, wherewith they doe both furniſh the place and the countrie about it.

BELLINGER-WOLDER-ZYEL.

IS a good village or rather a Borrough, at the end of the *Dullard*, where as the riuer of *Ems* growes narroweſt, by the which they muſt paſſe comming from *Emblen* by water to goe to *Boerentanghe*, leauing the caſtle of *Wedde* vpon the right hand: where the Eſtates haue made a fort to defend the county

of

of *Lingen*: yet is it not so well fortefied, but it must yeeld to the first enemy if he be Maister of the field.

As for the other forts dispersed here and there-vpon riuers, frontiers and passages, beeing many in number, throughout all the vnited Prouinces, I haue thought it superfluous to describe them here particularly, hauing onely vndertaken the chiefe.

By this description may be seene, that in the said eight vnited Prouinces, which make the Estates of the *Belgike* Common-weale, there are aboue sixe score townes, great and small, and aboue a hundred castles and forts of all sorts, entertained with ordi-narie garrisons, besides their troupes of reserue which they put into townes, especiallie in winter, or when they haue neede to refresh their compa-nies either of foote or horse, where they are well lodged and accommodated.

Touching the shippes of warre which the vnited Estates doe vsually entertaine, as well at sea, as vp-on the riuers of *Rhine*, *Meuse*, *Wahal*, *Ems* and o-thers, I cannot set downe the number, the which is great, some-times more, some-times lesse, accord-ing to the necessitie of their affaires: they haue some-times a hundred and twenty shippes of warre in paie, well armed and appointed with men and munition. Their nauigation and trafficke of mar-chandise extends to the East, West, North and South. I dare boldly saie, that the Common-weale of *Venice*, which is held so ritch and mighty an E-state, could not haue continued such intestine wars

three

three years, as they haue done many, and do yet like the ebbing and flowing of the sea, whom all the forces of *Spaine* could neuer vanquish.

Wherefore wee must conclude that the King of *Spaine* was ill aduised to intreate them with such rigor, as they haue beene forced to oppose themselues and to shake off his yoake. Whereas contrary-wise. the King his sonne now raigning, (for feare of some greater inconuenience) hath with good aduice, declared them free Estates, seeing that his father could not with all his forces and treasure, depriue them of their liberties and freedomes: offring then peace, without attending the preiudiciall euent of a warre of a hundred yeares: as the Princes of *Austria* his Predecessors had against the Cantons of *Suisses*, who almost for the like occasions, did shake off their yoake, neere three hundred yeares since. Let vs praie vnto God, that their vnion may continue: the which may restraine the insolency of some of their Neighbours and norrish peace among them.
Which God grant.

FINIS,